Vietnam: A New Middle Power in Asia

VIETNAM
A New Middle Power in Asia

Editors

Pankaj K Jha
Truong-Thu Doan
Thi-Hue Quach
Trong-Hung Vu

SHIPRA

Rs. 1500; US$ 60

ISBN: 978-93-88691-51-2

First Published in India in 2020

Vietnam: A New Middle Power in Asia

Published by:
SHIPRA PUBLICATIONS
LG 18-19, Pankaj Central Market
I.P. Ext., Patparganj, Delhi 110092, India
Tel.: +91 11 2223 5152/6152, 9650028065
E-mail: info@shiprapublication.com
www.shiprapublication.com

Preface

Vietnam has a glorious history and embedded mystery given the fact that the narratives with regard to Vietnamese history, economy and ethnic identities were subsumed under the Cold war narratives. Vietnam was seen as one of those countries in Southeast Asia which had intrinsically adopted the communist governance system. While China gained the international traction, Vietnam was seen as a country struggling with its structural endemic problems. However, in the mid-1980s the economic reforms programme (*Doi-Moi*) and subsequently its integration into ASEAN and other regional organizations in 1995/96 showed that Vietnam cannot be considered as the recalcitrant nation and has claimed its role as an important regional stakeholder. Following its integration in the ASEAN affiliated organizations and improved relations with its neighbours, in particular Thailand and Cambodia as well as US allies such as Japan, Korea and Australia showcased that Vietnam has the potential to be the next economic powerhouse of Asia. With a literacy rate of more than 80 per cent and relatively better economic productivity levels, Vietnam has seen a surge in FDI and incremental development of manufacturing centers within Vietnam. The opening up of the Microsoft chip fabrication unit in Ho Chi Minh city followed with research in collaboration in science and technology as well as Vietnam's urge to contribute to the regional economic integration network saw that the country became one of the first to join APEC, RCEP and also CPTPP (the new nomenclature of TPP after the withdrawal of US). Vietnam have started with gains in the field of infrastructure development, steel, cement and real estate sector. The automobile industry, telecommunications and consumer products have shown promise and a future in this country. Vietnam was also listed as the one of the promising economies when the VISTA was proposed (included the second tier economies including Vietnam, Indonesia, South Africa, Turkey, and Argentina) and these economies were seen as promising markets for future.

In the context of globalization and deep regional integration, every nation wants to maintain, develop and strengthen its position in international relations to have its own power. A nation's power exists in two forms: hard power and soft power, creating that nation's synergy. The concept of "soft power" was a term that appeared quite early in Western academic circles from the first half of the twentieth century but until 1990, American Professor Joseph S. Nye with his research works was first developed and clarified this concept. Through the practice of building and defending the Fatherland, the soft power of the nation has been gradually shaped, affirmed and had profound influence on countries in the region and the world. Vietnam's soft power is present in many aspects and is outstanding. An advanced culture imbued with national identity and strongly spreading in international forums. Vietnam's Peaceful foreign policy is based on patriotic traditions and the humanistic spirit. Impressive development was witnessed in all aspects of Vietnam after more than 30 years of renovation, especially economic growth and political stability. Social consensus is created from the personal reputation of Vietnam's political leaders. In particular, the national cultural identity is an important endogenous resource, strongly determining the sustainable development of the country, and a solid foundation for Vietnam's soft power. In the new context, the effective combination of "soft power" and "hard power" in the country's development has created a synergy for Vietnam, which contributed to enhancing its position and influence in international relations.

This book covers important aspect of Vietnam's history, economy, culture, defence and security relations as well as its ties with major powers and ASEAN. The book opens the latent discourse that whether with such important breakthroughs Vietnam can be considered as the new middle power of Asia. The book is expected to bridge the gaps in the literature from Vietnam and projects country's academic perspective. The contributors have sourced primary documents from the country to give a perspective about the Vietnam.

Editors

Acknowledgements

The editors thank all the contributors for different chapters and would like to acknowledge the guidance and help provided by those academic and policy luminaries who have been working in the field of Vietnam politics, economy and society. This includes the diplomats, strategic thinkers, academics and the new generation of young scholars. The rise of Vietnam at international level nurtured by the Vietnam's Ambassadors, commercial counselors, technical consultants, trade and industry associations. Our gratitude to all those people who have worked within their official commitments, and cultivated informal interactions to build modern Vietnam.

The editors and contributors would like to thank the publisher for showing a keen interest in the manuscript and bringing out the refined version in a very short time.

New Delhi and Hanoi
December 27, 2019

Pankaj K Jha, Truong-Thu Doan,
Thi-Hue Quach and Trong-Hung Vu

Contents

1 Introduction

Pankaj Jha and Thi-Hue Quach

Vietnam is located in very important strategic position in Southeast Asia with rich and diverse natural resources, and many famous landscapes in the world, especially Ha Long Bay (twice confirmed as UNESCO World Heritage Site) is one of the seven natural wonders of the modern world. Therefore, Vietnam has become an ideal destination for international tourists. The Vietnamese people have suffered three wars in the post Second war phase (1954, 1975 and 1979 with France, the US and China) and have committed themselves to rebuild the nation which had, suffered because of imperialistic policies of France and the US. It is especially interesting that the Vietnamese have developed their national character and have put aside hardships of the past which included medical effects of Napalm bombs and Agent Orange, and work towards a goal to build society to live together peacefully. This has been recognized by the international communities for many years.

In the process of national construction and development, Vietnam has shaped its own script, and built a rich and diverse culture of 54 ethnic groups, and fostered unity among all ethnic communities to develop Vietnam's identity. It has the tradition of ancestor worship, the existence and peaceful coexistence of localized religions. Vietnam has a rich and diverse cuisine culture of areas across the country with many attractive foods captivating people. With 54 ethnic groups, Vietnamese people's costumes have different designs and styles, but "*Ao Dai*" is the national costume of Vietnam. It has dignified and highlighted Asian-inspired characteristics of Vietnamese women. Vietnam is also a country of traditional festivals and world heritage sites, so it has received the attention of people around the world. Contemporary Vietnam exudes confidence and variety in its colourful traditional, cultural space and the warm affection of the Vietnamese people with the desire to build a peaceful and progressive country. With these interesting things and the impressive development in the socio-economic fields, the position of Vietnam is increasingly enhanced in the international arena.

The history of several thousand years of Vietnam is a history of struggle against foreign forces, reclaiming and protecting independence (the time of fighting against invaders up to 12th century). The patriotism of Vietnamese people has permeated into the feelings and thoughts of every people through the ages, creating a resilient society to help the Vietnamese people defeat all enemies. This has been summarized by President Ho Chi Minh: "Vietnamese people have passion and patriotism. It is our precious tradition. From the past to the present, every time the fatherland is invaded, the spirit of the patriotism is reinforced again. It formed a very strong, huge wave, it glided through all the dangers and difficulties, and it castigated all the invaders and traitors of the country". Therefore, during more than 1,000 years of North domination (179 BC.-938 AD), the Vietnamese people exerted a high patriotic tradition, uniting to fight strongly against the brutal rule of Chinese feudalism and ending with the victory of Bach Dang in 938 AD. Along with the victory on the military fronts, the Vietnamese people also defeated the annexation pursuit to turn Vietnam into a province of China. After more than 1,000 years of North domination, Vietnam still retains its national cultural identity while at the same time adopts the positive cultural elements from abroad to enrich people's culture. This acted as an important foundation to create synergy for Vietnam to continuously win resounding victories in the struggles against Chinese feudalism, such as: Le Hoan defeated Song Dynasty invaders, Tran Dynasty defeated the Mong, Nguyen, Le Loi defeated the Ming, Nguyen Hue defeated the Thanh.

Since 1930, under the leadership of the Communist Party of Vietnam (CPV), President Ho Chi Minh and generations of leaders; Vietnam continues to rewrite its heroic history. As a country that is not wide at the centre and Vietnamese cities are not overpopulated but they have the knowledge to multiply themselves under the rubric of the patriotic tradition, the spirit of solidarity and fighting, Vietnam has defeated the invasion wars of superpowers in the world like France, Japan, America. A typical example is the victory of the August Revolution in 1945, the Dien Bien Phu victory in 1954 and the victory of Spring General Offensive and Uprising in 1975. These victories of Vietnam have surprised the whole world. In the period between 1975-2019, Vietnam carried out the national construction under socialist fundamentals across the country, especially the implementation of the renovation policy (1986-2019) and Vietnam has achieved remarkable progress in all areas. From a country suffering heavy consequences of war, Vietnam has become a country with the strongest economic growth in Asia, with stable political structure, strong defence and security framework, and developed diplomatic ties with international recognition. As a result of these, Vietnam's position is increasingly consolidated and enhanced in the international arena. With the conducive natural and social conditions, especially the extremely important geostrategic location, Vietnam has become the "Pearl" that attracts attention of the countries in the world. Therefore, Vietnamese history of prolonged struggles to protect national independence, and territorial border against enemies have now helped to build the peace, cooperation and development.

Economic growth is one of the most important pillars of national development. So, to transform comprehensively, each country should recondition strategic thinking with economic priorities. Through the research and practical experimentation, Vietnam set a path of economic reform, which has been consistently revised to align with the country's actual situation and keep pace with the world. After 33 years of the "Doi Moi" (1986-2019), Vietnam came out of the crisis and gradually shifted from a centrally-planned subsidized economy to a socialist-oriented market economy. Particularly, the most outstanding achievements have been maintaining high economic growth rates in the Asia-Pacific region; constantly expanding the size of the economy; shifting the economic structure towards increasing industrial and services share, reducing agricultural contribution; and improving people's lives. Vietnam is member of many prestigious regional and global economic organizations; a reliable partner of many countries and territories; and a large market and an attractive destination for major investors in the region and in the world, especially for the leading economic powers. These achievements have paved the way for Vietnam's rapid and sustainable economic development, reinforcing Vietnam's position as a new mid-range economy in East Asia.

Vietnam has set a focus on stable politics through all the time of country's construction and development. From the period of feudal dynasties to modern times, adjustment has always been brought to the political system of Vietnam so that the system could be easily adapted to historic conditions and achieve more successes in adverse conditions. After August Revolution in 1945, the Democratic Republic of Vietnam was created. The Vietnamese, nevertheless, had to fight two resistance wars against French colonialism and American imperialism within 30 years (1945-1975) in order to protect the newly gained independence. After the Great 1975 Spring Victory, the Socialist Republic of Vietnam was born with the mission of establishing socialism, construction on a national scale, enhancing defence and reunification of the whole country. Under the new circumstances, the Communist Party of Vietnam remained custodian of single party politics which worked on the mission to build an independent and stable politics with the objective of integration and comprehensive development of the country.

Vietnam insisted on following the socialist political regime regardless of internal and external situations, including the collapse of the socialist model in the Soviet Union as well as in Eastern Europe; and counter embargo from imperialistic countries as well as intensification of activities causing political instability, and sabotaging covert operations from hostile forces. Under the leadership of the Communist Party of Vietnam, the Vietnamese revolution has achieved great success with stable politics, independence, sovereignty and the peaceful environment. Issues related to democracy, especially in the local level is increasingly promoted. Social issues are solved according to the Constitution and Laws; the Communist Party of Vietnam has been constantly innovating its leadership and enhancing the operational role of the political system associated with erasing corruption and administrative reforming to serve the interests of people.

Throughout thousands of years of history of national construction and defence, the Vietnamese nation has defeated many powerful invading enemies to firmly defend independence, autonomy and territorial integrity. Many lessons and experience against invading enemies, therefore, have been learned. The Communist Party of Vietnam since its establishment up till now, has inherited that tradition and always take construction of a strong defense as the mission so that invasion and destruction from hostile forces—inland and abroad could be prevented. One of the eloquent evidences for this point of view of the Party is the victory in the two wars against the French colonialists and the American imperialism, which is a solid foundation for innovation and development for the country and international integration at present also.

While inheriting the experiences from the previous generations including the theory of Marxism-Leninism and Ho Chi Minh's ideologies about national defence, the Party and State of Vietnam always set focus on national defense and security, especially the adjustment in accordance with practical conditions, revolutionary tasks in each specific historical period, in order to protect the Socialist Republic of Vietnam. Those achievements are described in conference documents of the Communist Party of Vietnam since the beginning of Innovation (*Doi Moi*) and in ongoing constitution as well as defence laws of Vietnam. The Communist Party of Vietnam advocates: "Constructing a national defense and a battle of the national defense associated with people's security and a battle of the people's security "(Clause 3, Article 3, Law of Defense 2018) with absolute leadership of the Communist Party of Vietnam. Strengthening national defense and security is upheld as a core and legitimate mission based on the synergy of entire nation and political system, in which the role of the people's armed forces is critical in defending the socialist Vietnam.

With peace and self-defense written on the national defense and security policies, Vietnam is opposed to any kind of war ("No participation in forces or military alliances of one party against another; No foreign military base or permission to use the territory of Vietnam against other countries; No threat or force using in international relations; Resolving any disagreement, dispute by peaceful measure on the principle of independent respect, sovereignty, unity, territorial integrity; No interference in the internal affairs of each other; balanced and equally beneficial"). Specially in the context of Vietnam's integration into the world, defence work and security is deemed to be proactive, active cooperation, international dialogue to create a favourable international environment serving the purpose of national development and protection in the new situation, which is regarded as the target of Vietnam's national defense and security policies at present.

Vietnam has thousands of years of history with subtle and celebrated diplomacy. Except for the 1,000 years of North domination, through dynasties from Hung, An Duong Vuong, Ngo, Dinh, Tien Le, Ly, Tran, Hau Le and Nguyen Kings, Vietnam mainly had diplomatic relations with feudal dynasties of China. After the career of fighting for independence, on September 2, 1945, the Democratic Republic of Vietnam was established, the modern Vietnam was born. President Ho Chi Minh was the first leader to head Vietnam's Diplomatic. In two fierce wars against French colonialism (1945-1954) and US imperialism (1954-1975), Vietnam enlisted the support of the United Nations and regional countries such as Thailand, Myanmar, Indonesia and other Socialist countries in Asia, Eastern Europe, especially forming an alliance with Laos and

Cambodia, establishing formal diplomatic relations with two important allies, the People's Republic of China and the Union of Soviet Socialist Republics (early 1950). After 1975, Vietnam gained independence, unified the country, moved on to build socialism. Vietnam actively establishes diplomatic relations with many countries and international organizations, especially joining the United Nations (September 20, 1977) to enlist the help of international friends to overcome the consequences of war, building and comprehensive development for the country. Up till now, Vietnam has established diplomatic relations with 189 countries in all continents, including all major countries, having economic relations with more than 220 foreign markets and being member of many international organizations and forums such as: French-speaking Community (1970), United Nations (1977), Non-Aligned Movement (1976), ASEAN (1995), Asia-Europe Meeting (ASEM) (1996), Asia-Pacific Economic Cooperation (APEC) (1998), and World Trade Organization (WTO) (2006).

After the end of the Cold War, the peaceful environment was established and strengthened, and the risk of a global war was repelled. International relations have developed to promote economic and political cooperation instead of conflicts in order to solve new emerging global issues without a single country having resources to deal with all by itself. Under these circumstances, countries with common interests will establish close relations with each other for the sake of peace, stability and development. The cohesion between India and Vietnam is a prominent example of sharing similar interests. Under the "Comprehensive Strategic Partnership", India and Vietnam identified economic-trade and defence–security cooperations as two main pillars in the relationship between the two countries. Thus, ensuring maritime security and safety in the East Sea is an important factor to ensure security and sustainable development of the two countries.

After nearly 50 years of official establishment of diplomatic relations (1972-2019), the relationship between Vietnam and India has made breakthroughs and officially been upgraded into a Comprehensive Strategic Partnership in 2016. This event marked an important milestone in the history of relations between the two countries, demonstrating the high political trust between the two nations, which is the important basis for the two countries to continue promoting the relationship in the fields of politics- diplomacy, economics-trade, security-defence, energy security and culture–education, etc. With efforts by the governments and people of the two countries, in recent years, Vietnam–India relationship has many achievements in all fields of cooperation, creating firm momentum for the outstanding development in the future.

Historically, Vietnam and China have had the relations lasting for thousands of years with many similarities in cultural traditions. The people of the two countries have built the deep-rooted, long-lasting, and strong friendship, supporting each other in national liberation and reconstruction. For the period after the normalization of relations between the two countries, Vietnam and China have resolved conflicts on the territorial boundary, started to restore the bilateral relations and trust, and strengthened their close cooperation in various fields. Since 2008, the relations between the two countries have been officially improved into "comprehensive strategic cooperative partnership" on the basis of respecting 16 golden words "*Láng giềng hữu nghị, hợp tác toàn diện, ổn định lâu dài, hướng tới tương lai* (Neighbourly friendship, comprehensive cooperation, long-term stability, future orientation)" and four good things of "*láng giềng tốt, bạn bè tốt, đồng chí tốt, đối tác tốt* (Good neighbours, good friends, good comrades, good partners)". Since then, the two countries have always made the best efforts to increasingly stabilize and build up the relations in many aspects. However, in the context of rapid and profound changes in the world and the Asia-Pacific region, resulted from the fierce strategic competition among the big countries, Vietnam and China both set out the changes in foreign policies. This poses great challenges, especially consequences of fierce history and unsolved conflicts on the Eastern Sea hampers the prospective development of relations between the two countries. Although some contentious issues still exist, in recent years, Vietnam-China relations have also had important achievements in term of politics-diplomacy, economic-trade cooperation, investment, and national security-defense, thereby contributing to the efforts made by both sides, especially the influence on Vietnam from China's foreign policy towards big countries.

Located in a dynamic development region as Southeast Asia, four neighbouring countries of Vietnam, Laos, Cambodia and Thailand are not only important in Vietnam's geopolitics and military strategy, but it is also geo-economic and geo-cultural microcosm to the world. In particular, the three countries of Vietnam-Laos-Cambodia have long-standing ties, with the land borders, adjacent waters and the Mekong river connecting the three countries and located on the majestic Truong Son mountain range. Three countries are adjacent to the world's leading maritime transport route, linking Northeast Asia and South Asia through the Atlantic Ocean and Indian Ocean. Vietnam, Laos, Cambodia and Thailand all share similar cultural traits coming from wet rice agriculture civilization in Southeast Asia and deeply influenced by Buddhism. During the building and developing process of nation, the four countries established diplomatic relations with each other on the basis of respecting the independence, sovereignty and territorial integrity. On June 15, 1956, Cambodian-Laos's diplomatic relations was established. On September 5, 1962, Vietnam and Laos established diplomatic relations. On June 24, 1967, Vietnam and Cambodia officially established diplomatic relations. On August 6, 1976, Vietnam and Thailand established diplomatic relations.

In the context of globalization, regionalization and integration with new opportunities and challenges, the four countries of Vietnam, Laos, Cambodia and Thailand all have to make major adjustments in foreign policy, which emphasizes the policy of multilateralization and diversification of international relations, attaching importance to the cooperation and integration among countries, the region and the world. The Vietnam-Laos-Cambodia-Thailand relationship has contributed positively to the stability and development of

ASEAN, reflected in the following areas: maintaining the environment of peace, stability, cooperation and development in the region; maintaining ASEAN's consensus, solidarity and unity; promoting the building of ASEAN Community; strengthening ASEAN's position in the international arena, maintaining ASEAN's central role in regional security structures and strengthening ASEAN's relations with the dialogue countries. In those relationships, Vietnam is an important partner and an indispensable link contributing to asserting the position of Vietnam's new middle power in Asia.

In the process of building, defending and developing the country, Vietnam wished to establish peaceful relations and development cooperation with other countries, territories and regional and international organizations. Vietnamese history has proved this goodwill of Vietnamese people in international relations. Notably, Vietnam has broken the siege, embargo and normalized relations with the United States, proceeding to establish Comprehensive strategic partnership with the United States; maintaining good traditional relations with Russia and developing strategic partnership with Japan after more than 45 years of establishing diplomatic relations. Vietnam has also received much attention from the European Union (EU), and EU member countries, and has built bilateral cooperation for mutual benefits on the most important fields such as economy, politics, diplomacy, defense, security, and culture interactions. In the new context, the superpowers of the United States, Japan and Russia, and the EU is constantly increasing diplomatic relations with Vietnam. This proves the position, influence and attraction of Vietnam increasing. In relation with superpowers and the EU, both Vietnam and the parties have achieved the desired results, creating the basis and the trust to bring cooperation and development across spectrum. In the current discourse related to regionalization and globalization, countries and organizations need to actively collaborate in new fields such as digital economy, cyberspace, renewable energy, etc. to meet the needs of the times. As Asia-Pacific becomes the most dynamic and attractive region in the world, Vietnam has become an important link and emerged as an indispensable player in regional and international relations. With its political position and important geostrategic position, Vietnam is fully qualified to be an important regional partner for superpowers and regional and international organizations. This contributes to the criteria for Vietnam to become a new middle power in Asia.

Under the leadership of the Communist Party of Vietnam, after more than 30 years of comprehensive innovation, Vietnam's economy, politics, culture, society, diplomacy and national defense and security have had impressive development. Vietnam ranks 46th in terms of economy size with the fastest growth in the region and the world. Vietnam is also one of the countries with leading military power in Asia-Pacific. Vietnam is an active member and plays an important role in regional and international organizations, such as the United Nations, ASEAN, WTO, especially Vietnam has been ASEAN Chair twice (in 1998 and 2010), and a non-permanent member of the UN Security Council twice (in the 1998-1999 and 2020-2021 periods), etc. With active diplomatic activities, Vietnam has become a catalyst and coordinator in relations between countries and organizations while proposing initiatives for resolving international disputes on the basis of respect for international laws, especially the settlement of international disputes with peaceful solutions. Therefore, Vietnam has received increasing trust from countries around the world, confirming the national brand with important regional and international influences. With these achievements, Vietnam has basically met the criteria of a new middle power in Asia.

2 Vietnam: Country, Society and Culture

Thi-Dung Nguyen

Vietnam is a nation what has a very important geostrategic position in Southeast Asia with great potential for development. Vietnam has total area of 329,314 km^2. The territory of Vietnam is on the eastern part of the Indochinese peninsula, China borders it to the north, Laos and Cambodia to the west, the Eastern Sea to the east and the Pacific Ocean to the east and south. Vietnam is a strip of land shaped like the letter "S", extending from latitude 23º23 'North to 8º27' North, the distance from north to south (along the flight path) is 1,650 km and the narrowest position to the east to west is 50 km, the widest part on the mainland is about 600 km long. Vietnam has three sides East, South and West-South over looking the sea with a coastline longer than 3,260 km, from Mong Cai in the North to Ha Tien in the Southwest. The sovereignty of the Vietnam in East Sea has expanded to east and southeast, with continental shelf having many islands and islands such as Hoang Sa, Truong Sa, Ha Long Bay, Bai Tu Long (Quang Ninh province); Cat Hai, Cat Ba, Bach Long Vi (Hai Phong city), Con Son, Phu Quoc and Tho Chu... In addition to the internal waters, Vietnam has 12 nautical miles, and additional 12 regional nautical miles of contiguous territorial sea, 200 nautical miles of exclusive economic zone and continental shelf. The sea area under sovereignty, sovereignty rights and jurisdiction of Vietnam is about 1,000,000 km^2 in East Sea[1]. Vietnam's coasts are attractive tourist destinations, especially Ha Long Bay in Quang Ninh province – the world natural heritage. In the sea and continental shelf of Vietnam, there are many precious resources. Vietnam has long affirmed sovereignty over the East Sea, Truong Sa Islands, the Hoang Sa Islands and many other islands on the sea. Due to its geostrategic location in the region, Vietnam is an important gateway connecting ASEAN countries and the world, linking the Indian Ocean and the Pacific Ocean. This is an extremely favourable condition to develop marine economic sectors, especially maritime trade to transport goods to many countries of the Greater Mekong Sub region (GMS) and the world.

Vietnam has a diverse terrain including mountains, hills, plain, coast and continental shelf. The area of hills and mountains accounts for three-quarters of the total area, but are mostly low hills[2] and form a large bow facing the East Sea with a length of about 1,400 km. Vietnam is famous for Phanxipang peak as the roof of Indochina with an altitude of 3,143 m and Tay Nguyen plateau, Truong Son mountain range. The area of plain occupies only 1/4 of the land area and is separated by mountains and hills into many areas. At both ends of the country there are two large, fertile deltas like the Northern Delta (Red River basin, 16,700 km^2 wide) and the Southern Delta (Mekong River basin or Cuu Long basin,

40,000 km^2 wide). In addition, Vietnam also has a narrow, small delta along the middle coast, from plains in the Ma river basin (Thanh Hoa) to Phan Thiet with a total area of 15,000 sq. km.

Vietnam is located in the tropical monsoon climate with air humidity of about 80 per cent, even over 90 per cent in the rainy season. The average temperature in Vietnam ranges from 21ºC to 27ºC and gradually increases from North to South. In summer, the average temperature across the country is 25ºC. Vietnam has a huge amount of solar radiation with the number of sunny hours from 1,400-3,000 hours/year. The average annual rainfall ranges from 1,500-2,000 mm[3]. Climate of Vietnam is not homogeneous throughout the territory but varies by seasons and areas from low to high, from North to South, from East to West. But it can be basically divided into two major climates: the North (from Hai Van pass out) is a tropical monsoon climate with 4 distinct seasons (spring, summer, autumn, winter); the South (from Hai Van pass onward) is due to less influence of the monsoon, the tropical climate is quite harmonious and hot all year and divided into two distinct seasons (dry and rainy seasons). In addition, Vietnam has sub-climate regions such as temperate climate in Sa Pa (Lao Cai), Da Lat (Lam Dong); continental climate in Lai Chau and Son La.

Vietnam has an interlacing network of rivers (about 2,360 rivers long over 10 km), flowing in two main directions: Northwest-Southeast and arc and over 3,000 km of canals. In particular, the two largest and longest rivers are the Red River (1,149 km, 510 km flowing into the territory of Vietnam) and the Mekong River (4,220 km, 220 km flowing into Vietnam territory), creating two large and fertile deltas. This is a favourable condition to promote Vietnam's agricultural economy to develop valuable products that dominate the world markets.

Vietnamese Society

In the territory of Vietnam, about 3000-4,000 years ago, there were people living and together building villages and ethnic communities. Over thousands of years of history, Vietnam's population has been growing. According to the 2009 national census, Vietnam had 85.85 million people, in 2018 increased to 96 million people. According to the latest figures from the United Nations, as of August 19, 2019, Vietnam's population is 97 million people, accounting for 1.27 per cent of the world's population and ranking 14th in the ranking of population of countries and territories[4]. The young population accounts for more than 50 per cent, which is a main resource in the construction and development of the country. Vietnamese people have a patriotic tradition, national pride, solidarity and heroism, resilience, intelligence and creativity in the struggle for national liberation, productive labour that is recognized in the world through historical periods. Wherever in Vietnam, people are gentle, tolerant, and open-minded with a friendly, warm attitude. Vietnamese has also respect for community that has become a characteristic, so the peoples of the world put trust in long-term cooperation with Vietnam.[5]

Vietnam has 54 ethnic groups, of which Kinh accounts for 86 per cent of the population. Each ethnic group has its own language but the official language of the entire nation is Vietnamese (the national language). Vietnam is a multi-religious and beliefs country. In addition to ancestor worship, in Vietnam there are also major religions of Buddhism, Catholicism, Cao Dai, Hoa Hao, Protestantism, and Islam. As a multi-ethnic nation, so Vietnamese culture is rich, diverse but bold national identity. Vietnam is proud of many intangible cultural heritages recognized by UNESCO as world heritage.

Features of Vietnam: Perspective about Vietnamese People

The Vietnamese people have very unique characteristics what have been deeply embedded in the daily life of Vietnamese people for many years, contributing to the Vietnamese national cultural identity. Some highlights:

- *National Anthem*: The national Anthem of Vietnam is the song "Tiến Quân Ca" by musician Van Cao–a song full of sacred emotions and proud of the heroic and indomitable tradition of the Vietnamese nation. Website: cracked.com of American reported that the National Anthem of Vietnam was ranked first among the most majestic national anthems in the world. This is a website specializing in making interesting statistics in the fields of culture, art, science and technology, society in the world with millions of readers every day.
- *National Flower:* Thanks to the humid monsoon climate and the Vietnamese hard-working people, this beautiful country has become the land of colourful flower fields and diverse species. On September 2, 2011, the Lotus has officially recognized as the National Flower of Vietnam, becoming a symbol of Vietnamese culture because this beautiful flower has the most similar characteristics to the mind and soul of the Vietnamese people.
- *National Costume:* Ao Dai is considered the national costume of the Vietnam. Ao Dai exalts the beauty of Vietnamese women body and is still luxurious, discreet and sophisticated in Eastern culture. During the feudal period, Ao Dai was used for both men and women. Nowadays, Ao Dai is mainly designed for women and has become a symbol of Vietnamese women, and is the cultural image and pride of Vietnamese women in the world.
- *Beliefs of Ancestor Worship:* Vietnam has a tradition of "When drinking water, think of its source", especially the respect for ancestors, parents, teachers and express deep gratitude to people who have contributed to the country, and communities. It is from this noble and fine tradition that the Vietnamese respect and retain ancestor worship. Every year, on the anniversary of the death of a deceased people and on the occasion of Tet holidays, Vietnamese people often prepare offerings to their ancestors to show their respect and gratitude to their ancestors and grandparents. The beliefs of ancestor worship has become an important part of the spiritual life of Vietnamese people.
- *A Multi-religious Country:* Vietnam has about 97 million people of 54

ethnic groups and includes many different religions such as Buddhism, Confucianism, Taoism, Christianity, Protestantism, and Islam. Therefore, in Vietnam, there are many religious infrastructure of Christianity, Buddhism, and Hinduism. Many of them are attractive tourist destinations such as Mariamman Hindu Temple, Notre Dame Cathedral in Ho Chi Minh City, One Pillar Pagoda, Temple of Literature etc.

- *Lunar New Year:* Vietnamese people also celebrate New Year like the Western people, however, the most important TET for them is the Lunar New Year. Lunar New Year also called Tet Ta, or Traditional Tet and Tet is about a month later than New Year. This is the most sacred holiday of Vietnamese people because it is the time of reunion and the day of hope. Tet is also a chance for Vietnamese people to remember their ancestral roots. Vietnamese people have a lot of customs during the Lunar New Year such as going to the temple to pray for peace and good luck, decorating ancestor worship, cooking traditional foods for Tet holidays, giving Tet gifts to relatives, Happy New Year to relatives, teachers, friends, giving lucky money for the elderly and children etc.
- *Vietnamese Cuisine:* Vietnam has a rich cuisine in the number of types, diverse in flavors and layout captivating the people. From delicacies to street food, there is always incredible appeal to the locals as well as the most discerning tourists visiting to Vietnam. Vietnamese dishes are typical of each regions and are delicately cooked with many flavors, such as salty, sweet, sour, spicy... associated with tropical agricultural produce. Vietnamese foods are nutritious with unique flavor and colour, different from Europe and China. Some Vietnamese famous dishes in over the world are Pho, Bun cha, spring rolls, Hue pancakes, Lam rice, Quang noodle, Cao Lau Hoi An etc. of which Pho has been repeatedly mentioned by CNN, BBC, Business Insider etc. voted in the top best food in Asia. In 2016, World Record Union-Wordkings has announced "Pho" is one of three Vietnamese dishes in the top 100 world famous delicacies.
- *Vietnam's Traditional Festivals:* Vietnam is a country of traditional festivals with over 8,000 festivals held in a year (According to statistics of the Committee for Ethnic Minorities). Festivals in Vietnam usually take place after the traditional Lunar New Year and across the country. Through the festivals, Vietnamese cultural identity is clearly shown, contributing to promotion of honouring the historical tradition, the strong mind, pride, and self-respect of the nation. Some typical festivals include: Hung King Temple Festival on the anniversary of the death of Hung Kings (The Hung Kings who had merit of building Van Lang state in the past, now is Vietnam). Saint Giong Festival–One of the four "immortals" of Vietnamese Nation–the Saint has merit in chasing the An invaders (from China) to save the country; Song Festival of the Tay people; Ban flower Festival, Flower Festival of Thai ethnic people, New Rice Festival of ethnic minorities in the Central Highlands, Hue Festival, Mid-Autumn Festival, Lim Festival, etc.

Vietnam: The Country of World Heritages

Along with the national culture, Vietnam is also famous for hundreds of heritage sites, including more than 20 world heritage sites honoured by UNESCO, such as world natural heritages, world cultural heritages, mixed cultural and natural heritage and intangible heritage, documentary heritage etc.

World's natural heritages

Nature has endowed Vietnam with many wonderful landscapes, including two world natural heritages as Ha Long Bay was recognized as a World Natural and World Geological Heritage in 1994 and 2000, and Phong Nha-Ke Bang National Park was recognized in 2003 and 2015.

Ha Long Bay is famous at home and abroad for its marvelous beauty. It forms a spectacular seascape of limestone pillars and is an ideal model of a mature Karst landscape developed during a warm and wet tropical climate. Ha Long Bay was voted as one of the seven natural wonders of the new world on November 11,2011 and is always on the list of the most beautiful bays in the world today.

Phong Nha-Ke Bang National Park (in Quang Binh province) is a cave kingdom in the world, in which, Son Doong cave is considered one of the most beautiful and largest caves in the world. Vietnam is also the most attractive tourist destination in the region and in the world with splendid beaches like Nha Trang–one of the most beautiful beaches in the world; Danang beach–one of the six most attractive bathing beaches on the planet.

In addition, Vietnam also has terraced rice fields in the Northwest region that stretches as far as the eye can see, and countless other beautiful landscapes and historical sites stretching from the North to the South of the country. Nature of Vietnam is like a sparkling gem with endless beauty.

World tangible cultural heritage

By 2018, Vietnam has 5 world tangible cultural heritages. They are: The Complex of Hue Monuments, Hoi An Ancient Town, My Son Sanctuary, Thang Long Imperial Citadel and Ho Dynasty Citadel.

- *Complex of Hue Monuments:* The complex of Hue Monuments is recognized by UNESCO as a World Cultural Heritage on September 11, 1993. These are historical-cultural relics built by the Nguyen Dynasty between the early 19th century and the first half of the 20th century in the ancient capital of Hue, (Thua Thien–Hue province, Vietnam). The massive complex features hundreds of monuments and ruins, such as the Forbidden Purple City, once the residence of the royal family and badly damaged during the Vietnam War, the Imperial City, royal tombs, flag tower, pagodas, temples, a library and museum[6].
- *Hoi An Ancient Town:* Hoi An Ancient Town is recognized by UNESCO as a world cultural heritage at the 23rd session on December 4, 1999. Hoi An

Ancient Town is an exceptionally well-preserved example of South-East Asian trading port dating from the 15th to the 19 century. Its buildings and its street plan reflect the influences, both indigenous and foreign that have combined to produce this unique heritage site. Most of the houses here are traditional architecture dating from the 17th century to the 19th century, the father along the narrow streets. Hoi An is also a land of many imprints of cultural mixing. Chinese guilds and temples are located next to traditional Vietnamese town houses and French architectural houses. With outstanding values, this relic is an attractive destination for domestic and international tourists.

- *My Son Sanctuary:* My Son Sanctuary in Duy Phu Commune, Duy Xuyen District, Quang Nam Province, is a complex of Cham temples in a valley about 2 km in diameter surrounded by hills and mountains. This was once the place of sacrifice as well as the tomb of the Kings of Champa. In 1999, My Son Sanctuary was selected by UNESCO as one of the modern world heritage sites.
- *Imperial Citadel of Thang Long:* Thang Long Imperial Citadel is a relic complex associated with the history of Thang Long-Dong Kinh citadel and Hanoi city starting from the pre-Thang Long period (An Nam dynasty covered in the seventh century) through the period of Dinh-Tien Le, thrived under the Ly, Tran, Le dynasties and Hanoi citadel under the Nguyen dynasty. This is a huge architectural work, built by the kings in many historical periods and has became the most important monument in the system of Vietnamese monuments. On July 31, 2010, UNESCO recognized the Thang Long Imperial Citadel as a world cultural heritage.
- *Citadel of the Ho Dynasty:* Ho Dynasty Citadel (in Thanh Hoa province) is a fortified citadel with a unique large-scale stone architecture rarely found in Vietnam. Ho Dynasty Citadel, built according to the Feng Shui principles, testifies to the flowering of neo-Confucianism in late 14th century Vietnam and its spread to other parts of east Asia. According to these principles it was sited in a landscape of great scenic beauty on an axis joining the Tuong Son and Don Son mountains in a plain between the Ma and Buoi rivers. The citadel buildings represent an outstanding example of a new style of south-east Asian imperial city[7]. On June 27, 2011, after 6 years of submitting the dossier, the Ho Dynasty was recognized by UNESCO as a world cultural heritage.

Trang An Relic Complex

Mixed World Heritage (both natural and cultural heritage): Trang An Relic Complex with its rich flora system, primeval forest and eco-system was recognized by UNESCO as a World Natural and Cultural Heritage on June 23, 2014, at the 38th session of the World Heritage Committee (Doha, Qatar). Now Trang An is a attractive tourist destination with a complex beauty–landscapes called as an "outdoor geological museum" with numerous caves, mountains, valley water, trees and the historic relic. This is the first and only mixed heritage of Vietnam to date.

World Intangible Heritage

Vietnam has hundreds of intangible heritages, of which 12 intangible heritages are UNESCO World Heritage Sites. These are: Space of gong culture, Nha Nhac, Hue royal court music, Quan Họ Bac Ninh folk songs, Ca trù singing, Giong festival of Phu Đong and Soc temples, Worship of Hung kings in Phu Tho, Art of Đon Ca Tai Tu music and songs in southern Vietnam, Vi and Giam folk songs of Nghe Tinh, Tugging rituals and games, practices related to the Viet beliefs in the Mother Goddesses of Three Tealms, Xoan singing of Phu Tho province, The art of Bai Choi in Central Vietnam [8].

Space of gong culture: The fame of Central Highlands gong culture has crossed national borders to become a property of all human beings. Specific values of the cultural space of the Central Highlands gong which is a part of Vietnam's cultural heritage and quintessence has been recognised by the international community. Space of Gongs Culture in the Central Highlands include: Gongs, gong songs, gong players, festivals using gongs (New rice celebration, Ben Nuoc worship ceremony...), venue of festivals (long houses, communal houses, fields, water wharves, tombs, forests next to the Central Highlands villages...). Cultural space of Gongs of the Central Highlands stretches throughout 5 provinces of Kon Tum, Gia Lai, Dak Lak, Dak Nong and Lam Don. On 25th November 2005, the UNESCO decided to recognize "the cultural space of gong in the Central Highlands" of Vietnam as "Masterpieces of the Oral and Intangible Cultural Heritage of Humanity".

Nha nhac-Hue royal court music is a kind of scholarly music of the monarchical dynasties in Vietnamese society for more than 10 centuries. This traditional music kind aims to create the solemnity for the court ceremonies. Nha nhac was born in the Ly dynasty (1010-1225) and settled in the Le dynasty (1427-1788) and actually developed in the Nguyen dynasty (1802-1945) performed on festivals (coronation, death, and other solemn festivals) in the year of the Nguyen Dynasty of Vietnam[9]. Hue royal court music was recognized by UNESCO as a masterpiece of oral and intangible human beings in 2003.

Quan ho Bac Ninh folk songs are one of the popular folk tunes of the Red River Delta region in Northern Vietnam. It was formed in the ancient Kinh Bac area, especially Bac Giang and Bac Ninh provinces. But now, people mention the Bac Ninh mandarin more than in Bac Giang. Quan Ho Bac Ninh Folk Songs, also called Quan Ho Bac Ninh singing, is an antiphonal singing tradition in which men and women take turns singing in a challenge-and-response fashion drawing on a known repertoire of melodies. Quan ho folk songs were recognized as an intangible cultural heritage of the world in 2009.

Ca Tru is a traditional art discipline in Northern Vietnam that combines singing with a number of ethnic instruments. Ca trù has been popular since the 15th century, once a type of court music and loved by nobility and intellectuals. Ca Tru is a fluent and peak combination between poetry and music. On October 1,

2009, at the 4th session of the UNESCO Intergovernmental Committee for the Protection of Intangible Cultural Heritage (from September 28 to October 2, 2009), Ca Tru has recognized as an intangible heritage requiring urgent protection.

The Giong Festival is held annually in Phu Dong Village, Gia Lam District, Hanoi and many other places on the 9th day of the 4th month of the lunar calendar, the date commemorates Saint Giong who defeated the An invaders. In order to show their gratitude to the hero of Giong Village who sacrificed his life to fight invaders, the people proclaimed him Saint Giong. In 2010, Giong Festival in Phu Dong Temple (Gia Lam District) and Soc Temple (Soc Son District) were recognized by UNESCO as an intangible cultural heritage of humanity.

Hung Vuong worship is a long-standing tradition in Vietnam, focusing on Phu Tho. This is a symbol of the sincerity and gratitude for the merits of Hung Kings who have contributed to the creation of Van Lang country. On major Hung Kings festival days, communities make offerings of rice-based delicacies such as square cakes (banh chung) and glutinous cakes (banh giay). People engage in verbal and folk arts and performances including reading of supplication petitions, praying, bronze drum beating and Xoan singing. With unique and distinct values, on 6 December 2012, in Paris (France), UNESCO officially recognized the worship of Hung Kings in Phu Tho Province as Intangible Cultural Heritage of Humanity. This is the first belief in Vietnam recognized as world heritage[10].

Art of Đon Ca Tai Tu music and song in southern Vietnam: A musical art with both scholarly and folk roots, it is an indispensable part of the spiritual activity and cultural heritage of the people of southern Vietnam. The music and songs evoke the people's life and work on the land and rivers of the Mekong Delta region. Art of Đon Ca Tai Tu is associated with five types of instruments: the dan tranh (16-chord zither), the cretan, the pianist, the stork, and the tam, with the addition of the flute usually the seven-hole flute. Performed at numerous events such as festivals, death anniversary rituals and celebrations, Art of Đon Ca Tai Tu music and song in southern Vietnam is thus intimately connected with other cultural practices and customs, oral traditions and handicrafts. Art of Đon Ca Tai Tu music and song in southern Vietnam was recognized by UNESCO as an intangible cultural heritage in 2013.

Vi and Giam folk songs of Nghe An – Ha Tinh are a type of folk performance art that plays an important role in the cultural life of people in Nghe An and Ha Tinh province and is recognized by UNESCO as an intangible cultural heritage in 2014. Vi and Giam folk songs of Nghe An – Ha Tinh are often associated with the moralities of life such as filiality to the mother and father, faithful fidelity, or good human characteristics such as honest..., that is very high value and educational.

Tugging rituals and games of Vietnam, Cambodia, the Philippines and the Republic of Korea were added to the UNESCO's Representative List of the Intangible Cultural Heritage of Humanity on December 2. Tugging rituals and games are prevalent in the rice-farming cultures of East Asia and Southeast Asia as a form for communities to pray for abundant harvests and prosperity. Typically held near a communal house or shrine, two teams on either end of a rope try to tug it from the other. In Vietnam, tug-of-war is a folk game that is practiced in a number of traditional festivals and community events. Tugging rituals and games is the 10th UNESCO-recognised Intangible Cultural Heritage of Humanity of Vietnam.

Practices related to the Viet beliefs in the Mother Goddesses of Three Realms (Tam phu) was recognized by UNESCO as a World Intangible Cultural Heritage in 2016. Practices related to the Viet beliefs in the Mother Goddesses of Three Realms is a mixture of indigenous religion of Vietnamese people and some elements of imported religions such as Taoism, Buddhism. the Mother Goddesses of Three Realms originated not only from the Kinh people, but also from ethnic minorities in Vietnam such as the Muong, Tay, Nung, Dao... That shows the cultural exchange, equal relationship and close ties among ethnic groups in Vietnam.

The art of Bai Choi in Central Vietnam was registered by UNESCO in the List of representative intangible cultural heritage of humanity in 2017. This is an important cultural activity in the village community, meeting the needs of entertainment and enjoy the art of the community. The stories in Bai Choi are moral lessons, demonstrating the love of the homeland and fatherland, the cohesion of the community and the experiences in people's lives.

Xoan Phu Tho singing is also known as Khuc Mon Dinh (singing at the communal house in the village), is a way of worshiping the god, which is said to have been dated from the Hung kings. In the olden days, Van Lang people organized Xoan singing in the springs to welcome the Lunar New Year. In 2017, Xoan singing was recognized by UNESCO as an intangible cultural heritage of humanity.

World Document Heritage

Vietnam is also recognized by UNESCO 4 World Document Heritage Sites. These are: Woodblocks of the Nguyen Dynasty, Doctoral steles at the Quoc Tu Giam Temple of Literature, woodblocks of Buddhist woodblocks of Vinh Nghiem pagoda and Chau dynasty of Nguyen dynasties. These are very valuable materials.

- *Woodblocks of the Nguyen Dynasty* are the first world heritage document in Vietnam recognized by UNESCO on July 31, 2009. It consisted of 34,618 plates of wood-blocks of the Nguyen Dynasty helped to record official literature and history as well as classic and historical books. Therefore, apart from their historical value, the wood-blocks also have artistic and technical merit as they mark the development of wood-block carving and printing profession in Vietnam. Their importance and high value led feudal dynasties and state regimes in history of Vietnam to pay considerable attention to preserving these records[11].
- *Doctoral steles at the Quoc Tu Giam Temple of Literature*: The 82 stone steles are carved with the names of 2,313 doctors who passed the court

examinations between 1442 and 1779 (some material recorded the period between 1484 and 1514) under the Early Le, Mac and Late Le dynasties. In July 2011, UNESCO recognized the 82 doctoral steles at the temple as a world documentary heritage. These steles were engraved with the names of over 2,000 doctors passing the royal examinations between 1442 and 1779.
- *Buddhist woodblocks of Vinh Nghiem Pagoda* in Bac Giang province has been officially recognized as a World Documentary Heritage by UNESCO. The valuable woodblocks have been made in the 13th, 14th, 15th, and 17th centuries, provides a wealth of information on the foundation, development and ideology of Truc Lam Zen Buddhism, founded by King Tran Nhan Tong in the 11th century.
- The Nguyen Dynasty's Chau Ban were documents of the royal court that the king signed in red ink. The Nguyen Dynasty's Chau Ban were administrative documents formed during the state management of the Nguyen Dynasty (1802-1945), the last dynasty in the feudal history of Vietnam. It includes documents of agencies in the central and local government apparatus submitted to the king for approval, documents issued by the kings and a number of diplomatic documents and poems of domination. The Nguyễn Dynasty Chau Ban was recognized by UNESCO as a world heritage site in 2014.

In short, Vietnam is located in an important geopolitical position, where is the gateway of Southeast Asia. In addition, Vietnam has many natural and social conditions that are favourable for comprehensive economic development and diversified and unique culture with many world heritage sites. Therefore, Vietnam has become an attractive and ideal destination for many investors in the world and global tourists. Besides, with its special important strategic position and increasing political status, Vietnam is contributing to the construction of a security, economy structure and political stability in the area.

Notes

1. http://www.gov.vn/portal/page/portal/chinhphu/NuocCHXHCNVietNam/Thong TinTongHop/dialy, accessed 7/12/2010
2. The terrain is less than 1,000 m accounting for 85 per cent, the high mountains over 2,000 m only account for 1 per cent of the territory
3. Led by the Open Encyclopedia: Climate of Vietnam, https://vi.wikipedia.org/wiki/Khí_hậu_Việt_Nam.
4. Led by https://danso.org/viet-nam/
5. Led by Vietnhathr.com.vn: *Introduction about Vietnam* http://vietnhathr.com.vn/gioi-thieu-ve-viet-nam.htm, accessed 3-8-2018.
6. http://www.vietnam-guide.com/hue/complex-of-hue-monuments.htm
7. https://whc.unesco.org/en/list/1358
8. https://ich.unesco.org/en/state/viet-nam-VN?info=elements-on-the-lists
9. http://www.vietnam-beauty.com/vietnam-world-heritages/oral-and-intangible-cultural-heritage-of-humanity/10-oral-and-intangible-cultural-heritage-of-humanity/12-royal-refined-music-of-hue.html

10. https://discoveryindochina.com/traveltip/worship-hung-vuong-phu-tho/
11. http://www.unesco.org/new/en/communication-and-information/memory-of-the-world/register/full-list-of-registered-heritage/registered-heritage-page-9/woodblocks-of-nguyen-dynasty/

References

TÀI LIỆU THAM KHẢO

1. Bách khoa toàn thư mở: *Khí hậu Việt Nam,* https://vi.wikipedia.org/wiki/Khí_hậu_Việt_Nam.
   (Open encyclopedia: Climate of Vietnam, https://vi.wikipedia.org/wiki/Khí_hậu_Việt_Nam).
2. Bách khoa toàn thư mở: *Lịch sử Việt Nam,* https://vi.wikipedia.org/wiki/Lịch_sử_Việt_Nam.
   (Open encyclopedia: History of Vietnam, https://vi.wikipedia.org/wiki/Lịch_sử_Việt_Nam).
3. Báo mới.com: *11 di sản văn hóa phi vật thể của Việt Nam được UNESCO vinh danh,* https://baomoi.com/11-di-san-van-hoa-phi-vat-the-cua-viet-nam-duoc-unesco-vinh-danh/c/20985084.epi, ngày truy cập 3-12-2016.
   (New newspaper.com: 11 intangible cultural heritage of Vietnam honoured by UNESCO, https://baomoi.com/ 11-di-san-van-hoa-phi-vat-the-cua-viet-nam-duoc-unesco-vinh-danh/c/20985084.epi, accessed on December 3, 2016.)
4. Cổng thông tin điện tử chính phủ nước Cộng hòa Xã hội Chủ nghĩa Việt Nam: Một số thông tin về địa lý Việt Nam, ngày truy cập 07-12-2010.
   (Website of Government of the Socialist Republic of Vietnam: Some information on Vietnam's geography, accessed 07-12-2010).
5. Hà Nội mới: *Tuổi thọ trung bình của người Việt Nam đạt 73,5 tuổi,* https://hanoimoi.com.vn/tin-tuc/Doi-song/924973/tuoi-tho-trung-binh-cua-nguoi-viet-nam-dat-735-tuoi, ngày truy cập 22-1-2019.
   (New Hanoi: The average life expectancy of Vietnamese people is 73.5 years, https://hanoimoi.com.vn/tin-tuc/Doi-song/924973/tuoi-tho-trung-binh-cua-nguoi-viet-nam-dat-735-tuoi, accessed on January 22, 2019).
6. Ngô Sĩ Liên và các sử thần triều Lê (1967-1968): *Đại Việt sử ký toàn thư (4 tập),* Nxb. Khoa học Xã hội, Hà Nội.
   (Ngo Si Liên and other courtiers in the Le dynasty (1967-1968): Dai Viet whole history (4 volumes), Social Science Publishing House, Hanoi).
7. Nghiên cứu quốc tế: *Tại sao VIệt Nam không bị đồng hóa sau 1.000 năm Bắc thuộc,* http://nghiencuuquocte.org/2015/09/07/viet-nam-khong-bi-dong-hoa-1000-nam-bac-thuoc/, ngày truy cập 7-9-2015.
   (International research: Why Vietnam is not assimilated after 1,000 years of colonization, http://nghiencuuquocte.org/2015/09/07/viet-nam-khong-bi-dong-hoa-1000-nam-bac-thuoc/, accessed on September 7, 2015).
8. Nhóm Ngân hàng thế giới, Bộ Kế hoạch và Đầu tư (2016), *Báo cáo tổng quan: Việt Nam 2035 hướng tới thịnh vượng, sáng tạo, công bằng và dân chủ,* Những thông điệp chính, Nxb. Hồng Đức.
   (World Bank Group, Ministry of Planning and Investment (2016), Overview Report: Vietnam 2035 towards prosperity, creativity, equity and democracy, Key messages, Hong Đuc Publishing House).
9. Phật giáo: Ý nghĩa hoa Sen và bí mật của Quốc hoa Việt Nam,

https://phatgiao.org.vn/y-nghia-hoa-sen-va-bi-mat-cua-quoc-hoa-viet-nam-d31036.html, ngày truy cập 5-6-2018.
(Buddhism: The meaning of the Lotus and the secret of the National Flower of Vietnam, https://phatgiao.org.vn/y-nghia-hoa-sen-va-bi-mat-cua-quoc-hoa-viet-nam-d31036.html, accessed June 5, 2018).

10. Tin tức: *Độc đáo 12 di sản văn hóa phi vật thể của Việt Nam*, https://baotintuc.vn/infographics/doc-dao-12-di-san-van-hoa-phi-vat-the-cua-viet-nam-20190227102213076.htm, ngày truy cập 27-2-2019.
(News: Unique 12 intangible cultural heritage of Vietnam, https://baotintuc.vn/infographics/doc-dao-12-di-san-van-hoa-phi-vat-the-cua-viet-nam-20190227102213076.htm, ngày truy cập 27-2-2019).
11. United Nations: *Vài nét về Việt Nam,* http://un.org.vn/index.php?option=com_content&view=article&id=19& Itemid=217&lang=vi
(United Nations: Overview of Vietnam, http://un.org.vn/index.php?option=com_content&view=article&id= 19&Itemid=217&lang=vi)
12. *Giới thiệu về Việt Nam,* http://vietnhathr.com.vn/gioi-thieu-ve-viet-nam.htm, ngày truy cập 3-8-2019.
(About Vietnam, http://vietnhathr.com.vn/gioi-thieu-ve-viet-nam.htm, accessed August 3, 2018).

3 Vietnamese History: A Background

Trong-Hung Vu

Vietnamese history from the beginning to 1858

The history of Vietnam has been tens of thousands of years, since the time of human existence, and taking cognizance of witten human history, it has only been around since 2879 BC. Around the seventh century BC appeared the first state of Vietnamese people in place located in northern Vietnam today. The historical remnants can be found in the Van Lang State of Hung kings, which is located in Phong Chau district, Phu Tho province. In the third century BC, Thuc Phan usurped the 18th Hung King throne and founded Au Lac state. In 179 BC, Trieu Da (an old general of the Qin-China Dynasty) captured Au Lac and merged Nam Viet. In 111 BC, Han Vu De's army invaded and annexed Nam Viet to the Han Empire. After that, Chinese feudal dynasties (Zhao, Han, Dong Han, Dong Ngo, Tao, Wei, Tan, Qi, Luong, Sui, and Tang) took turns to dominate Vietnam for over 1,000 years (179 BC-938 AD)[1].

Under the domination of Chinese feudalism, the Vietnamese people struggled and won many victories. Notably the Trung Sisters' Uprising against northern invaders in 40 AD established Linh Nam state, which was built in Me Linh, Hanoi (40-43 AD). In 541 AD, Ly Bi defeated the Luong Dynasty, claiming to be Ly Nam De, and founded the Kingdom of Van Xuan (544-602 AD). In 905, Khuc Thua Du rebelled, proclaimed himself the king, fought for the independence of Vietnamese people, and laid the foundation for Vietnam's independence. In particular, in 938 AD, Ngo Quyen defeated the Tang army and proclaimed himself king, ending more than 1,000 years of Northern domination. Along with the struggle to restore national independence, Vietnam has succeeded in fighting China's policy of national assimilation. China was defeated in assimilating Vietnamese people because the Vietnamese still retained the foundation of their inherent national culture after a thousand years of domination[2]; including preserving identity of their race, language and customs[3]. This is one of the most proud achievements of the Vietnamese, which is an important basis for the Vietnamese people to rewrite the majestic history of the fatherland.

From 938 AD, Vietnam carried out the construction of an independent and autonomous country under the Ngo dynasty (938-965), Dinh (968-980 AD)[4], Tien Le (980-1009 AD), Ly (1009-1225 AD), Tran (1225-1400 AD), Ho (1400-1407 AD)[5], Le So (1428-1527 AD), Mac (1527-1592 AD), Hau Le (Le Trung Hung 1533-1778 AD), Tay Son (1778-1802 AD), Nguyen during independence and autonomy (1802-1883 AD)[6], Nguyen depending on French (1884-1945 AD).

During the independent feudal period (X-XX), Vietnamese feudal dynasties led people to develop economy, culture and society and gained many important achievements, affirming position of Dai Viet state to other regional countries. Besides, Vietnamese people had repeatedly resisted the invasion of Chinese feudal dynasties from the Song, Ming and Mong Nguyen dynasties to the Manchu. Typically, Le Hoan defeated the Song Dynasty in 981 to establish Tien Le Dynasty; King Ly and the people defeated the aggression of Tong invaders in 1076. The Tran dynasty and Dai Viet people united to defeat Mongols army in 1258. Following years Nguyen Dynasty was established in 1285 and 1288 AD. Le Loi defeated the Ming invaders in the early fifteenth century (in 1428), and founded the Hau Le Dynasty. The Tay Son defeated 50,000 Siamese soldiers (in 1784 AD) in the South and 29,000 Manchu troops (in 1789) invaded in the North.

During the period of building an autonomous and independent feudal nation, together with affirming the sovereignty of the national border on the mainland, Vietnamese Kings have taken many wise measures to affirm and protect sovereignty for Hoang Sa and Truong Sa archipelagoes. Specifically, Le Thanh Tong King affirmed the sovereignty over Hoang Sa (Paracel islands) and Truong Sa (Spratly islands) through the historical maps. According to *"Dai Viet history"* book, since 1467 AD, King Le Thanh Tong gave the map of Dai Viet territory. *"The Hong Duc"* Map was completed at the end of 1469 and was added many times later, including the archipelagos of Hoang Sa and Truong Sa[7]. The presence Hoang Sa and Truong Sa archipelagos in Hong Duc Map shows that the two archipelagos were under the sovereignty of Dai Viet, and the Hau Le Dynasty was very interested in establishing the national border, affirming territorial sovereignty including the adjoining sea and islands.

During the time of Nguyen regime, Hoang Sa (Paracel islands) and Truong Sa (Spratly islands) were controlled by the "Hoang Sa" and "Bac Hai" teams. This is affirmed in the ancient bibliography of Vietnam, such as Phu Bien Tap Luc (written in 1776), Dai Nam Thuc Luc Tien Bien (in 1821), Thien Nam Tu Chi and Lo Do Thu Thu (in 1686). In Phu Bien Tap Luc, the scholar Le Quy Don made it clear: "the Nguyen Dynasty put the Hoang Sa team at 70 capacity, took the people of An Vinh commune to supplement, harvest the seasonal crops each year in March, to receive the administrative documents, and bring enough food to last six months. They used to go by five small fishing boats, travelling through the sea for three days and three nights to reach the islands". This is an important historical document affirming that the "Hoang Sa" and "Bac Hai" teams were assigned and implemented the Vietnamese sovereignty over the two archipelagos of Hoang Sa and Truong Sa from the second half of the seventeenth century.

Following the Nguyen regime is the Tay Son era. After four years of the uprising (1771), the Tay Son government restored the sovereignty over Hoang Sa (Paracel islands) to exploit abundant resources and controlled the Hoang Sa (Paracel islands) and Truong Sa (Spratly islands) archipelagoes. The Tay Son Dynasty also strengthened its power to exercise sovereignty by building large, powerful fire ships with the most advanced techniques of its time. In the book of Sacred Scripture (Thanh vu Ky), Wei Yuan (Ngụy Nguyên) (1794-1857) described, 'The Tay Son's boats were taller, bigger than the Qing ones, putting many guns, raging on the surface of the sea and it was difficult for the Qing troops to deal with Tay Son's boats'. This is a proof to confirm that the Tay Son naval forces had in fact controlled the maritime routes and were the owners of the islands in the East Sea, including the Hoang Sa (Paracel islands) and Truong Sa (Spratly islands) archipelagos.

By the end of Nguyen Dynasty, shortly after the emperor's reign, Gia Long King immediately re-established the Hoang Sa expedition. Under Gia Long's time, Hoang Sa sailors took over the task of reviewing and measuring the sea, mapping the Hoang Sa archipelago, spying, and guarding the sea, reporting about the pirates. In 1816, Gia Long king allowed the Vietnamese sailors to go to the island, raise the flag on the island and measure the adjoining sea-lanes. This is an important milestone on the re-establishment and enforcement of Vietnam's sovereignty over the islands. By the time of King Minh Mang, Vietnam became a prosperous country, which earned the respect of all neighbouring countries. Western countries also increased interactions with the regime. With that power and position, Minh Mang allowed his naval forces to continue to manage and affirm their sovereignty clearly on the islands, especially in the Paracel Islands (common names and previously popular about 2 archipelagoes Hoang Sa and Truong Sa). In particular, besides exploiting, patrolling on the sea, King Minh Mang also built a place of worship (pagoda, temple), planted trees, built masters (monks) houses and sovereignty in some islands in the years 1833, 1835 and 1836, at times, carrying out the rescue service, helping boats in distress in Vietnamese waters. Thus, King Minh Mang not only inherited but also developed the maritime strategy of previous dynasties to a new height, affirming Vietnam's sovereignty in the archipelagos of Hoang Sa (Paracel islands), Truong Sa (Spratly islands) and adjoining islands in the sea.

One of the major contributors to the military history of Vietnam was the person named Hung Dao Vuong Tran Quoc Tuan (1228-1300 AD). He was a famous politician and Supreme Commander of Vietnam during the Tran Dynasty. He was one of the main commanders in repelling three Mongol invasions and later the Mongol army–the world's most brutal army in the 13th century. This victory against the mighty power of the Mongols was one of the greatest victories in the history of the world. Therefore, he was listed as a great man and one of the most outstanding military men in human history. The British Royal family gave him the title of *"Man who defeated the Mongolian empire"*. In addition to military talents, Tran Hung Dao also left behind great thoughts, especially the thought of the people as the support base.

It is particularly interesting that Vietnam's military and defense power is not only in guns, swords, spears but also the strength of the people's support. Vietnamese people also affirmed the noble human spirit, always aspired for peace and conducted war in such a way to minimize damage to both sides during the war. In one of the instances when the Mong-Nguyen enemy lost the battle, the Tran court was ready to supply food to let the Nguyen Mong army retreat to China, quickly ending the war, avoiding much damage to both sides.

This is a rare and valuable thing in the world because Vietnamese people have repelled against foreign invaders but they were ready to create favourable conditions for the enemy troops to quickly withdraw, and make a harmonious atmosphere between the two nations. This has moved even the aggressive regimes wishing to wage war against Vietnam but at the same time, it affirmed the spirit of peace that it wants to live in harmony of the Vietnamese people with other countries. This has become a tradition of the Vietnamese people and recognized by international community.

Vietnam in the period of struggle for independence (1858-1945) and the war of resistance against French colonialism and American imperialism (1945-1975)

Vietnam during the period of struggle for independence (1858-1945)

Vietnam is located in a strategic position in Southeast Asia with rich natural resources, so it is easy to become the target for big powers to invade. In 1858, the French colonialists invaded Vietnam. The Nguyen Dynasty has gradually surrendered to the French colonialists. On June 6, 1884, the Nguyen Dynasty signed the Patenôtre Treaty to completely offer Vietnam to the French colonialists. By 1887, the French colonialists completed the process of colonising Vietnam.

Under the brutal and harsh domination of the French colonialists, the Vietnamese people's life was extremely miserable; the conflict between the Vietnamese people and the French colonialists (and Japanese Fascists since 1940) became increasingly harsh, so the struggle movements of Vietnamese broke out strongly. For instance, the patriotic movement aimed at restoring the feudal regime like the Can Vuong Movement (1885-1896) led by Ham Nghi King and Ton That Thuyet; Yen, the peasant uprising led by Hoang Hoa Tham (1884-1913). Patriotic movements according to the bourgeois democracy ideology led by Phan Boi Chau, Phan Chau Trinh; Dong Kinh Nghia Thuc movement and Yen Bai's uprising led by Vietnam Nationalist Party (2-1930). All of these movements failed[8] to show that the tendency to save feudalism and bourgeois democracy did not meet the objective of the national liberation. Meanwhile, the revolutionary movements of proletarian were strongly developing that led to the creation of communist organizations, such as the Indochinese Communist Party, An Nam Communist Party and Indochinese Communist federation. On that basis, "as an envoy of the Communist International who had full of right to decide all matters related to the revolutionary movement in Indochina", Nguyen Ai Quoc - Ho Chi Minh made a move from Siam (later called Thailand) to Hong Kong to convene and preside over the Conference on Consolidation of Communist Organizations into the Communist Party of Vietnam (CPV) in early 1930. The Communist Party of Vietnam was born out of the Vietnamese revolution. It is the first indispensable preparation to make a decisive decision for the development of the Vietnamese revolution.

Under the leadership of the Communist Party of Vietnam, after 15 years of arduous struggle (1930-1945), the Vietnamese revolution achieved one victory after another and the success of the August Revolution of 1945. On September 2, 1945, President Ho Chi Minh read the Declaration of Independence giving birth to the Democratic Republic of Vietnam at Ba Dinh square. The Declaration of Independence is a historical document with profound practical and theoretical value as well as an eloquent manifestation of indomitable spirit and vigor of the Vietnamese people, at the same time it contributed to enriching the thought of human rights of the world's peoples. It is the right to live in an independent country.

With the victory of the August Revolution of 1945, Vietnam became an independent country from a colonial one; Vietnamese people stood up to rescue their country from slavery. The Communist Party of Vietnam became a ruling Party; the name of "Vietnam" have been restored on the world political map. From here, the Vietnam's people entered a new era - the era of national independence associated with socialism. For the world, the victory of the August Revolution of 1945 encouraged and promoted the national liberation movements to develop and contributed end of the old-style colonialism around the world.

Vietnam's war of resistance against French colonialists (1945-1954)

After the win of the August Revolution of 1945, Vietnam faced serious challenges. The infrastructure was devastated; the economy was stagnated, thousands of hectares of fields were abandoned, most production facilities were stagnant, thousands of workers had no jobs, hunger and poverty increased. Besides, more than 90 per cent of the Vietnam's population being illiterate, social evils and backwardness of the earlier regimes were really burdensome for newly established revolutionary government. The strength of the armed forces to protect the revolutionary government were still small and they lacked experience of commanding and the use of weapons. Meanwhile, reactionary forces boosted activities against Vietnam revolution. Dozens of political parties had been appearing, such as "Nam Ky Party" led by Nguyen Tan Cuong, "Autonomous Indochina Party" led by Nguyen Van Ty, Dai Viet revolutionary Party and Vietnam Nationalist Party. According to the agreement at the Potsdam Conference of the countries that won the World War II, Allied troops entered Vietnam to disarm Japanese troops in the country. (Accordingly, the North (from the 16th parallel upward) was handed to Jiang Jieshi troops and the South (from 16th parallel southwards) to British troops.

On September 23, 1945, the French were supported by British forces to take over Saigon, then they attacked the provinces in the South and the South Central Coast, opening the war to invade Vietnam for the second time. In order to avoid confronting many enemies at the same time, President Ho Chi Minh on behalf of the Party and the Government implemented a strategy of making concession with Tuong Gioi Thach army in the North to concentrate on fighting the French in the South. But the French imperialists signed with Tuong Gioi

Thach, the China-France Treaty on February 28, 1946. Accordingly, Tuong Gioi Thach agreed to let France return to invade Vietnam and Indochina. As a result, President Ho Chi Minh on behalf of the Government of the Democratic Republic of Vietnam (DRV) signed the "Preliminary Agreement" with the French colonialists on March 6, 1946. According to this agreement, Vietnam entered an agreement with French to give 15,000 French troops to replace 20 thousand Tuong Gioi Thach's army, however French colonialists in return had to recognize Vietnam as a independent nation with its own parliament, government, army and finance in the Indochina Federation and within the French union.

Despite signing the Preliminary Agreement (March 6, 1946) with Vietnam, the French still intensified the activities against Vietnamese revolution by armed intervention. Therefore, in order to take advantage of the subsequent period to prepare for the long-term resistance, on behalf of the Government, President Ho Chi Minh agreed to sign the Vietnam - France Modus Vivendi on September 14, 1946. This showed Vietnam's peaceful gesture.

With a covert plot to invade Vietnam once again, the French intensified provocation and started encroachment. On November 20, 1946, the French army attacked provinces of Hai Phong, Lang Son and landed on Da Nang city. On 16, 17, and 18th December 1946, in Hanoi, the French forces massacred people at Hang Bun, and Yen Ninh streets. At the same time, French forces robbed weapons of Hanoi self-defense forces, demanded complete administrative control in the capital and sent an ultimatum to the Vietnamese revolutionary forces to surrender to French forces. Faced with blatant warfare actions caused by the French colonialists, the Vietnamese people forced to fight because if Vietnam had continued to make concessions, they would lose fatherland and Vietnamese people would return to slavery. In order to lead the struggle against the French colonialists, the Party set out the line of resistance as: *"All people, comprehensive, long-term, relying on our own strength"*[9].

Under the leadership of the Vietnamese Communist Party and President Ho Chi Minh, Vietnam's resistance war against the French colonialists was won like the Viet Bac Campaign in Autumn, 1947, the campaign of Border in 1950, and Hoa Binh 1951-1952, the winter-spring war of 1953-1954. Especially the victory of the Dien Bien Phu campaign in 1954. Due to consecutive and heavy defeats on the fronts, the French colonialists were forced to sign the Geneva Agreement on July 21, 1954 on the end of the war and the restoration of peace in Vietnam and Indochina. Accordingly, the North of Vietnam was completely liberated and this facilitated a legal basis for liberation of the South and the subsequent reunification of the Vietnam. The above successes showed that Communist Party of Vietnam gradually completed the right and creative way of resistance and national construction in accordance with the country's aspirations and conditions. At the same time, the Party also affirmed determination to protect independence, freedom and liberation of the nation before France–a great power of the world with the help of the America.

Vietnam's resistance war against America Imperialism to save country and unify the Fatherland (1954-1975)

America Imperialists wanted to turn the South of Vietnam into a military base of a new colonial master, formed a "dike"(wall) to prevent communism from falling into Southeast Asia, at the same time started march to the North and break the national liberation movements. So, as soon as the Geneva Agreement was signed (July 20-21, 1954), the US imperialists set up the puppet government of Ngo Dinh Diem and used the brutal weapons to terrorize Vietnamese people in the South. The provisions of the Geneva Agreement were not implemented. This led to Vietnam getting divided into the North and the South, and the southern revolution was crushed.

The Vietnamese people wanted to solve all of problems by peaceful methods according to the humanitarian principles. However, facing the thought of American imperialists, Vietnam once again had to fight the enemy. In this context, for the first time, the Communist Party of Vietnam led simultaneously two different strategic missions that were the Socialist revolution in the North and the Peoples democratic revolution in the South, towards unification of the country. In particular, the socialist revolution in the North has garnered large popular support, playing the most decisive role for the victory of the the peoples democratic revolution in the South. The southern people's democratic revolution was a big initiative, making direct decision to for liberation of the Southern part and resultant unification of country. The core content of the direction and thought of the resistance is *"All people, comprehensive, long-term, relying on our own strength and enlisting the supports of international friends".*

Under the leadership of the Party and President Ho Chi Minh, Vietnamese people in the North successfully carried out the task of building Socialism and defeated two invasion wars by Air Force and Navy of American imperialists. As a result, the achievements of the August revolution of 1945 and the Resistance War against French colonialists (1945-1954) were firmly protected. The Southern people also defeated strategies of American imperialists, such as the "Special War" strategy (1961-1965), the "Local War" strategy (1965-1968)," Vietnamization of The Vietnam War" strategy (1969-1975). The resistance war of Vietnam against the American Empire, rescuing the country, unifying Vietnam successfully with the Great Spring Victory of 1975. Then, Vietnam entered the new period of building socialism across the country.

Vietnamese people proved the highest level of patriotism, solidarity, heroism, resilience and the right way of resistance through resistance war against American Empire, especially the clever and wise leadership of the Party, President Ho Chi Minh and General Vo Nguyen Giap, Commander-in-Chief of the Vietnam Army. Therefore, a small nation with rudimentary weapons defeated the most powerful empire with the most modern and advanced weapons in the world. With the victories over the most powerful superpowers such as France, Japan, America, President Ho Chi Minh and General Vo Nguyen

Giap are two of the most revered individuals of Vietnam in the 20th century highly appreciated by international community.

President Ho Chi Minh and General Vo Nguyen Giap

President Ho Chi Minh (1890-1969) was the greatest national hero for the Vietnamese people. He devoted his whole life to the cause of liberation of the Vietnamese nation and made great contributions to the movement for peace and progress of mankind. By his energy, wisdom and talent, he found the right path of national liberation for the Vietnamese people as Proletarian revolution; established the Communist Party of Vietnam (1930) and led the Party and Vietnam to overcome all challenges to gain independence and moved forward to build socialism. President Ho Chi Minh was also a cultural man and a great thinker of the world. President Ho Chi Minh's beautiful revolutionary ideological heritage and moral example are always the precious asset of the Party and the Vietnamese people, a pride and a source of great encouragement to generations of Vietnamese people. Recognizing the contribution of President Ho Chi Minh to Vietnam and the world, UNESCO issued a Resolution honouring Ho Chi Minh as "a hero of national liberation and an outstanding cultural figure" (1987). In 1998, the Times named President Ho Chi Minh one of the 100 most influential people of the 20th century.

General Vo Nguyen Giap (1911-2013) is the first "5-star General" (when he was only 37 years old) who led Vietnamese soldiers and people to defeat the most powerful armies of the 20th century (French, Japanese and American troops), dubbed "Napoleon of Vietnam". He was one of the few Generals in the world to receive the admiration of the defeated generals at his hands. For example, General De Castries (in the Dien Bien Phu campaign) had to admit: "I am honoured to be a rival of General Giap, to be a direct opponent of a talented person like General Giap. I admire him". In the meeting with former US Secretary of Defense - Robert McNamara in 1997, General Chester Cooper of the United States told General Vo Nguyen Giap: *"Sir, I admire you 20 years ago. I'm still admiring"*. And even a former US soldier who fought in Vietnam, James G. Zumwalt, had to say: *"I can only say that he is the greatest general to belong to the greatest generation of Vietnam"* [10]. General Vo Nguyen Giap - the best student of President Ho Chi Minh was voted one of the top ten outstanding generals of the world by the Royal Council of Science of England (1984). He had contributed to developing the national security and defence strategy of the nation also.

Vietnam in the first 10 years of building Socialism and protecting national sovereignty (1975-1986)

Advantages of the Vietnamese revolution after 1975

After the great victory in the spring of 1975, Vietnam entered the era of independence, unity and transition to building socialism. During this period, Vietnam had rich natural resources, abundant labour resources of hard – working, creative people, material and technical bases of 21 years of building socialism in the North (1954-1975). This advantage helped Vietnam to enlist the support of its friends and the forces for national independence, democracy and peace in the world.

Difficulties of the Vietnamese revolution after 1975

Although there was a foundation of initial technical infrastructure in the North, in general, the starting point to transition to Socialism of Vietnam was very slow because Vietnam was still a poor and backward agricultural country; the consequences of the 30 years of war (1945-1975) for the whole country was long lasting, especially in the war of aggression and sabotage of the American empire that lasted 21 years. Besides, in the modern world, after 1975, the US did not abandon the conspiracy to destroy the Vietnamese revolution and conduct siege, isolation, and impose trade sanctions. The US vetoed Vietnam's accession to the United Nations; and mobilized most European Parliament countries to suspend economic aid for Vietnam. From the second half of the 1970s till the first half of the 80s, the socialist countries fell into a socio-economic sluggishness. The economic assistance of the Soviet Union, China and other socialist countries to Vietnam declined rapidly.

Under this situation, the requirements and tasks set for the Vietnam revolution in the 1975-1986 period were: to firmly protect the sovereignty and territorial boundaries; continue to fulfill the tasks of the national democratic revolution; quickly overcome the serious consequences of war, restore the economy, gradually stabilize people's lives; find patterns and transition paths to socialism to suit the country's historical circumstances.

Some achievements in the construction of socialism (1975-1986): Vietnam has achieved many successes in the first 10 years of building socialism across the country (1975-1986) thanks to highlighting the achievements, and managing difficulties as follows

Firstly, Vietnam completed the process of the State unification. On April 25, 1976, the general election for the National Assembly of Vietnam was unanimous and successful, with 98.77 per cent voters voted across the country. Subsequently, from June 24 to July 3, 1976, the first session of the 6th National Assembly was convened in Hanoi to decide formal name of the country as Socialist Republic of Vietnam; established a draft Constitutional Committee. The National Assembly elected Mr. Ton Duc Thang as President, Mr. Truong Chinh as Chairman of the National Assembly, and Mr. Pham Van Dong as the Prime Minister. In June 1976, following the guidelines of the Party Central Committee, mass organizations like the Ho Chi Minh Communist Youth Union, the Vietnam Women's Union, and the Vietnam General Confederation of Labour conducted a joint conference, bringing the leading agencies under one forum across the country. The unification of State was completed, creating a consensus in the society after 30 years of the resistance wars for national liberation.

Secondly, Vietnam gradually embarked on economic reforms known as "*Doi Moi*" and achieved many important results. Food production had grown, increasing from 13.4 million tons in 1976-1980 to 17 million tons in 1981-1985. Industrial production increased by an average of 9.5% compared to 0.6% annually in the period 1976-1980. The facilities of socialism continued to be strengthened nationwide with important infrastructure projects as a precursor for later reforms.

Thirdly, firmly protecting the independence and sovereignty of the national border and fulfilling international obligations towards Laos and Cambodia.

While the Vietnamese people were making efforts to develop the economy and society, the Pol Pot army started to cause problems and started military activities to fight against Vietnam on the southwestern border from the beginning of May 1975 until end of 1977. Specifically, landed on Phu Quoc Island on 3-5-1975; infringed on many places along the Vietnamese border from Ha Tien to Tay Ninh, took over Tho Chu Island on May 8, 1975 and caused other problems. The Government of Vietnam expressed its wish to resolve all problems by the way of peace through negotiations between the two sides, but the Pol Pot declined and continued to stubbornly conduct a war of aggression in Vietnam. On December 31, 1977, the Pol Pot unilaterally cut off diplomatic relations and waged a war to invade the southwestern border of Vietnam. In late 1978, the Pol Pot government mobilized 19/23 divisions to launch a large-scale invasion attack on Vietnam. On December 23, 1978, three Pol Pot army divisions attacked Ben Soi and Ben Cau areas of Tay Ninh province with the goal of occupying Tay Ninh and advancing to take Ho Chi Minh City. Faced with the stubborn action of the Pol Pot army, Vietnam conducted a successful self-defence war, firmly defending Vietnam's sovereignty and territorial integrity.

At the same time, the Khmer Rouge regime massacred Cambodian people. United Front for National Salvation of Cambodia called for the help of Vietnamese army and people. Volunteers of Vietnam supported by Cambodian people fought for the liberation of Phnom Penh Capital on January 7, 1979, and after 25 days, liberated all cities, towns and towns in Cambodia and saved the Cambodian people from the genocide. However, this good action of the Vietnamese military has been blamed by the anti-revolutionary forces to take action to invade Cambodia, making other countries and world organizations misinterpret Vietnamese action, adversely affecting relationship between Vietnam and the United Nations, and ASEAN.

On the northern border, since 1978, relations between Vietnam and China began to deteriorate. China unilaterally cut all economic and technical aid to Vietnam, withdrew experts working in Vietnam, publicly implemented the policy of hostility towards Vietnam. On February 17, 1979, Chinese troops of 60,000 people (including 11 main corps and 20 infantry divisions) with various weapons, tanks and planes attacked across the entire northern border of Vietnam, including provinces: Lai Chau (now Dien Bien province and Lai Chau province), Lao Cai, Ha Giang, Cao Bang, Lang Son and Quang Ninh. Before the invasion of Chinese troops, the Vietnamese army and people in the northern border provinces, determined to fight to protect the independence, sovereignty and territorial integrity of the fatherland and had solicited support of people who love peace and order in the world. Facing tough resistance of the Vietnamese people and strong worldwide rebuttal of Chinese action; on March 5, 1979, China announced its withdrawal. On March 18, 1979, Chinese troops completely withdrew from Vietnamese territory. The war to protect the northern border of the Vietnamese people ended with glorious victory.

Building and protecting the Socialist Vietnam Fatherland in the way of renovation (1986-2019)

In the early 80s of the twentieth century, capitalist countries increasingly developed thanks to effectively applying the achievements of the scientific and technological revolution and changing the management and production methods while the socialist countries in Eastern Europe, including the erstwhile Soviet Union were in serious crisis and collapsed in the late 1980s and early 90s of the twentieth century. Vietnam also fell into a serious crisis (1985-1986). Vietnamese society faced many difficulties: production efficiency was low; distribution and circulation were in confusion, high inflation (over 300% in 1985 and up to 774.7% in 1986), society was unstable due to the loose laws and discipline; some cadres, civil servants and public officials were in power and corruption that led to difficulties in people's lives and the confidence in the leadership of the Party and the State seriously decreased.

In this context, the Party and the State realized that it was necessary to conduct a comprehensive renovation of the country "renewing or dying". As the General Secretary of the Central Committee of the Communist Party of Vietnam, Mr. Truong Chinh initiated the renovation of the country. The 6th National Congress of the Communist Party of Vietnam met in Hanoi (December 15-18, 1986) to analyze the successes and limitations of 10 years of national transition to socialism (1975-1986) in the spirit of "looking at the truth, appreciating the truth and clarifying the truth". On that basis, the Congress set out to reform the country.

Economic structure reform: Identifying "an economy with a multi-component structure was a characteristic of the transition period", so it should be also used and properly reformed. These components were: socialist economy (state and collective); sub-economic production of goods; private capitalist economy; state capitalist economy and self-sufficient economy. In the immediate future, it was necessary to focus on three major economic programmes: food, consumer goods and export products.

Reforming the economic management mechanism: Resolutely eliminating the bureaucratic centralized mechanism, administration and subsidy; step by step brought the economy to operate under the market mechanism under the public management of the State. The essence of the new mechanism of economic management was the planning mechanism under the socialist business accounting method on the principle of democratic centralism.

Renovating external economic activities: To promote and expand investment cooperation with foreign countries through the announcement of investment encouragement policies in various forms, especially those requiring high technology and export goods; create conditions for foreigners and overseas Vietnamese to return to Vietnam for investment and business cooperation.

Renovating and enhancing the State's management and administration role in economy: Strengthening the state apparatus from the central to local levels into a unified body, with a clear distinction of duties, powers and responsibilities assign each level according to the principle of democratic centralism; Performing the function of state management on economy and society, implementing the mechanism of "Managing the country by law, not just morality".

Renovating the leadership of the Party on the basis of raising awareness of reasoning, properly applying the objective law, overcoming subjective, and conservative perceptions. Renovation begins from innovating thinking, firstly innovative economic thinking on the basis of mastering the revolutionary and scientific nature of Marxism-Leninism, inheriting President Ho Chi Minh's revolutionary ideology. The Party must thoroughly grasp the idea of "taking people as root", must grasp the reality and constantly improve the intellectual level and innovate the working style and methods.

Reform Socio-cultural policy: Issuing basic and long-term social policies and identifying tasks and objectives in line with requirements and capabilities in this time; focusing on promoting human factors and taking human was the highest purpose.

At the 6th National Congress of the Communist Party of Vietnam, Comrade Nguyen Van Linh was elected General Secretary of the Central Committee of the Communist Party of Vietnam and continued to steer the national renewal. The way of national renewal proposed at the 6th Congress continues to be supplemented, developed and completed by the 7th, VIII, IX, X, XI and XII congresses to make Vietnam soon to become an industrialized modern country. From 1986 to 2019, under the leadership of the Communist Party of Vietnam (through the life of the General Secretary of the Party Central Committee: Nguyen Van Linh, Do Muoi, Le Kha Phieu, Nong Duc Manh, Nguyen Phu Trong) Vietnam has achieved great achievements in all fields. From a poor country after the wars, after 33 years of reforming the country (1986-2019), Vietnam has an impressive development with the fastest economic growth in Asia-Pacific region. Vietnam's military and defense strength has constantly improved, becoming one of the top military power countries in the region, especially in Southeast Asia. The socio-political environment is stable, social order and safety are ensured, it should become a safe destination for countries around the world. With the achievements and high position of Vietnam in the world on the day, it is further enhanced and affirmed its position as a new middle power in Asia.

Notes

1. Dẫn theo Bách khoa toàn thư mở: *Lịch sử Việt Nam*, https://vi.wikipedia.org/wiki/Lịch_sử_Việt_Nam (Vietnamese version)
2. Đào Duy Anh: *Việt Nam văn hóa sử cương*, Nxb. Thế giới, 2014. (Vietnamese version)
3. Nghiên cứu quốc tế: *Tại sao VIệt Nam không bị đồng hóa sau 1.000 năm Bắc thuộc*, http://nghiencuuquocte.org/2015/09/07/viet-nam-khong-bi-dong-hoa-1000-nam-bac-thuoc/, ngày truy cập 7-9-2015. (Vietnamese version)
4. Đại Cồ Việt (大瞿越) là quốc hiệu của Việt Nam từ thời nhà Đinh đến đầu thời nhà Lý, do Đinh Tiên Hoàng thiết đặt năm 968 và tồn tại 87 năm. Năm 1054, đời vua Lý Thánh Tông, quốc hiệu Đại Cồ Việt được đổi tên thành Đại Việt. Quốc hiệu Đại Việt tồn tại lâu dài nhất, dù bị gián đoạn 7 năm thời nhà Hồ và 20 năm thời thuộc Minh, kéo dài đến năm 1804, trải qua các vương triều Lý, Trần, Lê, Mạc và Tây Sơn, khoảng 724 năm. (Vietnamese version)
5. Năm 1400, Hồ Quý Ly lên nắm quyền và đặt quốc hiệu là Đại Ngu (大虞), có nghĩa là *"sự yên vui, hòa bình"*, chứ không phải là từ "ngu" trong từ "ngu si" (愚癡). (Vietnamese version)
6. Năm 1804-1839, nhà Nguyễn đặt Quốc hiệu Việt Nam (越南), 1839-1945 đổi thành Đại Nam. Từ năm 1945-1976 là Việt Nam Dân chủ Cộng hòa; từ năm 1976 đến nay là Cộng hòa xã hội chủ nghĩa Việt Nam. (Vietnamese version)
7. Kienthuc.net.vn: "Chiến lược bảo vệ Hoàng Sa, Trường Sa của vua chúa Việt", ngày truy cập 8-2-2018. (Vietnamese version)
8. Đảng Cộng sản Việt Nam: *Văn kiện Đảng toàn tập*, Nxb. Chính trị quốc gia, Hà Nội, 2007, t.51, tr.14.
9. *Kháng chiến toàn dân*: Huy động toàn thể dân tộc và các tầng lớp nhân dân tham gia kháng chiến. Chủ tịch Hồ Chí Minh kêu gọi: Bất kỳ đàn ông, đàn bà, bất kỳ người già, người trẻ, không phân biệt tôn giáo, đảng phái, dân tộc, hễ là người Việt Nam thì phải đứng lên để đánh thực dân Pháp để cứu Tổ quốc, nhằm xây dựng một thế trận chiến tranh nhân dân sao cho mỗi làng xóm là một pháo đài, mỗi đường phố là một mặt trận, mỗi quốc dân là một chiến sĩ, đánh địch mọi lúc, mọi nơi, làm cho địch bị động, lúng túng, cuối cùng phải chịu thất bại.(Vietnamese version)

   Kháng chiến toàn diện: đánh địch bằng cả quân sự, chính trị, kinh tế, văn hóa, tư tưởng, ngoại giao, coi quân sự là mặt trận đấu tranh chủ yếu, đấu tranh vũ trang đóng vai trò quyết định... nhằm tạo nên sức mạnh tổng hợp lớn hơn địch để chiến thắng kẻ thù.(Vietnamese version)

   Kháng chiến lâu dài: Xuất phát từ sự so sánh lực lượng, ban đầu địch mạnh, ta yếu, nên Đảng chủ trương đánh lâu dài. Vừa đánh vừa xây dựng, phát triển lực lượng, đồng thời tích cực tiêu hao, tiêu diệt địch để so sánh lực lượng dần dần có lợi cho ta và ta sẽ chuyển từ yếu thành mạnh, tiến tới đánh thắng kẻ thù. Đảng khẳng định đánh lâu dài về chiến lược nhưng phải tạo thế chủ động để phát triển thế và lực, tạo thời cơ giành thắng lợi nhanh chóng trong từng giai đoạn kháng chiến, tiến lên giành thắng lợi quyết định. (Vietnamese version)

   Dựa vào sức mình là chính: là dựa vào sức lực của toàn dân, vào đường lối đúng đắn, độc lập, tự chủ của Đảng, vào các điều kiện thiên thời, địa lợi, nhân hoà của đất nước, đồng thời ra sức tranh thủ sự đồng tình, ủng hộ và giúp đỡ quốc tế để chiến thắng kẻ thù. (Vietnamese version)
10. http://scienceinfo.net/portrait-of-great-generals-in-world-history.html

References

1. Dao Duy Anh (2014), Vietnam historical culture, World Publishing House.
2. Open Encyclopedia: Vietnamese History, https://en.wikipedia.org/wiki/Calendar_Viet_Nam.
3. Central Executive Committee - Steering Committee for summarizing theory (2015), *Summary report on some theoretical and practical issues through 30 years of renovation (1986-2016),* National politics Publishing House, Hanoi.
4. The Steering Committee for summarizing wars under the Politburo (2000), *Vietnam Revolutionary War 1945-1975 - Victory and Lessons,* National politics Publishing House. Hanoi.
5. Ministry of Defense, Vietnam Military History Institute (2001-2017), *History of the resistance war against the French colonialists (1945-1954)*, 7 volumes, People's Army Publishing House, Hanoi.
6. Ministry of Defense, Vietnam Military History Institute (2014), *History of the resistance war against the US Army, 1954-1975*), including 9 volumes (reprinted with supplement and corrected), National politics Publishing House, Hanoi.
7. Truong Chinh (1976), *Revolutionary National People's Democratic Vietnam*, Volume 1, Volume 2, The truth Publishing House, Hanoi.
8. Phan Huy Chu (1960-1961), *Lunar New Year Charter* (4 volumes), History Publishing House, Hanoi.
9. The Vietnamese people: *The greatest Generals in the history of the world,* http://danviet.vn/dong-tay-kim-co/nhung-vi-tuong-vi-dai-nhat-trong-lich-su -the-gioi-800624 accessed August 30, 2017.
10. Le Duan (1975), Vietnamese Communist Party - organizer of all victories of the Vietnamese Revolution, The truth Publishing House, Hanoi.
11. Le Duan (1970), Under the glorious flag of the Party, for independence, freedom and socialism, to advance to new victories, The truth Publishing House, Hanoi.
12. Le Thai Dung, "*Strategy of protecting Hoang Sa and Truong Sa of Vietnamese kings*", https://baomoi.com/giai-ma-chien-luoc-bao-ve-hoang-sa-truong-sa- crab-king-vietnam-c/31602020.epi, accessed July 26, 2019.
13. The Communist Party of Vietnam (2011), *The Complete Party Document*, National politics Publishing House, Hanoi.
14. Great solidarity: *Comrade Truong Chinh - The one who started the renovation process*, http://daidoanket.vn/chinh-tri/dong-chi-truong-chinh---nguoi-khoi-xuong-cong-cuoc -doi-new-dat-nuoc-tintuc356363, access date 18-1-2017.
15. Le Quy Don (1978), Dai Viet history, Social Science Publishing House, Hanoi.
16. Kienthuc.net.vn: Hoang Sa and Truong Sa protection strategies of Vietnamese kings, access date 8-2-2018.
17. International research: *Why is Vietnam not assimilated after 1,000 years of colonization*, http://nghiencuuquocte.org/2015/09/07/viet-nam-khong-bi-dong-hoa-1000-nam -bac-thuoc/, accessed 7-9-2015.
18. Ho Chi Minh National Academy of Politics (2018), High School Curriculum on Political Theories, *History of the Communist Party of Vietnam*, Political Theory Publishing House, Hanoi.
19. Phan Huy Le, Tran Quoc Vuong, Ha Van Tan, Luong Ninh (1991), *Vietnamese History*, volume 1, Publisher of University and professional education.
20. Ngo Si Lien and other historians of the Le dynasty (1967-1968): *Dai Viet wrote the whole history* (4 volumes), Social Science Publisher, Hanoi.
21. Tran Huy Lieu (1956), 80-year history of fighting against the French, Hanoi.

22. Ho Chi Minh *Complete volume,* (2011), National politics Publishing House, Hanoi.
23. World Bank Group, Ministry of Planning and Investment (2016), *Overview Report: Vietnam 2035 towards prosperity, creativity, equity and democracy,* Key messages, Hồng Đức Publishing House.
24. Dang Phong (2009), *Breaking the economy in the eve of innovation,* Knowledge Publishing House, Hanoi.
25. Dang Phong (2009), *Vietnam Economic Thinking,* Knowledge Publishing House, Hanoi.
26. Nguyen Phu Trong (2009), *Innovation and Development in Vietnam - Some theoretical and practical issues,* National Political Publishing House, Hanoi.
27. Nguyen Trong Phuc (2007), *Innovation in Vietnam - Practical and cognitive theory,* National Political Publishing House, Hanoi.
28. Nguyễn Duy Quy (1998), *Theoretical issues on socialism and the path to socialism in Vietnam,* National politics Publishing House, Hanoi.
29. Finance Journal: *Foreign direct investment into Vietnam in the period of 1988-2018 and some solutions,* http://tapchitaichinh.vn/nghien-cuu-trao-doi/dau-tu-truc-tiep -nuoc-ngoai-viet-nam-phan-do-19882018-and-a-phase-phap-310154.html, accessed July 22, 2019.
30. *100 outstanding people of the century* The Times: No. 14 | Vol. 151 on April 13, 1998.
31. Journal of Propaganda: *The rate of participation in health insurance reaches 89% of the population,* http://tuyengiao.vn/bao-hiem-xa-hoi/ty-le-tham-gia-bao-hiem-y - te-dat-89-dan-so-121798, access date 3-6-2019.
32. Journal of Propaganda: *Achievements of hunger eradication and poverty reduction in Vietnam,* http://tuyengiao.vn/bao-ve-nen-tang-tu-tuong-cua-dang/thanh-tuu-xoa-doi- giam-ngheo-tai-nam-121047, accessed on 6 May-2019.
33. Tien Phong Online: *The Vietnamese army is a Buddhist army,* https://www.tienphong.vn/hanh-trang-nguoi-linh/thu-tuong-campuchia-hun-sen-bo-doi-viet- nam-la-do-nha-phat-1363075.tpo, accessed on 4-1-2019.
34. VnEconomy: *Average income per capita in 2018 reached 2,587 USD,* http://vneconomy.vn/thu-nhap-binh-quan-dau-nguoi-nam-2018-dat-2587-usd-2018122715235412.htm, access date updated 27-12-2018.

4 Doi-Moi and Economic Reforms: A Road to Growth

Le-Dung Phung

Driving force for Economic Reform in Vietnam

Vietnam's economic reform and transformation are transitional, reasonable and effective. Economic model based on collective ownership of the means of production and the centrally-planned mechanism positively impacted Vietnam during the period of independence struggle and national unification (1945-1975) by: ensuring the victory in the struggle for national liberation and defense, creating infrastructure foundations for the construction of socialism, giving people the right to social control, and improving people's lives materially and spiritually. However, during the socialist construction (1975-1986), this economic model was no longer appropriate, causing Vietnam to face great difficulties:

First, internal resources were managed while the economy was in severe crisis

Before 1986, economic growth did not reach the set target, internal resources were constrained, and the economy faced a serious recession. Particularly, an imbalanced economic structure; low performing infrastructure; low labour productivity; ineffectively exploited and utilized resources; and rising unemployment caused difficulties in people's lives, stressful and unstable social life.

It was attributed to the centrally-planned and subsidized model that progressively revealed shortcomings in handling economic tasks. The management mechanism that resisted the market, underestimated productivity and economic efficiency created potential instabilities to the economy. In addition, ownership relations were not built on the developmental levels of the production forces, but restrained them, eliminated the morale of employees, and destroyed people's activeness and creativity. The sixth Party Congress also stated: "In our awareness and actions, we have not really agreed that the multi-component economic structure has existed for a relatively long time, and not thoroughly grasped and applied the rules of conformity between the forces of production and relations of production"[1].

Second, external forces mobilization was challenging due to being "blocked" and "isolated".

Being "blocked", "isolated" and prolonged embargo with the lack of regular aid made it difficult to Vietnam to participate in international economic relations, and hindered the mobilization of external resources for domestic economic development and market expansion.

It was attributed to major changes in the world in the late 70s and early 80s of the 20th century that created great pressure on Vietnam's economy. First, the US Government imposed embargo on Vietnam, causing the economy to be "blocked", "isolated" and to face socio-economic recession. Second, by the late 1980s, the Soviet Union and the Socialist countries in Eastern Europe were also in deep crisis. As a result, aid from the socialist countries and trading plummeted, resulting in a large economic imbalance.

Third, the selection of a new development path created a miraculous transformation in some economies around the world, typically China and new industrialized countries (NICs)

Since 1978, China has carried out a comprehensive "market opening and reform" toward open market, creating foundational successes for the economy. Cooperation and competition are gradually replacing confrontation and conflict. Therefore, new industrialized countries (NICs) have taken advantage of this stage to promote industrialization, with the strategy: promoting internal strengths, opening markets, prioritizing export and attracting foreign investment. In addition, the scientific and technological revolution is fundamental to new developments of capitalist countries. This gave Vietnam an important practice example to carry out reform and bring the country out of crisis.

Vietnam was in an adverse socio-economic recession due to both internal and external reasons. In this situation, the key is to acknowledge the objective trend of the economy for appropriate policy and roadmap planning to help the country out of crisis. That trend includes development based on a modern, open market economy; developmental model transformation; formation of new socio-economic relations; new industrialization methods to remove institutional constraints and release developmental resources that drive Vietnam to comprehensively reform in all areas, but initially in the economy.

Breakthroughs in Reforming Economic Thinking in Vietnam

Reforming economic thinking in Vietnam with proven breakthroughs is reflected in the documents of the Communist Party from the sixth to the 12th National Congress. These breakthroughs laid the foundation to promote the formation and development of a socialist-oriented market economy in Vietnam. Based on that, the Party has planned socio-economic development strategies with orientations tailored to each area, industry and region by exploiting potentials and comparative advantages. The rapid, effective and sustainable economic development associated with progress, social justice and environmental protection has become the priority and foundation for a modern industrial country. Specifically:

Developmental methods: Transition from a centrally-planned and subsidized economy to an open multi-component commodity economy; and further, a socialist-oriented market economy controlled by the government. Given this transformation, the state and collective economy ceased to play an absolute role. All economic sectors are treated equally, in which the Party states that the state and collective economy together with the private economy are the key to development.

Growth model: Vietnam has gradually shifted the model of economic development on a large scale, i.e. outdated industrialization method, favouring heavy industry, the advantages of labour, land, natural resources and foreign aid to an open economic model, moving the economic structure towards industrial, services development and green growth that "effectively combine both breadth and depth of development, but more focus on depth, improve the quality of growth and competitiveness based on increasing labour productivity, scientific and technological advances and innovation, etc."[2], consider innovation as a strategic breakthrough. On the other hand, economic development was evaluated in relation to the progress, social justice and cultural development[3]. Moreover, economic growth is based on modern infrastructure to effectively use natural resources, reduce greenhouse gas emissions, respond to climate change, reduce poverty and incentivize sustainable economic growth, etc.[4]

Economic institution: The sixth National Party Congress (1986) stated: "Determine to abolish the centralized, bureaucratic, subsidized administrative management mechanism management, and build a new management mechanism"[5], a socialist-oriented market economy mechanism towards a government that constructs, develops and creates breakthroughs in market economy institution. Thus, from prioritizing the absolute role of planning, failing to acknowledge the existence of a market economy, Vietnam has identified effective planning with market under the State's instructions to develop the economy. Vietnam also prioritized breakthroughs in socialist-oriented market economy institutions to create favourable conditions for economic development and an attractive business environment for investors.

Developmental resources: "Improve the quality and competitiveness of the economy based on increasing labour productivity, quality of human resources while mobilizing, allocating and utilizing effectively resources under the market mechanism; gradually transition from investment and export-based growth model to rely on export, investment and the domestic market"[6]; "restructure the economy, promote industrialization and modernization associated with the knowledge economy"[7]. Thus, from neglecting labour productivity and manufacturing under self-service, the Party observed that combining the endogenous strength of the nation with the power of the times. Internal forces shall play a decisive role, implying a necessity to mobilize all resources of people and economic sectors, to focus on developing the domestic market. External resources also play an important role that require efforts to attract effective foreign investments. In particular, human resources development goes hand in hand with labour productivity elevation, considering human resources as a decisive factor for sustainable development.

Regarding *foreign economic relations*, from a "closed" country, Vietnam confirmed its foreign economic policy of multilateralization, diversification of international economic relations, and proactive integration into the world economy based on comparative advantages with the motto: Vietnam is willing to be a friend, a reliable partner of international economic organizations, countries and territories around the world. Foreign economic relations are an important external force and foundation of the country's economic development.

Thus, after 33 years of "*DOI MOI*", Vietnam's economic development path has been clearly defined. The economy has been restructured towards efficiency and great breakthroughs.

Impact of Reforming Economic Thinking on Vietnam's Economic Development (1986-2019)

First, the economic growth has remained high as compared to that of regional and global countries; the size of the economy has increasingly expanded.

From an outdated agricultural economy with 90% of the population employed in agriculture, Vietnam has had an impressive development with the economic growth remaining high and stable as compared to that in the region and in the world. During the period 1986-2015, Vietnam's economic growth rate reached 6.65%/year on average, over 7% in 12 years, and hit the record high of 9.54% in 1995[8]. In 2018, GDP increased by 7.08% which was the highest since 2008[9]. The rate is considered high not only in the Southeast Asia but also in the world. In Asia, Vietnam's economic growth rate ranking is second only to China and India, higher than South Korea, Thailand, Singapore, Indonesia, Malaysia and the Philippines.[10]. (*see* Fig. 1)

GDP growth has facilitated the expansion of the economy: The gross domestic product in 2005 reached VND 837.8 trillion, two times higher that in 1995[11]. In 2015, it reached about USD 204 billion, two times higher than that in 2010[12], and in 2018, it reached USD 245 billion, ranked 46th in the world, 14th in Asia and sixth in Southeast Asia[13]. The increasing scale of GDP has strengthened Vietnam's economic potentials, and enhanced the country's position as compared to other economies in the region and in the world. GDP measured by purchasing power parity is fairly impressive, surpassing many developed European countries such as Norway, Finland and Denmark. In 2012,

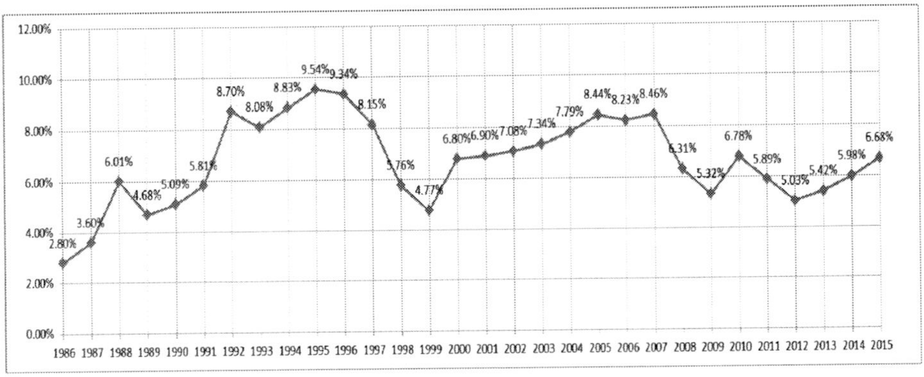

Fig. 1: Vietnam's economic growth rate in the period of 1986-2015.
Source: *Data consolidated from the General Statistics Office of Vietnam.*

Vietnam ranked 42th among 214 countries and territories; in 2016, Vietnam was the 32nd largest economy in the world and expected to rank 20th by 2050, surpassing Canada and Italy in terms of size of the economy[14]. Furthermore, Vietnam's national competitiveness increased from 60/138 to 55/137; business environment was also highly evaluated, increasing 14 levels from 82 to 69/190[15], reinforcing the position of the nation among other regional and global economies. Vietnam has currently been considered as one of the economies with good prospects and rapid growth as compared to those in the region and in the world.

Second, the economic structure has shifted positively towards industrialization and modernization

From a traditional agricultural country with low industrial and service development, after the "*Doi Moi*", the economic structure of Vietnam positively moved towards industrialization and modernization: the proportion in agriculture has declined but increased in industry and services sector. In 1986, agriculture, industry and services accounted for 38.06%, 28.88%, and 33.06%, respectively of total GDP; in 2000, 24.5%, 36.7%, and 38.7%, respectively; in 2014, 18.12%, 38.50% and 43.38%, respectively, and in 2018, 14.57%, 34.28% and 41.17%, respectively; (product tax minus subsidies accounted for 9.98%)[16].

Thus, after many years of development, Vietnam's services sector with 41.17% share has developed to acquire the highest proportion of GDP, aligned with the global development trends. The services sector also accounted for the biggest proportion in the economic structure. Despite the fast-paced growth in tourism, post and telecommunication, efficient and advanced growth in financial services, banking and legal consulting, traditional services are still dominant. However, 41.17% employed by the services sector is positive versus the target of 45-50%. Similarly, when comparing to modern industrial countries, the industrial sector must employ 40-45% of GDP. Considering the correlation of GDP growth rate, 34.28% (2018) contributed by the industrial sector versus the target is pretty close. Vietnam is described as the "new world's factory"[17]. Vietnam's agricultural sector has made great progress. From a frequent importer of million tons of foods, Vietnam has become one of the leading rice exporters in the world. In 1988, Vietnam had to import 50,000 tons of rice, but exported more than 6 million tons of rice in 2018, and became the world's third-largest rice exporter after India and Thailand[18]. Vietnam was also the world's largest exporter of robusta coffee, pepper, seafood, etc. The total export turnover of agricultural products increased rapidly from USD 7.16 billion in 2006 to USD 19.15 billion in 2010 and USD 30 billion in 2015 and hit the record high of USD 40 billion in 2018[19]. Vietnamese agricultural products are available in more than 180 countries and territories. Vietnam's agricultural exports rank second in Southeast Asia and 15th in the world[20]; more importantly, reinforcing the nation branding in large and potential markets such as the US, EU, Japan, Russia and China, etc.[21]

Third, abundant labour force and the labour structure are appropriately adjusted to the economic structural changes

Labour force: Vietnam's labour force is entering a period called "golden population structure" with the high working age population, accounting for over 65% of total population. These potentials and advantages are key to economic development, investment attraction and market expansion.

Vietnam's labour productivity has also improved significantly. In the period 2011-2015, the average annual increase was 4.35%, and that in the period 2016-2018 was 5.75%, particularly in 2018, it increased by 5.93% as compared to 2017[22]. These indicators confirm Vietnam's position in the group of countries with high labour productivity growth in ASEAN.

Vietnam's human capital index gradually improved and reached 0.67 points, ranking 48/157 countries in 2018; the talent competition index reached 33.41 points, ranking 92/125 countries, which was higher than the average score of low-middle income countries but still lower than many Southeast Asian nations[23].

In addition, employees acquiring higher education are ahead of the economic development. The literacy rate in the labour force of Vietnam hit 97.3% in 2015, equaling Thailand, Singapore and far ahead of middle-income (90%) and low-income countries (64%).[24]

Labour structure: Economic restructuring moved the labour structure of the economy toward declining labour force in agriculture and increasing labour force in industry and services. In 1990, employment in agriculture accounted for 73.02%, but decreased to 57% in 2005, employment in industry and construction accounted for nearly 18%, and 25% in services[25]. In 2015, employment in agriculture continued to decline to 44.3%[26]; and to 38.6% as of June 2018, dropped by half compared to that in 1990.

Fourth, science, technology and digital economy are gradually developing

The 2018 Global Innovation Index Performance Report recognized Vietnam's achievements in access to the global science and technology, indicating Vietnam's movements in terms of economic growth model and deeper participation in global value chains. In the period 2011-2015, the total factor productivity (TFP) contributed 33.6% to economic growth, and increased to 43.3% in the period 2016- 2018. According to WIPO, Vietnam's ranking of the global innovation index has shown consistent improvement, leading low-middle-income countries. Vietnam jumped 12 levels, ranking 59/126 countries in 2017, and two more levels to 45/126 countries in 2018, and particularly ranked 28th in terms of knowledge and technology outputs.[27]

Vietnam's digital economy reached USD 3 billion in 2015, rose to USD 9 billion in 2018 and estimated to reach over USD 33 billion by 2025. The percentage of GMV (Gross Merchandise Value) contributed by the Internet economy to the Gross Domestic Product (GDP) was 4% over total GDP, remaining the highest in Southeast Asia, followed by Singapore of 3.2%, Indonesia of 2.9%, Malaysia of 2.7%, Thailand of 2.7%, and the Philippines of 1.6%. Vietnam has the second largest e-commerce market (measured by GMV) in Southeast Asia, reaching USD 2.8 billion in 2018 and is forecast to reach USD 15 billion in 2025. In addition to e-commerce, Vietnam's CAGR in the period 2015-2018 ranked the second in Southeast Asia at 57%[28]. Vietnam is also evaluated as a growing digital economy, ranking 13/20 countries, and has the highest number of internet users in the world with 72% of the population using smartphones, ranking 14th in the cloud service coverage with 41/100 points (2018)[29]. Moreover, there are hundreds of thousands of digital startups with many high-tech projects every year. Therefore, by increasing investment in science and technology, especially digital technology, Vietnam will create breakthroughs in terms of economy, labour productivity, help the country escape the middle-income trap for developing countries, and transition quickly from the traditional economy to the digital economy.

Fifth, per capita income is on the rise and economic development is aligned with social progress and justice, and green growth

As a result of robust economic growth and the increasing size of the economy, *Vietnam's per capita income keeps rising*. Per capita GDP reached USD 640 in 2005, surpassing the average of low-income developing countries (USD 500)[30] and increased to USD 1,168 in 2010[31], USD 2,109 in 2015, a growth of 1.8 times against 2010 and USD 2,587 in 2018[32]. Therefore, Vietnam moved from low-income to lower middle-income group and is striving to obtain middle-income status.

Job creation, hunger eradication and poverty reduction were improved. At present, Vietnam has surpassed UN's Millennium Development Goals. Poverty rate was reduced over the years, in both rural and urban areas. Poverty rate according to the poverty line in 2005 dropped from 15.5% in 2006 to 10.7% in 2010. In 2011 the revised poverty line for 2011-2015 period was issued, doubling that in 2005. Accordingly, the poverty rate decreased from 12.76% in 2011 to 9.6% in 2012 and to well below 5% in 2015[33]. Besides, per capita GDP surged from USD 143 in 1991 to USD 1,334 in 2010 and approached USD 2,111 in 2015[34]. As a result, Vietnam moved from low-income to lower middle-income group and is striving to obtain middle-income status.

Vietnam's Human Development Index (HDI) followed an upward trend during economic renovation period: 0.439 in 1990; 0.534 in 2000; 0.573 in 2005; 0.611 in 2010; 0.666 in 2014 và 0.694 in 2017[35]. HDI 2017 enables Vietnam to join medium high HDI group and concurrently reflects the positive effects of Vietnam's economic growth on humand development.

Unemployment rate was significantly reduced, from 8.39% in 1990 – 2000 to 5.2% in 2001–2010 and under 4% in 2011–2015. In 2018, unemployment rate dipped to 2%, in particular, urban unemployment rate (2.95%) was higher than that in rural areas (1.55%). As a result, Vietnam is among the countries with the lowest unemployment rate, lower than that in Singapore and the U.S.[36]

Social welfare system was improved, satisfying the people's demand to a certain extent and enabling better access to cultural, healthcare and education services. In particular, social insurance, social support and community service were most enhanced. In 2009 Vietnam fulfilled the national goals of illiteracy eraducation and universal primary education. In 2018, vocational training exceeded the targets by 100%, etc.

Green growth strategy was well received and devised in view of the development of diferrent industries and sectors. The National Assembly issued, amended and supplemented several green growth-related laws, namely Law on economical and efficient use of energy; Law on natural disaster prevention and control; revised Law on environment protection; Law on Hydro-Meteorology. The government developed Strategy on renewable energy development in Vietnam till 2030 and with visions toward 2050; formulated a legal framework on the economical and efficient use of energy in production and everyday life, etc. In reality, numerous enviromental protection movements were widely spread and created positive effects.

The aforementioned achievements revealed that Vietnam did quite a great job in addressing the relationship between economic growth and social progress and justice.

Changes in the main Pillars of Vietnam Economy – Industry, Trade and FDI

Industry

Achievements: Vietnam industry was radically transformed during the renovation period. The industrial sector was modernized and associated with the development of knowledge economy.

From 1988 up to now, industrial sector maintained stable growth and increased its share in GDP from 21.6% in 1990 to 28.8% in 1995, 36.7% in 2000, 41% in 2005, 41.6% in 2008, 38.6% in 2012 and 32.72% in 2016.[37] Various industries applied modern and environment-friendly scientific and technological achievements and made considerable strides, such as mechanics and eletronics, consumer goods production and energy, etc.

Moreover, the share of processing and manufacturing industry was improved year over year and dependence on mining industry was reduced. In particular, the share of processing and manufacturing industry (in GDP) reached 13.28% in 2002, 13.34% in 2013, 13.18% in 2014, 13.69% in 2015, 14.27% in 2016 and 15.28% in 2017. In particular, such share increased more quickly in 2015-2017 than in 2012-2015 period. On the contrary, share of mining industry (in GDP) was on the wane, falling from 11.42% in 2012 down to 11.01% in 2013, 10.82% in 2014, 9.61% in 2015, 8.12% in 2016 and 7.47% in 2017[38]. This share dropped sharply by 1.5 times during 2012-2017 period. Possibly speaking, Vietnam paid great attention to the development of processing and manufacturing industries, as they are the key pillars of industrial sector and main drivers of economic growth.

The growth of industrial sector lays the foundation for economic growth. Industry acclerates urbanization and modernization, forms modern and synchronous infrastructure and drives economic structure change and trade growth, especially foreign trade.

Challenges: Apart from aformentioned achievements, the actual performance of Vietnam industrial sector has not lived up to its potential. Vietnam industrial sector still relies on natural resources and focuses primarily on manufacturing and assembling for foreign corporations and is even trapped by the application of outdated technologies with high commissions, for example, imports of vertical kiln cement plants, Chinese sugarcane production technologies or second hand compartments, etc. The added value in industrial products is quite low.

As a result, Vietnam should develop a concrete and long-term industrial strategy to create a breakthrough for this critical sector. Vietnam shall pursue green industry, which use less resources and sharpen its focus on a few key industries instead of spreading across industries.

Prospect of Vietnam's industrial sector: According to analysis on Vietnam's industrial sector, the potential and prospective industries are those facilitating industrialization, modernization and applying cutting-edge technologies; and supportive industry, namely mechanics (steel refining); petrochemistry; textile; processing; manufacturing; electronics, new and renewable energy.

Trade

Achievements: After the Cold War, exponential advancement of science and technology has enabled international economic connectivity to flourish and became the prevailing trend of modern international relation. Following such trend, since 1986, Vietnam has relentlessly "opened up", integrated and connected into the world economy, i.e. normalizing its relation with China (1991); joining Association of Southeast Asian Nations (ASEAN); normalizing its diplomatic relations with the U.S. (1995); participating in the Asia-Europe Meeting (ASEM-1996) as a founding member; joining Asia-Pacific Economic Cooperation (APEC-1998) and most importantly, becoming an official member of World Trade Organization (WTO-2007), etc. Vietnam also proactively signed a number of bilateral and multilateral free trade agreements, such as entering into FTA with 15 countries within the framework of 6 regional FTAs, namely ASEAN Free Trade Area (AFTA), ASEAN-China FTA, ASEAN-Korean FTA, ASEAN-Australia–New Zealand FTA, ASEAN-India FTA[39]. Additionally, Vietnam also signed a number of multilateral trade agreements, such as Vietnam- Japan Comprehensive Economic Partnership (2008), Vietnam-Chile FTA (2011), EU-Vietnam FTA and EU-Vietnam Investment Protection Agreement (EVIPA), etc.

As a result, in recent years Vietnam trade witnessed remarkable progress. Vietnam established trade relation with over 200 countries and territories, including 70 markets in which its export turnover surpasses USD 100 million, such as the U.S., Japan, China, Germany, the U.K., etc.

In 1995, *Vietnam's total import and export turnover* was only USD 13.4 billion. It increased to USD 100 billion 12 years later, when Vietnam joined WTO (2007) and reached USD 300 billion in 2015, an increase of 22.3 times. In 2007, it amounted to USD 400 billion.

Vietnam's export turnover increased from USD 0.7 billion in 1986 to USD 5 billion in 1995 and surpasssed USD 20 billion in 2003, USD 60 billion in 2008, USD 100 billion in 2012 and reached USD 162.11 billion in 2015[40]. Export grew by 17.8% in 2001-2005 period[41], 17.3% in 2006-2010 period and 17.5% in 2011-2015 period[42].

Vietnam recorded current account deficit for many years. However, from 1999, Vietnam current account started to post surplus and this trend continued in the next 3 years. After that, Vietnam current account became unstable[43]. Nevertheless, from 2012 up to now, it was further improved. In 2018, Vietnam recorded trade surplus with 150 countries and territories and trade deficit with 85 countries and territories. 2018 was also the third consecutive year that Vietnam posted a record high surplus at USD 6.8 billion, given USD 2.11 billion in 2017 and USD 1.78 billion in 2016.[44]

Vietnam's trade market was further expanded to numerous countries and territories in the world. To date, Vietnam has markets in 5 continents and established trade relations with 230 countries, in which Asia is the biggest one. In 2018 Vietnam's biggest trade partners are in Asia (accounting for 54% of total export and 80.3% of total import), followed by America (accounting for 23.8% of total export and 8.6% of total import); Europe (accounting 19% of total export, of which EU28 made up 17.2% and 7.5% of total import, of which EU 28 made up 5.9%); Atlantic (accounting for 2% of total export and 1.9% of total import) and Africa (accounting for 1.2% of total export and 1.7% of total import)[45]. However, Vietnam's dependence in Asia market tends to decrease in its im-export market mix.

Vietnam's strategic partners include China, the US, Japan, Korea, India, etc. These key partners have close and diversified economic relations with Vietnam across different industries. In 2018, Vietnam's 10 biggest trade partners made up 72% of its total trade value. In particular, its trade value with China was the highest, reaching USD 106.7 billion and accounting for 22.2% of total trade value. Vietnam posted trade value of USD 65.7 billion with Korean (13.7%), USD 37.8 billion with Japan (7.9%), USD 17.3 billion with Thailand (3,6%); USD 11.5 billion with Malaysia (2,4%); USD 10.7 billion with India and Germany (2.2%) and nearly USD 9.5 billion with Hong Kong (2%)[46]. Particularly, India is considered among the biggest and most potential market. Vietnam-India bilateral turnover in 2018 doubled that in 2016[47], increasing by 16% per annum over the last decade (2008-2018)[48], and is likely to reach USD 15 billion in 2020.

Regarding the structure of export and import goods, Vietnam tends to increase the export share of processed products, materials, parts and components for production and reduce that of raw product and resource. In particular, for 2001-2010 period, the share of agro-forestry-fishery products dropped by 6.07% from 29.37% (in 2001) to 23.3% (in 2010), share of mineral decrease by 7.12% from 34,92% (2001) to 27.8% (2010). On the contrary, export share of light industrial products and handicrafts grew by 13.18% from 35.72% (2001) to 48.9% (2010). In 2018 most exported goods were mobile phone and its components, given a value of USD 49.1 billion, one-fifth of total export value. Most imported goods were computers, electronic devices and its components, with a value of USD 42.2 billion, accounting for 17.8% of total import value. In particular, the value of 20 most imported and exported goods made up 80% of total goods trade value[49]. As a result, import structure was changed in accordance with the priorties in export production.

In particular, according to WTO, in 2017 Vietnam's goods export ranked 27th and goods import ranked 25th in the world.[50]

Vietnam's *maritime trade* plays an important role in economic development. Vietnam has the advantages of geo-economic development and long coast as a part of East Sea, connecting the Indian Ocean and the Pacific Ocean. This is the strategic position as the gateway to the sea of Southeast Asian mainland and the bridge from maritime Southeast Asian countries to all countries around East Sea; one of the most important and bustling international trade routes in the world. Vietnam has 45 seaports with 272 ports, including 2 international gateway ports (Cam Ranh-Khanh Hoa and Cat Hai-Hai Phong); 12 regional hub ports with total cargo volume of 550 million tons per year[51]. Vietnam has signed maritime trade agreements with 26 countries; built 18 coastal economic zones[52]. In 2018, Vietnam's shipping fleet ranked fourth in ASEAN and 30th in the world with 1,593 ships with total transported volume of 144.6 million tons of cargo, accounting for 55.6% of total volume of all transport modes[53]. Vietnam's maritime trade finds a lot of development potential.

Challenges: Despite these achievements, Vietnam's trade still faces many challenges. First, the export turnover is still small. Rapid increase in the export of processed and assembled products from imported raw materials leads to unsustainable export. Second, it is much dependent on certain markets such as the Chinese market that limits the activeness of Vietnam's economy. Third, the majority of businesses in the trade sector are small and low-tech; poor logistics infrastructure creates bottleneck, etc.

Therefore, Vietnam should have a comprehensive and sustainable trade development strategy in the future to move traditional economic structure towards modern one, apply high technology, create a modern distribution system, and aggregate high value supply chains.

Vietnam's trade prospects: In the next period, Vietnam has a higher trade prospects than other countries in the region. A series of effective FTAs, especially EVFTA, will increase 20% of Vietnam's export turnover to the EU by 2020[54]. The US-China Trade War will lead to production and export shifting of some products from China to Vietnam. Many foreign companies will consider locating their factories in Vietnam instead of China.

Foreign Direct Investment

Achievements: Vietnam has made clear and positive progress in attracting foreign direct investment. UNCTAD selected Vietnam as one of the 12 most successful countries in FDI attraction.[55]

Regarding the volume, the total cumulative registered FDI capital in the period 1988-2015 reached USD 313.56 billion, total realized capital reached USD 138.7 billion, hitting 44.23%[56]. The amount of registered capital increased rapidly since the early 2000s. Specifically, the total FDI registered in 10 years of 2006-2015 reached around USD 241 billion, in which realized capital was about USD 102 billion, accounting for 42%[57]. From 2006-2016, Vietnam steadily had better and more consistent FDI efficiency than other regional countries such as Indonesia, Malaysia, Thailand, and the Philippines[58].

From 2016 to date, FDI inflows has constantly increased. In 2016, the total new and additional registered capital, capital contribution, and shares purchase reached USD 24.4 billion, disbursing USD 15.8 billion, increasing significantly compared to that of 2015[59]. In 2018, the amount increased to USD 35.46 billion with an estimated disbursement of USD 19.1 billion which was nearly five times higher than that in 2006, 1.5 to 1.7 times higher than that in the period 2008-2015[60]. Many multinational corporations invested in Vietnam, creating a strong investment wave, including the projects of Posco - USD 1.1 billion (Korea, 2006), Intel Corporation-USD 1 billion (United States, 2006); Keangnam - USD 500 million (Korea, 2007); Nghi Son Oil Refinery Project - USD 6.2 billion (Japan and Kuwait joint venture, 2008); Sam Sung Thai Nguyen, Phase 2 - USD 3 billion (Korea, 2014), electronic equipment factory, USD 260 million (Hong Kong, 2019), and Vinhtex-USD 200 million (Singapore, 2019)[61], etc.

Regarding the coverage, FDI projects cover in almost all provinces of Vietnam; however, the majority of projects are mainly concentrated in Hanoi and Ho Chi Minh City.

Regarding investment partners, the leading investors include South Korea, Japan, Singapore, Taiwan, Hong Kong, Malaysia, United States, China, India, etc. Particularly, India's investment are progressing significantly. India is Vietnam's largest FDI partner in Central and Western Asia[62]. Many big Indian corporations such as TATA, ONGC, Essar, etc are investing in Vietnam. Total FDI capital has reached USD 877.48 million, ranking 26/126 countries and territories (measured by the registered capital) with 206 projects, focusing mainly on information technology, processing technology, manufacturing, pharmacy,[63] etc.

Regarding investment structure by economic sectors, FDI projects are mainly on processing, manufacturing and real estate with the total capital of USD 253.2 billion, accounting for 74.4% of total investment. Accordingly, agriculture and mineral industries account for a small proportion in total FDI.

Vietnam has achieved positive results in attracting FDI after 33 years of reform and proved to be an attractive investment environment.

Challenges: First, in terms of enterprise size measured by number of employees, most FDI enterprises are small and micro enterprises that arerising in numbers. In 2000, small and micro enterprises accounted for 62%, and increased to 71.59% in 2016[64]. Second, foreign investors bring capital to Vietnam to target at combining land, cheap labour, preferential policies to maximize profits under their business strategy, but lack of factors to increase productivity such as technology, scientific and technical progress or advanced management. The impacts of the FDI such as increasing labour productivity and exports are mainly based on the development on the broad scale. Third, there are negative impacts on the environment: global warming caused by greenhouse gas emissions, river pollution, marine pollution, impacting flora and fauna ecosystem. The dramatic environment disaster in Ha Tinh caused by the Formosa Group is a typical example.

Therefore, improving the efficiency of FDI attraction by adjusting FDI policies in line with in-depth and sustainable development orientations; lowering FDI to low technology industries that require a great number of employees and large infrastructure. Priority should be given to industries that can form a collabouration of production with domestic enterprises such as manufacturing and automobile industry, etc.

Vietnam's FDI attraction prospects: Abundant labour force, stable macro economy, actively improved investment environment, proactive and deep integration into the world economy are Vietnam's great advantages. Therefore, it is forecast that Vietnam shall continue to be an attractive destination for international investors in the next coming years. FDI inflows shall increase together with an increasing volume of USD 100 to 500 million. FDI also tends to transition and increase significantly in high-tech areas that create great value added such as electronics, processing and manufacturing industries. Besides, labour-intensive industries such as textiles and garments also appeal to investors.

Conclusion

Economic reform is the right step Vietnam embarked to find a path to development for the nation which has positively changed the economy. The landmark of "Doi Moi" (1986) has created a turning point for the economy, laying the foundations for new economic thinking in Vietnam on the path, methods, and steps to move the economy out of crisis. The pathway to Vietnam's economy in the next stages are clear as an open, modern, dynamic and efficient economy represented by many achievements, reinforcing Vietnam's position in the international arena. In 2019, Vietnam is ranked as one of the 10 best places in the world for foreigners to work and live thanks to low cost of living, good and stable income, beautiful nature and friendly people. This motivates Vietnam to improve and perfect its economic criteria. Vietnam shall also innovate the growth model towards modernity, prioritizing in-depth and sustainable development, and comprehensive economic restructure. Moreover, Vietnam also contributes its responsibility to the global community, and proactively and positively integrates, confirming the position of a "Middle power" in the region and in the world.

Notes

1. ĐảngCộngsảnViệt Nam, VănkiệnĐạihộiĐạibiểutoànquốclầnthứ VI, tập 1, NXB Sựthật, HN 1987 (Communist Party of Vietnam, Document of the sixth National Representative Congress, Volume 1, Truth Publishing House, HN 1987).
2. ĐảngCộngsảnViệt Nam, VănKiệnĐạihộiĐạibiểutoànquốclầnthứ XII, Nxb CTQG, HN 2011, tr 87 (Communist Party of Vietnam, Document of the 12th National Representative Congress, National Political Publishing House, HN 2011, p. 87).
3. ĐảngCộngsảnViệt Nam, VănKiệnĐảngToàntập, tập 51, Nxb CTQG, HN 2007, tr 160 (Communist Party of Vietnam, Complete Party Document, National Political Publishing House, HN 2007, p. 160).
4. ThủtướngChínhphủ, Chiếnlượcquốcgiavềtăngtrưởngxanhthờikỳ 2011-2020 vàtầmnhìnđếnnăm 2050, Quyếtđịnhsố 1393/QĐ-TTgngày 25/09/2012, 2012 (Prime Minister, National strategy on green growth for the period 2011- 2020 with vision to 2050, Decision No. 1393/QĐ-TTg dated September 25, 2012).
5. ĐảngCộngsảnViệt Nam, BáocáoTổngkếtMộtsốvấnđềlýluận-thựctiễn qua 20 nămđổimới (1986-2006), Nxb CTQG, HN 2005, tr 49-50 (Communist Party of Vietnam, Summary report on some theoretical and practical issues after 20 years of "Doi Moi", National Political Publishing House, HN 2005, pp. 49-50).
6. ĐảngCộngsảnViệt Nam, VănKiệnĐạihộiĐạibiểutoànquốclầnthứ XII, Nxb CTQG, HN 2011, tr 87 (Communist Party of Vietnam, Documents of the 12th National Representative Congress, National Political Publishing House, HN 2011, p. 87).
7. ĐảngCộngsảnViệt Nam, *VănKiệnĐạihộiĐạibiểutoànquốclầnthứ XII*, Nxb CTQG, HN 2011, tr 22
(Communist Party of Vietnam, Documents of the 12th National Representative Congress, National Political Publishing House, HN 2011, p. 22).
8. TổngcụcThốngkê, *Tìnhhìnhkinhtếxãhội 2018*, truycậpngày 29/7/2019 *(General Statistics Office, Socio-economic situation in 2018, retrieved on July 29, 2019)*, https://www.gso.gov.vn/default.aspx?tabid=382&idmid=2&ItemID=19041

9. TổngcụcThốngkê, *Tìnhhìnhkinhtếxãhội 2018*, truycậpngày 29/7/2019 *(General Statistics Office, Socio-economic situation in 2018, retrieved on July 29, 2019)*, https://www.gso.gov.vn/default.aspx?tabid=382&idmid=2&ItemID=19041
10. Trung tâm thông tin và dự báo Kinh tế - xã hội quốc gia (2015), *"Một số điểm nhấn trong tăng trưởng kinh tế giai đoạn 2011 – 2015"*, http://www.ncseif.gov.vn/sites/vie/Pages/motsodiemnhantrongtang-nd-17232.html
11. VõHồngPhúc,*Nhữngthànhtựuvềkinhtế - xãhội qua 20 nămđổimới (1986-2005)"*, Việt Nam 20 nămđổimới, NxbChínhtrịquốcgia, HN 2006, tr. *146 (*National Center for Socio-Economic Information and Forecast (2015), Some highlights of economic growth in the period 2011 – 2015)*;*
12. Dântrí, KinhtếViệt Nam qua lăngkínhcủacáctổchứcquốctế, truycậpngày 27/7/2019 (Dan tri, Vietnam's economy through the lens of international organizations, retrieved on July 27, 2019),
https://dantri.com.vn/kinh-doanh/kinh-te-viet-nam-qua-lang-kinh-cua-cac-to-chuc-quoc-te-20151218175005893.htm
13. Ngânhàngthếgiới (WB), Báocáo GDP củacácquốcgiatrênthếgiới, 2018 (World Bank (WB), Reports on GDP reports of countries around the world, 2018).
14. Ngânhàngthếgiới (WB), Báocáoxếphạng GDP (PPP) củacácquốcgiavàvùnglãnhthổ, 2012, 2016.(World Bank, List of countries and territories by GDP (PPP), 2012, 2016).
15. HoàngXuânHòa, Chủđộnghộinhậpkinhtếquốctếsau 5 nămnhìnlại, TạpchíCộngsản, số 150, 2019, tr 25.(Hoang Xuan Hoa, review on proactive economic integration into global economy after 5 years, Communist Review, issue 150, 2019).
16. TổngcụcThốngkê, *Tổngquantìnhhìnhkinhtếxãhộinăm 2018*, truycậpngày 27/7/2019 *(General Statistics Office, Socio-economic situation in 2018, retrieved on July 29, 2019)*, https://www.gso.gov.vn/default.aspx?tabid=382&idmid=2&ItemID=19041
17. Vietnambiz, BáochíthếgiớiđánhgiácaosựtăngtrưởngcủanềncôngnghiệpViệt Nam (International press impresses with Vietnam's industrial growthretrieved on August 18, 2019), https://vietnambiz.vn/bao-chi-the-gioi-danh-gia-cao-su-tang-truong-cua-nen-cong-nghiep-viet-nam-63364.htm, truycậpngày 18-8-2019.
18. DẫntheoĐầutư Online, *Giátăng, xuấtkhẩugạothuvề 3,03 tỷ USD trongnăm 2018*, https://baodautu.vn/gia-tang-xuat-khau-gao-thu-ve-303-ty-usd-trong-nam-2018-d93938.html, ngàytruycập 12-1-2019 *(Vietnam earned USD 3.03 billion from rice exports in 2018 thanks to higher price, retrieved on January 12, 2019).*
19. Dẫn theo số liệu thống kê của Bộ Nông nghiệp và Phát triển Nông thôn (Statistics consolidated from the Ministry of Agriculture and Rural Development).
20. Đánh giá của Bộ Nông nghiệp và Phát triển nông thôn tại "Hội nghị Tổng kết 10 năm thực hiện Nghị quyết Trung ương 7 khóa X về nông nghiệp, nông dân, nông thôn", Hà Nội, ngày 7-9-2018 (Review of the Ministry of Agriculture and Rural Development at "The 10-year review of implementing the Resolution of the seventh Congress by the Session X Central Executive Committee on agriculture, farmers and rural areas", Hanoi, September 7, 2018).
21. Hồ sơ Sự kiện, Chuyên san của Tạp chí Cộng sản, số 306, ngày 10-7-2015, tr.1 2 (Event profile, special issue of Communist Review, issue 306, July 10, 2015, p. 12).
22. Tổng cục Thống kê, Tổng quan tình hình kinh tế xã hội năm 2018, truy cập ngày 27/7/2019 ((General Statistics Office, Socio-economic situation in 2018, retrieved on July 29, 2019) https://www.gso.gov.vn/default.aspx?tabid=382&idmid=2&ItemID=19041
23. Ngân hàng thế giới (WB), Báo cáo tại Diễn đàn Kinh tế thế giới (2018).(World Bank, Report of the World Economic Forum (2018)).
24. Nguyễn Thị Miền, Nâng cao chất lượng nguồn nhân lức đáp ứng yêu cầu đổi mới mô hình tăng trưởng kinh tế Việt Nam, Tạp chí Lý luận Chính trị, số 5, 2019, tr 97

(Nguyen Thi Mien, Improving human resources quality to meet the requirements of reforming Vietnam's economic growth model, Journal of Political Theories, issue 5, 2019).

25. Đảng Cộng sản Việt Nam, Báo cáo tổng kết một số vấn đề lý luận – thực tiễn qua 20 năm đổi mới (1986-2006), Nxb CTQG, HN 2005, tr 74 (Communist Party of Vietnam, Summary report on some theoretical and practical issues after 20 years of "Doi Moi" (1986-2006), National Political Publishing House, HN 2005, p. 74).
26. Đảng Cộng sản Việt Nam, Văn kiện Đại hội Đảng toàn quốc lần thứ XII, Nxb CTQG, HN 2016, tr 231 (Communist Party of Vietnam, Documents of the 12th National Congress, National Political Publishing House, HN 2016, p. 231).
27. Hải Vân, Phát huy vai trò của khoa học và công nghệ trong phát triển kinh tế nhanh, bền vững, truy cập ngày 30/7/2019 (Hai Van, Promoting the role of science and technology in rapid and sustainable economic development, retrieved on July 30, 2019), http://www.tapchicongsan.org.vn/Home/kinh-te/2019/55000/Phat-huy-vai-tro-cua-khoa-hoc-va-cong-nghe-trong-phat.aspx
28. Google & Temasek, Báocáo e-Conomy SEA, 2018 (Google & Temasek, E-Conomy SEA report, 2018).
29. PhạmViệtDũng, Kinhtếsố - Cơhội "bứtphá" choViệt Nam, TạpchíCộngsản, Số 921, tr 54 (Pham Viet Dung, Digital Economics - An opportunity for Vietnam to make a breakthrough, Communist Review, issue 921, p. 54).
30. VõHồngPhúc, *Nhữngthànhtựuvềkinhtế - xãhội qua 20 nămđổimới (1986-2005)"*, Việt Nam 20 nămđổimới, NxbChínhtrịquốcgia, HN 2006, tr. 146 (Vo Hong Phuc, Socio-economic achievements after 20 years of "Doi Moi" (1986-2005), Vietnam - 20 years of "Doi Moi", National Political Publishing House, Hanoi 2006, p. 146);
31. DiễnđànkinhtếViệt Nam, *GDP đầungườinăm 2010 là 1168 USD*, truycậpngày 27/7/2019 *(Vietnam Economic Forum, GDP per capita in 2010 was 1,168 USD, retrieved on July 27, 2019)*, https://vef.vn/2010/12/31/2010-12-31-gdp-dau-nguoi-nam-2010-la-1-168-usd/
32. Vneconomy, Thu nhậpbìnhquânđầungườinăm 2018 đạt 2.587 USD, truycậpngày 27/7/2019 (Vneconomy, Per capita income in 2018 reached USD 2,587, retrieved on July 27, 2019) http://vneconomy.vn/thu-nhap-binh-quan-dau-nguoi-nam-2018-dat-2587-usd-20181227152354l2.htm
33. Chính phủ (2015), Báo cáo kết quả thực hiện các chương trình MTQG giai đoạn 2011-2015 và định hướng xây dựng các chương trình MTQG giai đoạn 2016-2020 (Government (2015), Report on the results of the implementation of NTPs in the period 2011-2015 and their development orientations in the period 2016-2020).
34. World Bank, *http://data.worldbank.org*
35. UNDP, Báo cáo phát triển con người năm 2015, 2018 (UNDP, Human development report 2015, 2018).
36. Bộ Lao động-Thương binh và Xã hội, Bản tin cập nhật thị trường lao động Việt Nam số 21, 2019 (Ministry of Labour, Invalids and Social Affairs, Newsletters for Vietnam's Labour Market Update, volume 21, 2019).
37. Võ Văn Đức-Đinh Văn Trung (đồng chủ biên), Tái cấu trúc nền kinh tế Việt Nam - Lý luận và thực tiễn, Nxb LLCT, HN 2015 và Tổng cục thống kê(Vo Van Duc – Dinh Van Trung (co-author), Vietnam's economic restructuring – Theory and practice, Publishing House of Political Theory, HN 2015 and General Statistics Office of Vietnam).
38. Báo Điện tử Chính phủ nước CHXHCNVN, Tăng trưởng công nghiệp chế biến, chế tạo và dịch vụ là động lực thúc đẩy GDP tăng cao, truy cập ngày 25/7/2019 (Online newspaper of the Government of the Socialist Republic of Vietnam, Growth in processing, manufacturing and services industries is the driver to GDP increase, retrieved on July 25, 2019), http://baochinhphu.vn/Thu-tuong-va-Thanh-vien-Chinh-phu-tra-loi-chat-

van/Tang-truong-cong-nghiep-che-bien-che-tao-va-dich-vu-la-dong-luc-thuc-day-GDP-tang-cao/346480.vgp

39. Bộ Ngoại giao Việt Nam, Những thành tựu trong tiến trình hội nhập kinh tế quốc tế của Việt Nam, truy cập ngày 29/7/2019 (Ministry of Foreign Affairs of Vietnam, Vietnam's achievements in international economic integration, retrieved on July 29, 2019), http://www.mofahcm.gov.vn/vi/mofa/nr091019080134/ns120222162217/
40. Nguyễn Thị Hải Bình, Trần Thu Thuỷ (2015), Phát triển kinh tế giai đoạn 2011-2015 và định hướng 2016-2020 (Nguyen Thi Hai Binh, Tran Thu Thuy (2015), Economic development in the period 2011-2015 and the 2016-2020 orientation), http://tapchitaichinh.vn/nghien-cuu--trao-doi/trao-doi-binh-luan/hoi-nhap-kinh-te-quoc-te-cua-viet-nam-sau-gan-30-nam-doi-moi-57479.html
41. Đinh Văn Ân, Kinh tế Việt Nam năm 2001-2005 và kế hoạch phát triển kinh tế-xã hội 2006-2010, Viện Nghiên cứu Quản lý kinh tế trung ương, Báo cáo khoa học, 2005, tr 9 (Dinh Van An, Vietnam's economy in 2001-2005 and socio-economic development plan for 2006-2010 period, Central Institute for Economic Management, scientific journal, 2005, p. 9).
42. Báo Công thương, Ngành Công thương Việt Nam: 65 năm phát triển và hội nhập, 16/5/2016 ((Industry and Trade Newspaper, Vietnam Industry and Trade Sector: 65 years of development and integration, May 16, 2016).
43. Võ Văn Đức – Đinh Văn Trung (chủ biên), Tái cấu trúc nền kinh tế Việt Nam – Lý luận và thực tiễn, Nxb Lý luận chính trị, HN 2015, tr 111 (Vo Van Duc – Dinh Van Trung (Co-author), Vietnam's economic restructuring – Theory and Practice, National Political Theory Publishing House, Hanoi 2015, p. 111).
44. Hải quan Việt Nam, Xuất nhập khẩu hàng hóa năm 2018 của Việt Nam: Những nét nổi bật qua ghi nhận các con số thống kê của Tổng cục Hải quan, truy cập ngày 29/7/2019 (Vietnam Customs, Vietnam's export and import in 2018: Highlights by statistics of the General Department of Vietnam Customs, retrieved on July 29, 2019), https://www.customs.gov.vn/Lists/ThongKeHaiQuan/ViewDetails.aspx?ID=1560&Category=Ph%C3%A2n%20t%C3%ADch%20chuy%C3%AAn%20%C4%91%E1%BB%81&Group=Ph%C3%A2n%20t%C3%ADch
45. Hải quan Việt Nam, Xuất nhập khẩu hàng hóa năm 2018 của Việt Nam: Những nét nổi bật qua ghi nhận các con số thống kê của Tổng cục Hải quan, truy cập ngày 29/7/2019 (Vietnam Customs, Vietnam's export and import in 2018: Highlights by statistics of the General Department of Vietnam Customs, retrieved on July 29, 2019). https://www.customs.gov.vn/Lists/ThongKeHaiQuan/ViewDetails.aspx?ID=1560&Category=Ph%C3%A2n%20t%C3%ADch%20chuy%C3%AAn%20%C4%91%E1%BB%81&Group=Ph%C3%A2n%20t%C3%ADch
46. Hải quan Việt Nam, Xuất nhập khẩu hàng hóa năm 2018 của Việt Nam: Những nét nổi bật qua ghi nhận các con số thống kê của Tổng cục Hải quan, truy cập ngày 29/7/2019 (Vietnam Customs, Vietnam's export and import in 2018: Highlights by statistics of the General Department of Vietnam Customs, retrieved on July 29, 2019). https://www.customs.gov.vn/Lists/ThongKeHaiQuan/ViewDetails.aspx?ID=1560&Category=Ph%C3%A2n%20t%C3%ADch%20chuy%C3%AAn%20%C4%91%E1%BB%81&Group=Ph%C3%A2n%20t%C3%ADch
47. ThờibáoTàichính, ThươngmạiViệt Nam - ẤnĐộđạtgần 10,7 tỷ USD trongnăm 2018, truycậpngày 30/7/2019 (Vietnam Financial Times, Vietnam-India trade reached nearly USD 10.7 billion in 2018, retrieved on July 30, 2019), http://thoibaotaichinhvietnam.vn/pages/kinh-doanh/2019-01-15/thuong-mai-viet-nam-an-do-dat-gan-107-ty-usd-trong-nam-2018-66695.aspx

48. NguyễnVăn Lan, Quan hệViệt Nam - ẤnĐộ: TừĐốitácchiếnlượcđếnĐốitácchiếnlượctoàndiện, TạpchíCộngsản, truycậpngày 30/7/2019 (Nguyen Van Lan, Vietnam-India relation: From strategic partner to comprehensive and strategic partner, Communist Review, retrieved on July 30, 2019), http://www.tapchicongsan.org.vn/ Home/Doi-ngoai-va-hoi-nhap/2018/53393/ Quan-he-Viet-Nam- An-Do-Tu-Doi-tac-chien-luoc.aspx
49. HảiquanViệt Nam, Xuấtnhậpkhẩuhànghóanăm 2018 củaViệt Nam: Nhữngnétnổibật qua ghinhậncác con sốthốngkêcủaTổngcụcHảiquan, truycậpngày 29/7/2019 (Vietnam Customs, Vietnam's export and import in 2018: Highlights by statistics of the General Department of Vietnam Customs, retrieved on July 29, 2019), https://www.customs.gov.vn/Lists/ThongKeHaiQuan/ViewDetails.aspx?ID=1560&Category=Ph%C3%A2n%20t%C3%ADch%20chuy%C3%AAn%20%C4%91%E1%BB%81&Group=Ph%C3%A2n%20t%C3%ADch
50. HảiquanViệt Nam, Xuấtnhậpkhẩuhànghóanăm 2018 củaViệt Nam: Nhữngnétnổibật qua ghinhậncác con sốthốngkêcủaTổngcụcHảiquan, truycậpngày 29/7/2019 (Vietnam Customs, Vietnam's export and import in 2018: Highlights by statistics of the General Department of Vietnam Customs, retrieved on July 29, 2019), https://www.customs.gov.vn/Lists/ThongKeHaiQuan/ViewDetails.aspx?ID=1560&Category=Ph%C3%A2n%20t%C3%ADch%20chuy%C3%AAn%20%C4%91%E1%BB%81&Group=Ph%C3%A2n%20t%C3%ADch
51. BáoGiaothông, CảngbiểnViệt Nam "lộtxác" saugầnhaithậpkỷquyhoạch, BộGiaothôngvậntải, truycậpngày 22/8/2019 (Transportation newspaper, The "makeover" of Vietnam seaports after nearly two decades of planning, Ministry of Transport, retrieved on August 22, 2019), http://mt.gov.vn/vn/tin-tuc/59994/cang-bien-viet-nam-%E2%80%9Clot-xac%E2%80%9D-sau-gan-hai-thap-ky-quy-hoach.aspx
52. TTXVN, Biển, đảoViệt Nam: Tiềmnăngvàlợithế *(VNA, Vietnam's sea and islands: Potentials and advantages retrieved on August 22, 2019)*, https://sonoivu.hanoi.gov.vn/thong-tin-tuyen-truyen/-/view_content/2386499-bien-dao-viet-nam-tiem-nang-va-loi-the.html, truycậpngày 22/8/2019
53. UNCTAD, BáocáoĐánhgiáVậntảiHànghải 2018 (UNCTAD, The 2018 Review of Maritime Transport).
54. Vũ Anh Tú, BáocáochuyênđềTriểnvọngthươngmạivàdòngvốnđầutưnướcngoài (FDI) vàoViệt Nam, 17/7/2019 (Vu Anh Tu, Seminar report on trade Prospects and foreign direct investment (FDI) inflows into Vietnam, July 17, 2019, retrieved on August 22, 2019), https://vdsc.com.vn/vn/downloadRptAttachment.rv?rptId=619D37DF7BABB1017538BAB727784586A, truycậpngày 22/8/2019
55. LiênHiệpQuốc, DiễnđànLiênHiệpQuốcvềThươngmạivàPháttriển (UNCATAD), 2018 (United Nations, United Nations Forum on Trade and Development (UNCTAD), 2018).
56. Ngô Quang Trung (2015), Đầu tư trực tiếp nước ngoài ở Việt Nam giai đoạn 1988-2015: Thực trạng và vấn đề (Ngo Quang Trung (2015), Foreign direct investment in Vietnam during 1988-2015: Situation and problems), http://www.ipd.org.vn/nghien-cuu-truong-hop-noi-bat/dau-tu-truc-tiep-nuoc-ngoai-o-viet-nam-giai-doan-1988-2015:-thuc-trang-va-van-de-tac-gia:-ngo-quang-trung-a452.html
57. TổngcụcHảiquanTổngcụcHảiquan, Báocáo FDI qua cácthờikỳ (General Department of Vietnam Customs, Report on FDI over the periods).
58. NgânhàngthếgiớivàBộKếhoạchvàĐầutư, Dựthảochiếnlượcthuhút FDI giaiđoạn 2018 – 2030, HàNội (World Bank and Ministry of Planning and Investment, Draft strategy of FDI attraction in the period 2018-2030, Hanoi).

59. CụcĐầutưnướcngoài, Tìnhhìnhthuhútđầutưnướcngoài 12 thángnăm 2016, truycậpngày 27/7/2019 (Foreign Investment Agency, Actual situation of foreign direct investment attraction in 12 months of 2016, retrieved on July 27, 2019), http://fia.mpi.gov.vn/TinBai/5177/Tinh-hinh-thu-hut-Dau-tu-nuoc-ngoai-12-thang-nam-2016
60. CụcĐầutưnướcngoài, Tìnhhìnhthuhútđầutưnướcngoài 12 thángnăm 2016, truycậpngày 27/7/2019 (Foreign Investment Agency, Actual situation of foreign direct investment attraction in 12 months of 2016, retrieved on July 27, 2019), http://fia.mpi.gov.vn/TinBai/5177/Tinh-hinh-thu-hut-Dau-tu-nuoc-ngoai-12-thang-nam-2016
61. CụcĐầutưnướcngoài, BộKếhoạchđầutư, Báocáotìnhhìnhkếhoạchđầutư qua cácnăm (Foreign Investment Agency, Ministry of Planning and Investment, report on investment situation over the years).
62. Economic Time, KinhtếViệtKinhtếlàmộttrọngtâmtrongquanhệViệt Nam-ẤnĐộ, BộNgoạiGiaoViệt Nam (Economic Time, Vietnam's economy is a key focus of Vietnam-India relations, Ministry of Foreign Affairs of Vietnam), https://ngkt.mofa.gov.vn/kinh-te-la-mot-trong-tam-trong-quan-he-viet-nam-an-do/truycậpngày 22/8/2019
63. Khánh Lan, Quan hệViệt Nam - ẤnĐộngàycàngpháttriểnsâurộngvàthựcchất, BáoĐiệntửĐảngCộngSảnViệt Nam, truycậpngày 22/8/2019 *(Khanh Lan, Vietnam - India relations are deeply and substantially developing, Communist Party of Vietnam Online Newspaper, retrieved on August 22, 2019),* http://dangcongsan.vn/chao-xuan-ky-hoi-2019/xuan-que-huong/quan-he-viet-nam-an-do-ngay-cang-phat-trien-sau-rong-va-thuc-chat-512209.html
64. Lê QuốcHội-TrươngNhưHiếu-VũMạnh Linh, Khuvựcdoanhnghiệpcóvốnđầutưtrực tiếpnướcngoàitạiViệt Nam-thựctrạngvànhữngvấnđềđặt ra, TạpchíKinhtế&Phá ttriển, số 263, 2019, tr16 (Le Quoc Hoi - Truong NhuHieu - Vu Manh Linh, Foreign direct investment enterprises in Vietnam - actual situation and issues, Journal of Economics and Development, issue 263, 2019).

References

1. An ninhthủđô, Việt Nam và EU chínhthứckýkếthiệpđịnhthươngmạitự do EVFTA, truycậpngày 29/7/2019 (An ninhthu do, Vietnam and EU officially signed the EU - Vietnam Free Trade Agreement (EVFTA), retrieved on July 29, 2019), https://anninhthudo.vn/chinh-tri-xa-hoi/viet-nam-va-eu-chinh-thuc-ky-hiep-dinh-thuong-mai-tu-do-evfta/816030.antd
2. Nguyễn Thị Hải Bình, Trần Thu Thuỷ (2015), Phát triển kinh tế giai đoạn 2011-2015 và định hướng 2016-2020 (Nguyen Thi Hai Binh, Tran Thu Thuy (2015), Economic development in the period 2011-2015 and the 2016-2020 orientation), http://tapchitaichinh.vn/nghien-cuu--trao-doi/trao-doi-binh-luan/hoi-nhap-kinh-te-quoc-te-cua-viet-nam-sau-gan-30-nam-doi-moi-57479.html
3. BộNgoạigiaoViệt Nam, Nhữngthànhtựutrongtiếntrìnhhộinhậpkinhtếquốctếcủa Việt Nam, truycậpngày 29/7/2019 (Ministry of Foreign Affairs of Vietnam, Vietnam's achievements in international economic integration, retrieved on July 29, 2019), http://www.mofahcm.gov.vn/vi/mofa/nr091019080134/ns120222162217/
4. Bộ Lao động - ThươngbinhvàXãhội, Bản tin cậpnhậtthịtrường lao độngViệt Nam, số 21, 2019 (Ministry of Labour, Invalids and Social Affairs, Newsletters for Vietnam's Labour Market Update, volume 21, 2019).
5. Chính phủ (2015), Báo cáo kết quả thực hiện các chương trình MTQG giai đoạn

2011-2015 và định hướng xây dựng các chương trình MTQG giai đoạn 2016-2020 (Government (2015), Report on the results of the implementation of NTPs in the period 2011-2015 and their development orientations in the period 2016-2020).

6. Báo Công thương, Ngành Công thương Việt Nam: 65 năm phát triển và hội nhập, 16/5/2016 (Industry and Trade Newspaper, Vietnam Industry and Trade Sector: 65 years of development and integration, May 16, 2016).
7. CụcĐầutưnướcngoài, Tìnhhìnhthuhútđầutưnướcngoài 12 thángnăm 2016, truycậpngày 27/7/2019 (Foreign Investment Agency, Actual situation of foreign direct investment attraction in 12 months of 2016, retrieved on July 27, 2019), http://fia.mpi.gov.vn/TinBai/5177/Tinh-hinh-thu-hut-Dau-tu-nuoc-ngoai-12-thang-nam-2016
8. CụcĐầutưnướcngoài, Tìnhhìnhthuhútđầutưnướcngoàinăm 2018, truycậpngày 27/7/2019 (Foreign Investment Agency, Actual situation of foreign direct investment in 2018, retrieved on July 27, 2019), https://dautunuocngoai.gov.vn/tinbai/6108/ Tinh-hinh-thu-hut-Dau-tu-nuoc-ngoai-nam-2018
9. CụcĐầutưnướcngoài, BộKếhoạchđầutư, Báocáotìnhhìnhkếhoạchđầutư qua cácnăm (Foreign Investment Agency, Ministry of Planning and Investment, report on investment situation over the years).
10. BáoĐiệntửChínhphủnước CHXHCNVN, Tăngtrưởngcôngnghiệpchếbiến, chếtạovàdịchvụlàđộnglựcthúcđẩy GDP tăngcao, truycậpngày 25/7/2019 (Online newspaper of the Government of the Socialist Republic of Vietnam, Growth in processing, manufacturing and services industries is the driving force to increasing GDP, retrieved on July 25, 2019), http://baochinhphu.vn/Thu-tuong-va-Thanh-vien-Chinh-phu-tra-loi-chat-van/Tang-truong-cong-nghiep-che-bien-che-tao-va-dich-vu-la-dong-luc-thuc-day-GDP-tang-cao/346480.vgp
11. TạpchíCộngsản, Nhữngthànhtựunổibậttrongpháttriểnkinhtế qua 30 nămđổimới, truycậpngày 27/7/2019 (Communist Review, Outstanding achievements in economic development after 30 years of "Doi Moi", retrievedon July 27, 2019), http://www.tapchicongsan.org.vn/Home/PrintStory.aspx?distribution=36945&print=true
12. Dântrí, KinhtếViệt Nam qua lăngkínhcủacáctổchứcquốctế, truycậpngày 27/7/2019 (Dan tri, Vietnam's economy through the lens of international organizations, retrieved on July 27, 2019), https://dantri.com.vn/kinh-doanh/kinh-te-viet-nam-qua-lang-kinh-cua-cac-to-chuc-quoc-te-20151218175005893.htm
13. DiễnđànkinhtếViệt Nam, *GDP đầungườinăm 2010 là 1168 USD,* truycậpngày 27/7/2019 *(Vietnam Economic Forum, GDP per capita in 2010 was 1,168 USD, retrieved on July 27, 2019),* https://vef.vn/2010/12/31/2010-12-31-gdp-dau-nguoi-nam-2010-la-1-168-usd/
14. PhạmViệtDũng, Kinhtếsố - Cơhội "bứtphá"choViệt Nam, TạpchíCộngsản, Số 921 (Pham Viet Dung, Digital Economics - An opportunity for Vietnam to make a breakthrough, Communist Review, issue 921).
15. ĐảngCộngsảnViệt Nam, VănkiệnĐạihộiĐảngtoànquốclầnthứ VI, VII, VIII, XI, X, XI, XII, Nxb CTQG, HN 1987, 1991, 1996, 2001, 2006, 2011, 2016 (Communist Party of Vietnam, Documents of the sixth, eighth, ninth, 10th, 11th, 12thNational Congress, National Political Publishing House, HN 1987, 1991, 1996, 2001, 2006, 2011, 2016).
16. ĐảngCộngsảnViệt Nam, Báocáotổngkếtmộtsốvấnđềlýluận – thựctiễn qua 20 nămđổimới (1986-2006), Nxb CTQG, HN 2005 (Communist Party of Vietnam, Summary report on some theoretical and practical issues after 20 years of "Doi Moi"

(1986-2006), National Political Publishing House, HN 2005).
17. VõVănĐức–ĐinhVănTrung (chủbiên), Táicấutrúcnềnkinhtế Việt Nam – Lýluậnvàthựctiễn, NxbLýluậnchínhtrị, HN 2015 (Vo Van Duc – Dinh Van Trung (Co-author), Vietnam's economic restructuring – Theory and Practice, National Political Theory Publishing House, Hanoi 2015).
18. Economic Time, KinhtếViệtKinhtếlàmộttrọngtâmtrongquanhệViệt Nam-ẤnĐộ, BộNgoạiGiaoViệt Nam *(Economic Time, Vietnam's economy is a key focus of Vietnam-India relations, Ministry of Foreign Affairs of Vietnam),* https://ngkt.mofa.gov.vn/kinh-te-la-mot-trong-tam-trong-quan-he-viet-nam-an-do/ truycậpngày 22/8/2019
19. Google & Temasek, Báocáo e-ConomySEA, 2018 (Google & Temasek, E-Conomy report SEA, 2018)
20. BáoGiaothông, CảngbiểnViệt Nam "lộtxác" saugầnhaithậpkỷquyhoạch, BộGiaothôngvậntải, truycậpngày 22/8/2019 (Transportation newspaper, The "makeover" of Vietnam seaports after nearly two decades of planning, Ministry of Transport, retrieved on August 22, 2019), http://mt.gov.vn/vn/tin-tuc/59994/cang-bien-viet-nam-%E2%80%9Clot-xac%E2%80%9D-sau-gan-hai-thap-ky-quy-hoach.aspx
21. HảiquanViệt Nam, Xuấtnhậpkhẩuhànghóanăm 2018 củaViệt Nam: Nhữngnétnổibật qua ghinhậncác con sốthốngkêcủaTổngcụcHảiquan, truycậpngày 29/7/2019 (Vietnam Customs, Vietnam's export and import in 2018: Highlights by statistics of the General Department of Vietnam Customs, retrieved on July 29, 2019), https://www.customs.gov.vn/Lists/ThongKeHaiQuan/ViewDetails.aspx?ID=1560&Category=Ph%C3%A2n%20t%C3%ADch%20chuy%C3%AAn%20%C4%91%E1%BB%81&Group=Ph%C3%A2n%20t%C3%ADch
22. HoàngXuânHòa, Chủđộnghộinhậpkinhtếquốctếsau 5 nămnhìnlại, TạpchíCộngsản, số 150, 2019 (Hoang Xuan Hoa, review on proactive economic integration into global economy after 5 years, Communist Review, issue 150, 2019).
23. Lê QuốcHội - TrươngNhưHiếu - VũMạnh Linh, Khuvựcdoanhnghiệpcóvốnđầutư trựctiếpnướcngoàitạiViệt Nam-thựctrạngvànhữngvấnđềđặt ra, TạpchíKinhtế& Pháttriển, số 263, 2019 (Le Quoc Hoi - Truong NhuHieu - Vu Manh Linh, Foreign direct investment enterprises in Vietnam - actual situation and issues, Journal of Economics and Development, issue 263, 2019).
24. HSBC, Báocáo HSBC expat, 2019 (HSBC expat report, 2019)
25. ViệtHùng-BảoTrung, Việt Nam xuấtsiêu sang thịtrườngChâuMỹ, https://bnews.vn/viet-nam-xuat-sieu-sang-thi-truong-chau-my/127863.html, truycậpngày 22/8/2019 (Viet Hung - Bao Trung, Vietnam's trade surplus to America market retrieved on August 22, 2019).
26. Khánh Lan, Quan hệViệt Nam - ẤnĐộngàycàngpháttriểnsâurộngvàthựcchất, BáoĐiệntửĐảngCộngSảnViệt Nam, truycậpngày 22/8/2019 (Khanh Lan, Vietnam - India relations are deeply and substantially developing, Communist Party of Vietnam Online Newspaper, retrieved on August 22, 2019), http://dangcongsan.vn/chao-xuan-ky-hoi-2019/xuan-que-huong/quan-he-viet-nam-an-do-ngay-cang-phat-trien-sau-rong-va-thuc-chat-512209.html
27. V. Lênin, Toàntập, t44, NxbTiếnbộMát-xcơ-va, 1979 (V. Lenin, complete volume, p. 44, Progress Publishers Moscow, 1979).
28. LiênHiệpQuốc, DiễnđànLiênHiệpQuốcvềThươngmạivàPháttriển (UNCATAD), 2018 (United Nations, United Nations Forum on Trade and Development (UNCTAD), 2018).

29. NguyễnThịMiền, NângcaochấtlượngnguồnnhânlứcđápứngyêucầuđổimớimôhìnhtăngtrưởngkinhtếViệt Nam, TạpchíLýluậnChínhtrị, số 5, 2019 (Nguyen Thi Mien, Improving human resources quality to meet the requirements of reforming Vietnam's economic growth model, Journal of Political Theories, issue 5, 2019).
30. Ngân hàng thế giới (World Bank), http://data.worldbank.org
31. Ngânhàngthếgiới (WB), BáocáotạiDiễnđànKinhtếthếgiới (2018) (World Bank, Report of the World Economic Forum (2018)).
32. Ngânhàngthếgiới (WB), Báocáoxếphạng GDP (PPP) củacácquốcgiavàvùnglãnhthổ, 2012, 2016 (World Bank, List of countries and territories by GDP (PPP), 2012, 2016).
33. VõHồngPhúc, Nhữngthànhtựuvềkinhtế - xãhội qua 20 nămđổimới (1986-2005), Việt Nam 20 nămđổimới, NxbChínhtrịquốcgia, HN 2006 (Vo Hong Phuc, Socio-economic achievements after 20 years of "Doi Moi" (1986-2005), Vietnam - 20 years of "Doi Moi", National Political Publishing House, Hanoi 2006).
34. TTXVN, *Biển, đảoViệt Nam: Tiềmnăngvàlợithế,* https://sonoivu.hanoi.gov.vn/thong-tin-tuyen-truyen/-/view_content/2386499-bien-dao-viet-nam-tiem-nang-va-loi-the.html, truycậpngày 22/8/2019 *(VNA, Vietnam's sea and islands: Potentials and advantages retrieved on August 22, 2019).*
35. Tổng cục Thống kê, *Tình hình kinh tế xã hội 2018*, truy cập ngày 29/7/2019 *(General Statistics Office, Socio-economic situation in 2018, retrieved on July 29, 2019)*, https://www.gso.gov.vn/default.aspx?tabid=382&idmid=2&ItemID=19041
36. Ngô Quang Trung (2015), Đầu tư trực tiếp nước ngoài ở Việt Nam giai đoạn 1988-2015: Thực trạng và vấn đề (Ngo Quang Trung (2015), Foreign direct investment in Vietnam during 1988-2015: Situation and problems), http://www.ipd.org.vn/nghien-cuu-truong-hop-noi-bat/dau-tu-truc-tiep-nuoc-ngoai-o-viet-nam-giai-doan-1988-2015:-thuc-trang-va-van-de-tac-gia:-ngo-quang-trung-a452.html
37. Trung tâm thông tin và dự báo Kinh tế - xã hội quốc gia (2015), Một số điểm nhấn trong tăng trưởng kinh tế giai đoạn 2011 – 2015 (National Center for Socio-Economic Information and Forecast (2015), Some highlights of economic growth in the period 2011 – 2015). http://www.ncseif.gov.vn/sites/vie/Pages/motsodiemnhantrongtang-nd-17232.html
38. ThươngvụViệt Nam tạiẤnĐộ, ThươngmạiViệt Nam - ẤnĐộđạt 10,69 tỷ USD trongnăm 2018 tănggấp 2 lần so vớinăm 2016, BộCôngThương (Vietnam's trade in India, Vietnam - India Trade hit USD 10.69 billion in 2018, two times higher that that in 2016, Ministry of Industry and Traderetrieved on August 22, 2019), https://www.moit.gov.vn/tin-chi-tiet/-/chi-tiet/thuong-mai-viet-nam-an-%C4%910-%C4%91at-10-69-ty-usd-trong-nam-2018-tang-gap-2-lan-so-voi-nam-2016-13585-401.html, truycậpngày 22/8/2019.
39. Vũ Anh Tú, BáocáochuyênđềTriểnvọngthươngmạivàdòngvốnđầutưnướcngoài (FDI) vàoViệt Nam, 17/7/2019 (Vu Anh Tu, Seminar report on trade Prospects and foreign direct investment (FDI) inflows into Vietnam, July 17, 2019, retrieved on August 22, 2019) https://vdsc.com.vn/vn/downloadRptAttachment.rv?rptId=619D37DF7BABB101753 8BAB727784586A, truycậpngày 22/8/2019.
40. UNDP (2015), Báo cáo phát triển con người năm 2015 (UNDP (2015), The 2015 Human Development Report).
41. Vneconomy, Thu nhậpbìnhquânđầungườinăm 2018 đạt 2.587 USD (Vneconomy, Per capita income in 2018 reached USD 2,587, retrieved on July 27, 2019).http://vneconomy.vn/thu-nhap-binh-quan-dau-nguoi-nam-2018-dat-2587-usd-20181227152354 12.htm, truycậpngày 27/7/2019.

5 Political Reforms and Democracy Innovation in Vietnam

Tuan-Thuy Nguyen

Vietnam's Politics in the colonial and non-reunited period

On September 1st, 1858, the French imperialists ordered an attack at Da Nang harbor, which started the invasion of France in Vietnam. The Nguyen regime was powerless and gradually abided France. Since 1884, France established a protectorate and colonial regime throughout the territory of Vietnam. From the early days, mass resistance movements under the leadership of patriotic scholars erupted everywhere, however they failed all eventually.

President Ho Chi Minh, on the way to save the country, founded the Communist Party of Vietnam on February 3rd, 1930. Under the leadership of the Communist Party, the Vietnamese fought against the French colonialists and Japanese fascists, with the Victory in August 1945, which set a ground to the establishment of the Democratic Republic of Vietnam on September 2nd, 1945. Right from the beginning, however, Vietnam had to cope with the intrigue and aggression from France and the United States, so it had to wage a war of national liberation for 30 years (1945-1975). Initially, the resistance war against the French invaders lasted for 9 years (1945-1954) and ended with the victory of Dien Bien Phu and the signing of the Geneva Agreement. Under this Agreement, the country of Vietnam was temporarily divided by the 17th latitude into two South - North regions. The North belonged to the Democratic Republic of Vietnam, led by the Labour Party with Hanoi as the capital. The South was named the Republic of Vietnam governed by the pro-French and pro-American, located in Saigon and called Saigon Government. The Saigon government has tried everything but could not prevent the people's aspiration to unify the country, especially since the Establishment of National Liberation Front of South Vietnam (December 20th, 1960).

In order to maintain the Saigon regime, the United States has increased its aid in various ways, especially in the military. In the mid-1960s onwards, the United States sent half a million troops to South Vietnam to directly participate in the war. From August 5, 1964, the US began to bomb North Vietnam. In the spirit of "Nothing is more precious than independence and freedom", the Vietnamese people have stood firm and won many victories in both the regions. On January 27, 1973, the Paris Agreement on Restoration of Peace in Vietnam was signed; accordingly, the United States agreed to withdraw all troops from

Vietnam. On April 30, 1975, the general offensive to liberate the South and reunify achieved a resounding victory.

Through painful yet majestic historical periods of the nation, the leading role of the Communist Party of Vietnam has been increasingly asserted. During the period 1930-1945, the Communist Party of Vietnam led the Vietnamese revolution to victory in the struggle for power, culminating in the victory of the August Revolution in 1945, leading to the birth of the Democratic Republic of Vietnam. This event opened a new era in national history - an era of independence, freedom, happiness and socialism.

During the 30-year-long resistance war (1945-1975) in order to liberate the people from the yoke of French colonialism and American imperialism, the Communist Party of Vietnam was the one and only force with political mission to lead Vietnam's Revolution. Although there were also two other parties in the Communist Party (the Democratic Party of Vietnam and the Socialist Party of Vietnam) besides the Communist Party during this period; both of these parties expressed their unity with the Communist Party of Vietnam, supported and acknowledged the leadership of the Communist Party of Vietnam. On the opposing side, there were pro-French and US parties opposed to the Communist Party of Vietnam, contrary to the interests of the nation and the interests of the working people, that's why they were also eliminated by the Vietnamese people.

The victory of the General Offensive and Rebellion in 1975 was one of the greatest victories of the Vietnamese nation and the victory of the national liberation movement worldwide. This victory of the Vietnamese army and people attributed to the leadership of the Communist Party of Vietnam and President Ho Chi Minh with revolutionary ways and methods of independence, autonomy, rightness, creativity and highlight national independence and socialism, simultaneously carrying out two different revolutionary strategies in the two regions with a common goal of liberating the South, protecting the North and reuniting the country.

Vietnamese Politics in the period of 1975-1991

On July 2, 1976, at the first session of the National Assembly of reunified Vietnam, the Assembly decided to name the country the Socialist Republic of Vietnam. On September 20, 1977, Vietnam became a member of the United Nations.

During the period 1976-1980, the task of the state institution of the Socialist Republic of Vietnam was to successfully build socialism on a national scale, and to defend national independence and unity. From 1980 to 1989, the institution of the Socialist Republic of Vietnam was built on the 1980 Constitution basis, which was structured into the National Assembly. The National Assembly is the highest representative organ of the people, the highest organ of state power of the Socialist Republic of Vietnam, has the right to make constitutional and legislative decisions on internal policies and foreign affairs, decide economic and cultural development goals, the main guidelines about the organization and operation of the state apparatus with respect to social relations and the activities of citizens, take supreme supervision over the entire state's activities. The term of the National Assembly is five years. The National Assembly elects the President and Vice Presidents.

The State Council carries out tasks and uses the powers assigned by the Constitution, implements laws and passes resolutions in the National Assembly; decides important issues on building socialism and protecting the Nation, supervise the implementation of the Constitution, ordinances, resolutions of the National Assembly and State Council, oversee the operation of the state apparatus. The State Council delegates are elected among the National Assembly deputies, including the President, Vice Presidents, the Secretary General and other members. The State Council and the President of the State Council stand for the Socialist Republic of Vietnam when dealing with domestic and foreign affairs. The President of the State Council dominates the people's armed forces nationwide and holds the position of Chairman of the National Defense Council. The term of the State Council is counted following that of the National Assembly.

The Ministers Council is the highest executive organ and State administration of the highest state authority. The Ministers Council collectively manages the implementation of the State's political, economic, cultural, social, security, defense and foreign affairs. The Ministers Council is composed of President, Vice Presidents, Ministers and Heads of State Committees. The term of the Ministers Council is counted following that of the National Assembly.

The People's Courts and the People's Council have the task of protecting the socialist legislation, protecting the socialist regime and the collective ownership of labour class, and protecting socialist properties, ensuring respect for the life, property, freedom, honour and dignity of citizens.

From 1975 to 1986, Vietnam encountered multiple challenges caused by the war, such as social evils, the flow of refugees, the war on the southwest border against the Khmer Rouge genocide and border war in the North, the siege and embargo from the United States and Western countries, natural disasters, constraining reasons and the will to rebuild the country without taking into account historical and other conditions. In the early 1980s, the socio-economic crisis in Vietnam became severe.

From December 1986, under the leadership of the Communist Party, Vietnam began to carry out the *Doi Moi* reforms to overcome development challenges and gradually integrate into the regional and the international scale. At the 6th Congress, the Vietnamese Communist Party strictly reviewed its leadership process, affirmed its achievements, pointed out the mistakes and based on that, laid out the renovation policy in all aspects of life, in which, economic innovation is put on top with the policy of developing a multi-sector commodity economy operating under the state-controlled market mechanism and socialist orientation, along with strengthening the legal basis, reforming Party and State organizations.

The 6th Conference of the Party Central Committee (March 1989), the Communist Party of Vietnam used the concept of political system instead of the concept of the dictatorship of the proletariat. This was an important turning point of the central task of the Vietnamese political process that has been shifted towards building and promoting socialist democracy and thereby, marking a higher development step of the *Doi Moi*.

Vietnamese Politics from 1991 to 2019

The comprehensive reforms objective required transformation, both economically and politically. The 7th Congress (June 1991) of the Communist Party of Vietnam reaffirmed its determination to continue the *Doi Moi* policy with the goal of overcoming challenges, addressing stability and socio-economic development, strengthening political stability, eliminating negative social justice, and pulling the country out of a crisis. The Meeting also set out foreign policy of based on independent policy, strategic autonomy, openness, diversification and multilateralisation of relations with the goal "Vietnam wants to be friends with all countries in the international community, strive for peace, independence and development ". The political reforms undertaken in Vietnam is essentially the renewal of the political system, which is the renewal of relations between the Party, the state and socio-political organizations with the people.

"Simultaneously with economic innovation, it is necessary to gradually renovate the organization and mode of operation of the political system; promote the people's mastery and creative capacity much greater in all major fields including political, economic, cultural and social. Because politics is related to particularly complex and sensitive relationships in society, the renewal of the political system must necessarily be based on serious research and preparation without allowing any instability leading to confusion. However, it is not the reason for delaying the renovation of the political system, especially in terms of organizational structure and cadres, the relationship between the Party, the State and mass organizations because it is a condition to promote social as well as economic development and implementation of democracy"(Communist Party Declaration, 7th Congress).

In the context of a profound impact from the collapse of the socialist model in the Soviet Union and Eastern Europe, instable domestic markets, extended hardships because of embargoes and confrontation with covert activities causing political instability and violent overthrow by hostile forces, Vietnam gradually overcame challenges and continued to the renewal process in this period. Political stability, independence, sovereignty and peaceful environment of Vietnam are maintained, national defense and security were strengthened. The political system from the central to local levels and the apparatus of the rule of law is incrementally completed. The foreign policy of independence, multilateralization and diversification of Vietnam's relations has achieved excellent results.

For more than three decades (1986-2019), Vietnam's economy has continuously grown and developed thanks to the implementation of the socio-economic development strategy. Gross domestic product (GDP) grew steadily, in 2018, the growth rate reached 7.08%. It is estimated that in the first 9 months of 2019, the growth rate reached 6.98% over the same period last year. Culture and society have made progress in many aspects; the association of economic development with the resolution of social problems has improved, especially in the work of hunger elimination and poverty reduction; living-conditions of people from all social class have been improved. Political - social stability, national defense and security were strengthened; Foreign Relations have got a new development. The building of a socialist rule-of-law State has made progress in all 3 areas of legislative, executive and judicial. The strength of the great unity bloc of the nation was promoted.

The victories that Vietnam obtained has been affirmed in the 8th Congress (1996): "Incorporating from the beginning economic reform with political innovation, economic innovation as the focus, at the same time political innovation step-by-step". The main objective of renewing the political system is to implement socialist democracy well, promote the full ownership of the people, and the path of socio-economic development as "Economic growth associated with associated with social progress and justice, preserving and promoting the national cultural identity and protecting the ecological environment".

With the achievements, and the goal of building a Vietnam "Rich people, strong country, democracy, justice, civilization", Vietnam has established an extensive international relationship with 189 countries. National, economic and trade relations with more than 200 countries and territories, has established more than 80 diplomatic missions abroad, the position of Vietnam is increasingly asserted in the region and the world.

Entering the 21st century, from the 9th Congress (2001), the Party introduced the concept of "Socialist-oriented market economy" and affirmed the policy of building and developing a commune-oriented market economy. Socialism is a general model, a consistent strategic path of Vietnam in the transition to socialism. The way of economic management in the direction of developing a socialist-oriented market economy should be under the state management. The State manages the economy with laws, strategies and policies, uses the market mechanism to free up production capacity, promotes positive aspects, creates a limit against negative aspects of market economy and protects benefit of the whole people.

In the 10th Congress (2006) with the spirit of inheriting the achievements of the renovation process, the Party proposed a strategy to "continue completing the socialist-oriented market economy institution". The socialist orientation in the market economy in Vietnam is the realization of the objective "rich people, strong country, fair, democratic and civilized society", strong liberation of production and development capacity, economic development of various forms of ownership and various economic sectors, of which, the state economy plays a leading role, the state economy and the collective economy are becoming a solid foundation of the national economy. Along with economic development, social progress and justice are made right in every step and every development policy.

The people's sovereignty has been promoted, the management and regulatory role of the socialist rule-of-law economy under the leadership of the Party has been steadily guaranteed.

The 11th Congress (2011) has adopted the Credo for supplementing, developing, raising the overall goal when the transition period in our country ends. The Credo emphasizes: "Perseverance and drastic implementation of innovation. The political reform must get along with the economic renovation in accordance with the proper agenda and a focus on completing the socialist-oriented market economy institution, renewing the Party's leadership and building a socialist rule of law state, expanding democracy in the Party and in society associated with strengthening discipline and discipline to promote comprehensive innovation and promote the synergy of the entire nation for the purpose of building a rich Socialist Vietnam, a strong, democratic, fair and civilized country.

The 12th Congress of the Party (1-2016) with the theme "Strengthening building a clean and strong Party; promote the strength of the entire nation, socialist democracy; promote comprehensively and synchronously the renovation process; firmly defending the Fatherland, maintaining a stable and peaceful environment; to strive to soon turn our country basically into an industrialized country towards modernization.

The 12thCongress made a big step: defined the basic characteristics of the socialist-oriented market economy of Vietnam as follows: "The socialist-oriented market economy of Vietnam is an economy that operates fully and synchronously in accordance with the rules of the market economy and at the same time ensures the socialist orientation suitable to each stage of development of the country, which is a modern and international integrated market; under the management of the Socialist rule of law State, led by the Communist Party of Vietnam, aims at "rich people, strong country, democracy, justice and civilization".

From the Party's new undertakings, the 2013 Constitution concretized the legal status of the Communist Party of Vietnam, in addition to continuing to define the Party's state and social leadership, the 2013 Constitution has added provisions: "The Communist Party of Vietnam closely goes with the people, serves the people, is under the supervision of the people, and is accountable to the people for its decisions." At the same time, it added "members of the Communist Party of Vietnam make actions within the framework of the Constitution and Laws". These regulations define the obligations of the Communist Party's organizations and members of the Communist Party of Vietnam for a close association with the people, service for the people, submission to their supervision, and responsibility about their decisions. These regulations are a legal basis for people to ensure that Party organizations and Party members operate in accordance with the requirements of the socialist rule of law state;

"State power is the division, coordination and control among state agencies in the exercise of legislative, executive and judicial rights." Compared to the 1992 Constitution, the 2013 Constitution, besides the provisions on division and coordination, has added control of power among state agencies in the exercise of legislative, executive and judicial powers. This supplement is essential to eliminate the weaknesses in the control of the state power of the Vietnamese apparatus according to the 1992 Constitution (which was amended and supplemented in 2001).

Regarding the forms of exercising people's power, Article 6 of the 2013 Constitution stipulates: "The people exercise their state power by means of direct and representative democracy through the National Assembly and the People's Council and other state agencies." Compared to the 1992 Constitution, this provision of the 2013 Constitution shows a clear improvement in Vietnam's constitutional thinking. The 1992 Constitution only prescribes representative forms of democracy, while the 2013 Constitution provides for two forms of direct democracy and representative democracy in the Constitution.

Regarding the political regime, there are also new and supplemented regulations on the role of the Vietnam Fatherland Front, which is "the role of social criticism, participation in building the Party, the State, the people's external activities, contribution to construction part and national defense". The social critic role of the Vietnam Fatherland Front is an important addition in the 2013 Constitution. The unitary political regime of the socialist countries has the advantage of high political unity and stability. However, there is also the limitation that there is a lack of proper critical analysis so sometimes decisions have not been viewed and considered in many different aspects objectively and fully. The addition of the above provisions on the role of the Front is entirely consistent with the current conditions of international integration and globalization in Vietnam.

The 2013 Constitution expresses the reasonable reception of the principles of power division theory in the organization of the state apparatus when establishing the position and nature of the National Assembly, the Government, the People's Court and Procuracy clearly. The 2013 Constitution clearly states that the National Assembly is the agency exercising constitutional rights, legislative rights (Article 69) the Government is the agency exercising executive powers (Article 94), and People's Courts exercise private rights. France (Article 102); The People's Procuracy (functions such as acting as the prosecutor) set the right to prosecute and control judicial activities (Article 107).

Regarding the institution of the President, the 2013 Constitution clearly defines the President's powers when determining the President's decision to bestow, promote and demote the rank of general, the rank of admiral, deputy admiral, naval director, appoint, and dismiss the Chief of the General Staff, Chairman of the General Department of Political and Military of Vietnam instead of stipulating the decision of the rank and rank of "senior officers" in the armed forces page as specified in the 1992 Constitution.

The task is also to organize local state powers according to the 2013 Constitution: The 1992 Constitution, Chapter IX is the People's Council and the People's Committee still in the 2013 Constitution, Chapter IX is the "Local Government". The affirmation in the Constitution of local government including People's Council and People's Committee is necessary. Because the

1992 Constitution did not specify which agencies the local government consisted of, the concept of the People's Court in some localities and the local People's Procuracy were also local governments, since then interference interferes with the Court's independence in trial.

Another new and notable point is that in addition to the three levels of provincial and municipal administrations; districts, towns, provincial cities; new communes, wards and townships and the new Constitution also stipulate a special administrative-territorial unit established by the National Assembly. On the other hand, in order to create favourable conditions for the diversification of local governments, Clause 2, Article 111 stipulates: "Local governments include the People's Council and People's Committee organized in accordance with the characteristics of rural areas, urban areas, islands, special administrative - economic units determined by law".

About the organization of implementation and control of state power, the 2013 Constitution provides for two independent constitutional bodies, the Central Election Council and the State Audit. Independent constitutional bodies, as defined by the Constitution, should show a high degree of independence in their organizations and activities, so that these institutions can operate effectively, efficiently and without depending on other institutions in the state apparatus, ensuring that state power is strictly controlled.

The model of political leadership of the Communist Party of Vietnam

There are two important aspects: the leadership content and the leadership mode in the Party's leadership over the state. The leadership content of the Party is the policy on socio-economic development issues; and the Party's leadership is the way to realize that policy. In order to improve the effectiveness of the Party's leadership, the leadership content of the Party must be right and the mode of leadership must be appropriate. In Vietnam, the issue of determining the Party's leadership mode is extremely important and considered the basic viewpoint of the Party and is presented in the Party Congress Documents and some Party Central Conferences.

The political leadership method of the Communist Party of Vietnam is understood as a system of methods, forms, measures, working processes, working styles employed by the Party to influence social forces, organizations and individuals to turn the Party's lines, policies and policies into the awareness and actions of the target subjects, thereby fulfilling the revolutionary tasks set by the Party.

The basic content of the Party's leadership method was determined in the Credo 1991, including:

- The Party leads the society with guidelines, strategies, policies and guidelines.
- The Party leads by propaganda, persuasion, mobilization, organization, inspection and by exemplary actions of party members.

- The Party introduces elite party members who are qualified and qualified to operate in government leadership agencies and mass organizations.
- The Party does not replace the work of other organizations in the political system.
- The Party leads the political system and is a part of that system. The Party is closely connected to the people, subject to the people's supervision, operating within the framework of the Constitution and laws.

In addition to the points mentioned above, the Party leads the State, the Fatherland Front and socio-political organizations and the people from the Party's prestige, from promoting and respecting the role of the State and organizations in the political system and the whole society. The true leadership of the Party is not only through decisions and directives but also by prestige, by the ability to inspire and persuade in words, in actions and in the working style of organizations. Party and of each individual leader, party member.

The way of leadership of the Party has always been changed in accordance with the requirements and revolutionary tasks, with the Party's lines, guidelines and policies in each specific historical period. Renewing the Party's leadership is always an objective requirement, an important task in the Party's construction work and improving the Party's ruling capacity. This objective requirement is always thoroughly and emphasized by the Communist Party of Vietnam in the Congress and Conference of the Central Executive Committee documents.

In the pre-*Doi Moi* period, some party members and people were simply aware of the handling of the relationship between the ruling party and the state affecting the determination of the Party's leadership mode for the State and society. Therefore, from the 6th Party Congress (1986), the Party has advocated to renovate the way of leadership. The document of the Party Congress VI affirmed: The Party need to renovate working styles, conduct in depth, go closely to reality, capture information quickly and accurately, and have inspection programmes; officials must go deep to the base; leadership must master the centralized and unified leadership; It is necessary to strengthen collective leadership, expand democratic activities, research creative experiences from the local levels and listen to the opinions of the masses; important guidelines need to be discussed and decided collectively; leaders must listen to their opinions against them. The Party Congress VI has not used the concept of "leadership mode" yet but already the concept of "working style".

The reform of the Party's leadership to the State was made more clearly and urgently at the 7th Party Congress. In the "Platform for building the country during the transition to socialism" (1991), which was adopted at the 7th Party Congress, the Party determined that the direction of renewing the Party's leadership method was by credo and strategies, policies and guidelines; by propaganda, persuasion, mobilization, inspection organization and by exemplary actions of party members. The Party introduced elite party members who are competent and qualified to operate in government leadership agencies and mass organizations. The Party does not do the job of other organizations in the political system; "The party leads the political system and is part of that system. The Party is closely connected with the people, under the supervision of the people, operating within the framework of the Constitution and laws."

Under the spirit of the 7th Party Congress and the National Delegation Conference between the term of 7th Congress, the 8th Party Congress determined the direction of renewing the Party's leadership method as follows: "The Party leads through party organization not just through individual party members; lead by collective decisions and by monitoring, giving direction, inspecting implementation, encouraging good sides, rectifying deviations. The Party leadership promotes the role and effectiveness of the State rather than operating on behalf of the State. The Party and all party members operate within the framework of the Constitution and laws and take responsibility for their own activities."

The Document of the 9th Party Congress affirmed: "Strengthening the leadership role and continuing to renovate the Party's leadership method for the State through setting guidelines, guidelines, major policies and orientations for the development and inspection of the organization and implementation of the Party's lines and undertakings and the Constitution and laws of the State. The Central Executive Committee, the collective committee, the party cadres, delegation discuss on a basis of democracy, vote and make resolutions according to the majority of important issues on guidelines, guidelines, policies and organization, officials. Strengthen the collective leadership system in combination with promoting the spirit of initiative, creativity and personal responsibility".

The 10th Party Congress affirmed: "Focus on renewing the Party's leadership method towards the State. The Party leads by way, viewpoint and resolutions; leadership institutionalized, concretized into the Constitution, laws, plans, major work programmes of the State; properly arranging officials and regularly inspecting the organization of implementation"; "The Party leads but does not advocate or change the State; on the contrary, promoting the active and creative role of the State in the management of the country and society".

The 11th Party Congress continued the spirit of the congresses before emphasizing: "Overcome the situation of justification, change or loosen of Party leadership with state agencies. Innovate the Party's leadership method for the Fatherland Front and socio-political organizations to renew the way of issuing resolutions, focusing on leading, directing the implementation, checking, reviewing and summarizing the implementation of the Party's resolutions; promote reform of administrative procedures in the Party".

The document of the 12th Party Congress wrote: "Improve the effectiveness of the implementation and continue to strongly renew the Party's leadership method for the political system, especially the State. The Party leads the State with major guidelines and policies, institutionalizes the Party's views, guidelines and policies into policies, laws, and leaders to build up a sufficient number of qualified officials and public employees. quality and capacity, leading to effective implementation of guidelines, policies and the legal system;

attaching importance to leading the renovation, improving the quality of law, administrative reform and judicial reform; Party organizations and party members must be exemplary in compliance with the Constitution and laws"; "To clearly define the authority and responsibilities of the Central Executive Committee, the Politburo, the Secretariat, the Party Committee and the Standing Committee at all levels."

Addressing corruption and public sector reform

Corruption is an alien phenomenon of state power, lack of democracy, undermining the confidence of the people in the Party and the State. In the context of the ruling Communist Party, cadres and party members are easy to fall into the lure of power and money, easy to lose themselves, vulnerable to political, moral and political ideology. It discredits the Party in front of the people, libel the title of a Communist Party member. To prevent and fight against corruption, there must be a mechanism for supervision and control from within the state itself and from the society.

Not only aware of the risk of corruption, but to address the challenges of corruption, the 2018 Anti-Corruption Law has been enacted. The law identifies acts of corruption occurring both in the state sector by persons with positions and power centres in agencies, organizations and units of the state sector and outside the state by persons with positions and rights. In non-state sector enterprises and organizations. The law has built a comprehensive and extensive anti-corruption mechanism in order to contribute to building a public and transparent state management and social management mechanism so that "corruption cannot occur"; at the same time, create a synchronous legal basis for timely detection and handling of acts of corruption so as to "not dare to be corrupt". Ensure that the constitutionality, legality and consistency of the Anti-Corruption Law 2018 with the 2013 Constitution and other relevant laws, ensure the feasibility of the Law; take appropriate steps to improve the compliance with the requirements of the United Nations Convention against Corruption of which Vietnam is a member state.

The law specifies ways of perceiving corruption, specifically addressing corrupt practices in all areas of life. Create unity and uniformity in the Vietnamese legal system, namely the unity and consistency between laws and related policies and legal documents. The enactment of the anti-corruption law also promotes publicity, transparency and accountability, thereby, to control conflicts of interest, to prevent corruption in the private sector, to control assets, income, especially assets, income generated without explaining the source of cadres and civil servants, as well as sanctions to strengthen compliance with anti-corruption laws.

Regarding Public Sector Reform

In the context of the development of a market economy and administrative reform, the State must not only organize and manage society through legal institutions but also through satisfying the essential needs of the people - supply. The State of Vietnam has rightly established its nature from the people, by the people and for the people, from the time of its establishment, always putting the interests of the people and the people first. In the historical periods, the Party and the State of Vietnam always uphold the responsibility of caring for the lives of the people in every aspect, promoting the development of production, health care, education, etc., improving material and spiritual lives of the people. However, there is still a certain distance between desire and reality. Vietnam is still an underdeveloped country, and the demand for services is still very limited.

In the context of developing a socialist-oriented market economy and opening up international integration, Vietnam should further promote the reform of public services (state administration), contribute to building and completing improve the socialist rule of law state. The contents of administrative reform are aimed at building a democratic, clean and strong administration; step by step modernizing in order to better serve basic and essential needs, ensure basic rights and obligations of the people. In particular, the renewal of the role and responsibilities of the Government and the state administrative apparatus in the management and organization of public service delivery is really an important task to focus on. Administrative reform, therefore, must come from specific conditions of Vietnam, with reference to the experience of countries in the world, which will make an important contribution to the success of the administrative reform in Vietnam today.

In the upcoming time, the public sector reform in Vietnam will mainly focus on the following:

- Reform state administrative institutions to create a system of legal corridors for state administrative activities. Building and perfecting the legal system, along with the process of building and perfecting the institutional system, mechanisms and policies, ensuring fairness in accessing the fruits of the development process; Perfecting the institution of ownership, ensuring the legitimate rights and interests of different owners in the economy. Continue to build and improve the institutional system on the organization and operation of state administrative agencies; amend, supplement and complete legal documents on the organization and operation of the Government, People's Councils and Committees at all levels. Formulate and complete the provisions of the law on the relationship between the State and the people, with a focus on ensuring and promoting the people's mastery, obtain the people's opinions before deciding on undertakings, important policies and the people's right to supervision of activities of state administrative agencies.
- Reform administrative procedures to resolve the relationship between state agencies with each other and state agencies with citizens and organizations in society in the direction of simplicity, compactness and publicity and transparency. Reduce and improve the quality of administrative procedures in all areas of state management, administrative

procedures related to people, businesses and between state agencies. Strictly control the issuance of new administrative procedures in accordance with the law and make all administrative procedures transparent and practical in appropriate and appropriate forms; uniformly performing the method of calculating expenses that individuals and organizations must pay when settling administrative procedures at state administrative agencies; maintain and update the national database on administrative procedures; expanding democracy, promoting the role of independent organizations and consultants in building institutions and national standards on administrative procedures; sharply reducing the current administrative procedures; public administrative standards and regulations for people to supervise the implementation; Receive, handle feedback and recommendations of individuals and organizations on administrative regulations to support the improvement of the quality of administrative regulations and supervise the implementation of administrative procedures of administrative agencies at all levels.

- Reforming the state administrative apparatus: The field of reforming the organization of the state administrative apparatus aims to build a simple, compact and smooth administrative apparatus. Specifically, conducting a general review of the existing positions, functions, tasks, powers, organizational structures and payrolls of ministries, ministerial-level agencies, government-attached agencies and People's Committees of levels, professional agencies under provincial-level People's Committees, other agencies and organizations attached to the central and local state administrative apparatus on which basis to adjust their functions and tasks, powers and organization, rearrangement of agencies and units in order to overcome the overlap, vacancy or duplication of functions, tasks and powers; transfer the work that should not be done or ineffective to state-run society, social organizations and non-governmental organizations; proper identification of functions and tasks of rural and urban government models. Strengthen the autonomy and self-responsibility mechanism of public service delivery units, etc.
- Building and improving the quality of the contingent of cadres, civil servants and public employees with good ethical qualities, political ability, professionalism and dedication to the people through various forms, suitable and effective training and retraining methods; Complete the system of legal provisions on titles and professional standards of cadres, civil servants and public employees, including leading and managing cadres and civil servants. Build an active structure of cadres, civil and public employees.

Complete the provisions of the law on recruiting, arranging and assigning tasks in accordance with the qualifications, capabilities and forte of successful recruited civil servants and public employees; implement the regime of rank promotion examinations on the principle of competition; competitive contests for appointment to leadership and management positions. Complete the provisions of the law on assessment of cadres, civil servants and public employees based on the performance of assigned tasks; implement the mechanism of eliminating and dismissing people who fail to fulfill their tasks, violate discipline and discredit people; clearly define tasks and powers of officials, public employees and employees corresponding to their responsibilities and set severe punishment for law violation, violation of discipline, violation of public service ethics of officials and employees; reform the salary regime and improve accountability, administrative discipline and public service ethics of cadres, civil and public employees.

Conclusion

As a country encountering with foreign invasion and domination throughout its history, Vietnam has still defeated all enemies. The reasons for that success are various, of which, notably, Vietnam has built a stable politics, promoted the strength of the great national unity bloc in the Party, the political system and in the whole people. In the process of leading the Vietnamese revolution and building the country, the Communist Party of Vietnam has set out the right revolutionary way, suitable to the country's situation and constant innovation the appropriate leadership method with vivid practical conditions of the country and the development trend of the times. Associated with each historical period with specific revolutionary tasks, the task of building Vietnamese politics was clearly defined and achieved great results. Especially since the country was reformed from 1986 up to now, Vietnam's politics has become more and more stable, creating trust among the people and recognized by international friends. Therefore, many countries and organizations around the world have chosen Vietnam as the ideal place to conduct their important events. Along with the continuous renewal of politics, Vietnam is also interested in promoting democracy throughout the Party and the entire people and achieving great results. Achievements create more motivation for the civil classes to be confident and make efforts to contribute efforts to successfully implement the goal of building a stable and sustainable Vietnam – a rich, strong country with democracy, justice, civilization and international integration.

References

1. Đảng Cộng sản Việt Nam: Văn kiện Đại hội Đảng thời kỳ đổi mới (Đại hội VI, VII, VIII, IX), NXB Chính trị Quốc gia, Hà Nội, 2005.
   (The Communist Party of Vietnam: Document of the Renewal Party Congress (the 6th, 7th, 8th and 9thCongress, National Political Publishing House, Hanoi, 2005)
2. Đảng Cộng sản Việt Nam: Văn kiện đại hội đại biểu toàn quốc lần thứ X, XI, XII, NXB Chính trị Quốc gia, Hà Nội, 2006, 2011, 2016.
   (The Communist Party of Vietnam: Documents of the 10th, 11th and 12th National Congress, National Political Publishing House, Hanoi, 2006, 2011, 2016.)
3. Đảng Cộng sản Việt Nam: Văn kiện Đảng toàn tập, t.47, NXB Chính trị quốc gia, Hà Nội, 2006.

(The Communist Party of Vietnam: Comprehensive Party Document, p. 47, National Political Publishing House, Hanoi, 2006)

4. Đảng Cộng sản Việt Nam: Văn kiện Đảng toàn tập, t.51, NXB Chính trị quốc gia, Hà Nội, 2007.
   (The Communist Party of Vietnam: Comprehensive Party Document, p. 51, National Political Publishing House, Hanoi, 2007.)
5. Nguyễn Văn Giang: Các nguyên tắc tổ chức và hoạt động của Đảng Cộng sản Việt Nam hiện nay - Lý luận và thực tiễn, NXB Lý luận chính trị, Hà Nội, 2017.
   (Nguyen Van Giang: The principles of organization and operation of the current Communist Party of Vietnam - Theory and practice, Political Theory Publishing House, Hanoi, 2017.)
6. Nguyễn Long Hải: Thể chế pháp lý về kiểm soát quyền lực nhà nước ở Việt Nam, NXB Chính trị Quốc gia Sự thật, Hà Nội, 2017.
   (Nguyen Long Hai: The legal institution on the control of state power in Vietnam, National Political Publishing House Truth, Hanoi, 2017.)
7. Hiến pháp Việt Nam 2013.
   (Vietnamese Constitution 2013.)
8. Dương Xuân Ngọc (Chủ biên): Quan hệ giữa đổi mới kinh tế và đổi mới chính trị ở Việt Nam, NXB Chính trị Quốc gia, Hà Nội, 2012.
   (Duong Xuan Ngoc (Editor): The relationship between economic innovation and political innovation in Vietnam, National Political Publishing House, Hanoi, 2012.)
9. Nhóm Ngân hàng Thế giới và Bộ Kế hoạch và Đầu tư: Việt Nam 2035 - Hướng tới Thịnh vượng, Sáng tạo, Công Bằng và Dân chủ, NXB Hồng Đức, Hà Nội, 2016.
   (World Bank Group and Ministry of Planning and Investment: Vietnam 2035 - Towards Prosperity, Innovation, Justice and Democracy, Hong Duc Publishing House, Hanoi, 2016.)
10. Nguyễn Trung Thanh, Ngô Huy Tiếp, Dương Trung Ý: Nội dung và phương thức cầm quyền của Đảng Cộng sản Việt Nam, NXB Lý luận chính trị, Hà Nội, 2018.
    (Nguyen Trung Thanh, Ngo Huy Tiep, Duong Trung Y: Contents and ruling method of the Communist Party of Vietnam, Political Theory Publishing House, Hanoi, 2018.)
11. Nguyễn Đăng Thành, Vũ Hoàng Công, Nguyễn An Ninh: Đối mới bộ máy của Đảng, bộ máy của nhà nước trong điều kiện mới, NXB Lý luận Chính trị, Hà Nội 2017.
    (Nguyen Dang Thanh, Vu Hoang Cong, Nguyen An Ninh: Renewing the apparatus of the Party, the apparatus of the state in new conditions, Political Theory Publishing House, Hanoi 2017.)
12. Bùi Thị Nguyệt Thu: Giám sát của Mặt trận Tổ quốc Việt Nam đối với hoạt động của chính quyền cấp xã, NXB Tư pháp, Hà Nội 2018.
    (Bui Thi Nguyet Thu: Supervisor of the Vietnam Fatherland Front on the activities of communal authorities, Justice Publishing House, Hanoi 2018.)

6 Vietnam's Defense and Security Policy

Truong-Thu Doan

Concept of National Defence and Security

National defence and security have been discussed under various aspects for a long time by many military commanders. Strengthening and constructing a national defence and security outlook is main task of every country in order to protect homeland from any aggression. According to the Vietnam Military Encyclopedia: National Defence "is the protection for the country including the overall military, politics, economy, science activities internally and externally... of the state and people to defend the country so as to create a comprehensive and balanced strength, in which military strength is characteristic, in order to maintain peace, repel and prevent war activities of the enemy and ready to defeat the aggression war in any form and scale"[1]. Vietnam Defence law 2018 affirmed: National defence is the country's defending task with the combined strength of the entire nation, of which the military strength is the characteristic, the people's armed forces act as the core. Security, in general, is recognized by the military theorists, strategists and scholars as a stable and safe state of a country. National Security is: "...a capacity to control those domestic and foreign conditions that the public opinion of a given community believes necessary to enjoy it's all self-determination or autonomy, prosperity and well-being"[2]. That is the basis to ensure sustainable development, inviolability to sovereign independence, territorial integrity of a nation.

From the two concepts above, it can be understood that national defence and security are the strength and ability to resist domestic and foreign threats to a nation to protect its independence, sovereignty and integrity, political regimes and peaceful environment for the stable development of a country. Therefore, constructing strong national defence and security is important for the existence and development to every nation in the world, including Vietnam.

Marxism–Leninism and Ho Chi Minh's ideology about defending the home country

Marxism–Leninism classics assume that during the process of implementing the socialist revolution, capitalist countries will take many anti-sabotage measures and methods, therefore the proletariat of countries must make wars to protect the revolution. From the experience of the Paris Commune in 1871, Marx and Engels considered that in order to protect the revolutionary achievements, the proletariat first had to establish and consolidate the dictatorship of the proletariat and the people must be armed and form civil police teams right after gaining power. These forces play an important role in protecting the young revolutionary government, against the anti-sabotage and protesting actions from the bourgeoisie. These ideas are considered as the original ideas of Marx and Engels on building armed forces to protect the socialist state and they have been inherited as well as developed by later generation theorists to be more complete.

In his doctrine about the protection of the Socialist Homeland, Lenin argued that constructing socialism must go together with protecting the nationalist homeland, which is an indispensable and objective rule. The task of protecting the revolutionary achievements must be taken as the focus of the revolutionary government and must be carried out resolutely, regularly, permanently and uphold the revolutionary vigilance spirit[3]. Resolution means no chance for the bourgeoisie and reactionary forces to protest; Frequency, long-term and upholding the spirit of revolutionary vigilance is against the nature, the conspiracy of the enemy for always desiring to sabotage the revolutionary results of the proletariat, in order to establish the governorship by the private class as well as derivative from practical conditions of the world revolution. In addition, Lenin also said that in order to firmly defend the Socialist Fatherland, the revolutionary states should take advantage of the peaceful time to focus on strengthening the national economic, political and military potentials, science-technology to increase national power, ready to protect the country in all situations. Meanwhile, he also emphasized the absolute leadership of the Communist Party with the armed forces, considered it as an important factor to ensure the success of the revolutionary career.

During his revolutionary career, President Ho Chi Minh mentioned the task of protecting the Socialist Republic of Vietnam many times. According to Ho Chi Minh, defending the country is the responsibility of the generation for the previous generations, who sacrificed their blood and bones for the peace and independence of the Vietnamese nation. Ho Chi Minh once emphasized: "The Hung Kings once established our country, we have to keep it free"[4], and this sentence is regarded as a declaration of determination to protect the country. Therefore, in order to protect the revolutionary government, "Any peace or war must be mastered proactively, foreseen and prepared in advance"[5], always be alert to the country not to be surprised, to take advantage of the time of peace, peace to consolidate, build forces. He asserted: "We must have an army to fight against the enemy"[6] and seriously the task of building an armed force being capable enough for protecting the revolutionary government, which consisted of the main army, the local army and the militia and self-defence force. According to Ho Chi Minh, defending the Vietnamese Fatherland the socialist south is not the task for any individual but it is the duty of the entire Vietnamese citizens, people must have the spirit and responsibility to protect Vietnam as long as they are Vietnamese. In the Declaration of Independence of the Democratic Republic of Vietnam, Ho Chi Minh affirmed: "The whole Vietnamese people are determined to bring all their spirit, power, destiny and wealth to maintain freedom and independence"[7], which is considered an important theoretical premise, and also an inspiration for the formation of the national defence and security posture of the Party and State of Vietnam today.

In summary, the views of Marxism-Leninism and Ho Chi Minh's ideologies on defending the Fatherland are the important ideological and theoretical foundation to orient the Vietnamese Party and State plan defence policies and security phase at present. The above opinions have been supplemented and applied creatively by the Communist Party of Vietnam, an important contribution to the cause of building and defending the Socialist Republic of Vietnam.

The viewpoint of the Communist Party of Vietnam on current national defence and security outlook.

The viewpoint of the Communist Party of Vietnam on national defence and security is based on the creative application of Marxism – Leninism, Ho Chi Minh's ideologies and experiences gained over thousands of years of fighting against foreign aggressors and specific requirements for Vietnam. In recent years, the views and policies of the Party and the State of Vietnam on national defence and security have been constantly renovated, supplemented and perfected through historical periods. The current viewpoints and policies on defence and security of Vietnam are aimed at building national defence and security to become a pioneer in the task of protecting the Socialist Republic of Vietnam in the period of Innovation, which is also consistent with the inevitable development trend of mankind.

Since the 3rd Congress (1960), the Communist Party of Vietnam has affirmed that the renovation and building of socialism must "focus on strengthening national defence and constructing the powerful armed forces of the people"[8] besides economic and cultural development, in order to smash all the protests and invasions of the enemy, especially in the context that Vietnam Revolution was still facing with the fierce resistance of the domestic and foreign enemy forces and the South had not been liberated yet. Therefore, national defence and security must have been strong enough to protect the cause of building socialism in the North and liberating the South to unite the country.

Particularly, at the 5th Congress (1982), the Communist Party of Vietnam set a demand: Building an all-inclusive and comprehensive national defense. The guiding viewpoint at this Congress of the Communist Party of Vietnam has become a principle orientation in the development of Vietnam's national defence and security policy in the next and current period, which is to construct national defence and entire national defence posture tied to national security and national security posture.

The year 1986 was an important milestone in the development history of the Vietnamese nation, which was a change of mindset and create awareness about the country's development orientation under the leadership of the Communist Party of Vietnam. National defence and security along with renovating the economy and a number of other important fields have always been specially concerned by the Party and State of Vietnam. The Communist

Party of Vietnam affirmed that defending the Fatherland is not an individual task but a duty of the entire nation under the leadership of the Party. At the 6th Congress (1986), the Communist Party of Vietnam affirmed: We must fully understand and implement the viewpoint: "All people build the country and defend the country; the whole army defends the country and builds the land"[9] and emphasized the absolute leadership of the Communist Party of Vietnam to the military and defense.

After the 6th National Congress, the views of the Communist Party of Vietnam on leading and directing the cause of national defence and security have been supplemented and completed in accordance with the domestic and international contexts. Especially in the context of the late 80s and early 90s of the twentieth century, when the socialist system in the Soviet Union and Eastern European countries in crisis led to collapse, which impacted Vietnam's Revolution. Besides, hostile forces always took chance to destroy the Vietnamese revolution in order to abolish the socialist regime in our country. In this context, at the 7th. National Congress (1991), the Communist Party of Vietnam affirmed: "Strengthening national defence and maintaining national security is an important and regular task of the people"[10]. National defence and security forces must be closely associated with economic development and must take advantage of favourable conditions to serve the cause of national construction and defense.

Inheriting perspectives from previous People's Congresses, the leadership based their action on practical reviews and evaluation of the global trends. Since the 7th National Congress, the Communist Party of Vietnam has always affirmed: Consolidating national defence and security is an important and frequent task of the Party, the State, the political system and the entire people. Vietnam affirms that: The focus of the contemporary period has been on constructing socialism, however, protecting the revolutionary results and build successful socialism means "we are not a little loose in the task of protecting national defense, always attaching importance to national defence and security, considering these as two closely linked strategic tasks"[11] to promptly detect and smash every conspiracy, method and action against Vietnam's revolution from hostile forces.

Therein, the Vietnamese Communist Party emphasizes the objectives and tasks of national defence and security is to firmly defend the independence, sovereignty, unity, territorial integrity, sovereignty of the country, protect the Party, defending the socialist regime is the task of the entire nation under the exclusive and absolute leadership of the Party. Therefore, in order to accomplish the above-mentioned objective, it is necessary to build a national all-people defence and strong and comprehensive people's security so that the country will not be surprised in every situation. In particular, at the 12th National Congress (2016), the Communist Party of Vietnam also emphasized: "Building a popular people's posture, creating a solid foundation for the national defence and all national security"[12] meanwhile promoting international cooperation on national defence and security at the same time.

In short, the views of the Communist Party of Vietnam on national defence and security are the succession and development of theories of Marxism-Leninism, Ho Chi Minh's ideologies on defending the Fatherland, experiences in fighting foreign invaders of the country over thousands of years of history in order to protect national independence and socialism in Vietnam. Therefore, strengthening defence and security potentials is necessary and suitable to the development in the context of international and regional situations with complicated and unpredictable happenings as hostile forces are taking advantage of the peaceful environment to implement the strategy of "Peaceful Evolution" and carrying out many activities against the revolution of the Party, State and People of Vietnam.

International and regional context

After the end of the Cold War (1991), the volatile regional and world situation witnessed the collapse of socialist system in Eastern Europe and the Soviet Union, which created certain advantages for the US to become world hegemony and establish unipolar world order led by the United States. However, after the Cold War, the United States weakened relatively, while a number of countries have risen and flourished such as Japan, Western Europe (EU), China, etc. these countries advocated for establishing a multipolar world, which changes the world situation and international relations fundamentally. The general trend in international relations is to take economic-political competition instead of political-military confrontation; economic power becomes a measure of strength of a nation. In this context, all countries have adjusted the national development strategy. The risk of a global war has decreased, yet local conflicts still occur in many parts of the world and tend to be more complicated and unpredictable, which has been and directly affects the Vietnamese revolution. The trend of peace and cooperation, nonetheless, is still the current mainstream in international relations, creates a favourable environment for economic cooperation and increasing national synergy. In this context, major countries have made important strategic adjustments in economics, politics and military, which stands for both cooperation and collabouration, mutual competition, parallel mutual restraint in order to protect the national interests in the international arena.

The 4th scientific and technological revolution (better known as Industrial Revolution 4.0) has been continuing in order to develop rapidly and affecting all areas of social life, the field of national defence and security is not out of this change. Military scientists around the world predict that future war will be a war with high-tech weapons. That requires countries around the world and Vietnam to make appropriate policy adjustments for development and modernization of defence and security.

In particular, in the current period, ethnic, religious conflicts, territorial disputes and the emergence of more non-traditional security issues such as the emergence of terrorism (Islamic State–ISIS is a typical example) that has seriously threatened security, stability and development for all countries in the world. In Asia, the current sovereignty disputes over islands in the East Sea such as: disputes between Vietnam and China; China with the Philippines, or the expansion of IS terrorism to Southeast Asia in countries like Indonesia, the arms race between countries in the region has been setting new demands and heavy duty. It is applicable also for Vietnam in the field of defence and security, in order to protect the independence, sovereignty, security and territorial integrity.

In the context of Vietnam

After more than 30 years of reforming, Vietnam has achieved many achievements in national construction and development. Vietnam has risen to become a middle-income country, improving the material and spiritual life of the people. In addition, the opening of international integration has helped Vietnam to take advantage of many external resources for the country's development. Economic development helps enhance Vietnam's position and role in the international arena.

Along with the achievements in socio-economic development in recent years, the field of national defence and security of Vietnam has achieved many important achievements. The potential of national defence and security has been constantly strengthened and developed in the direction of elite and modernity. The posture of national defence and people's security has been further strengthened, the economic integration associated with national defence and security has been increasingly tightened. Vietnam has been active and proactive in expanding its defence and security cooperation with traditional partners such as the Federal Republic of Russia, the Republic of India and other partners in the world such as Japan and the US.

On the other hand, hostile forces taking advantage of the precarious international environment are aggressively taking actions against Vietnam's communist regime with many sophisticated endeavours. They urgently implement the strategy of "peaceful evolution" in order to claim pluralism and multi-party in Vietnam, proceed to change political regimes, abolish the leadership of the Communist Party of Vietnam and overthrow the regime. Meanwhile, a number of strategic and key areas such as the Central Highlands, Northwestern and Southwestern regions still pose a great risk of political insecurity. In addition to many evils, many types of crimes such as trans-national crime, drug trafficking, human trafficking which requires advancement in the field of national defence and security.

However, under the leadership of the Communist Party of Vietnam, the attention and attention of the Vietnamese State to the field of defence - security, in recent years, most of the strategic and political areas - stable society, national defence and security are maintained and strengthened, making an important contribution to the task of maintaining peace, stability and safety in order to create a favourable environment for the country's development.

Current Defence Potential and Current National Defense amd Security Policy

Vietnam is a country with an important role and position in the region. Along with the increase in economic and political influence, Vietnam has also implemented many measures to increase its military strength and defence potential. The recent efforts of Vietnam in developing and modernizing defence are aimed at improving the combat capability and defending the country in the context of the most complicated and regional developments in the region and the world. There are tensions between Vietnam and China over the issue of sovereignty over sea and islands in the East Sea in recent years.

According to the assessment of Global Firepower Organization, in 2019, Vietnam is a country with 23/137 military power ranking countries in the world (with Vietnam's military strength index (Power Index–PI)). The South is 0.3988 (the smaller the PI is, the stronger the military power of that country) and 2nd in Southeast Asia after Indonesia (16/137-Indonesia's military strength (PI) is 0.2804). With a population of over 97 million people in 2019, Vietnam has 51,043,216 million people capable of fighting when a war occurs, including 41,804,394 million people of suitable age, the number of people up to the annual age of military enlistment is 1,651,274 million. According to Global Firepower, Vietnam currently has about 5,482,000 troops (the standing army is 482,000 and the reserve is 5,000,000). Regarding the air force, Vietnam has 318 types of aircraft (excluding unmanned aerial vehicles - UAV (Unmanned aerial vehicle)) ranked 33/137 countries in which: fighter aircraft is 108 (ranked 21/137), attack helicopter is 25 (rank 22/137), transport helicopter is 38 (rank 24/137). Regarding the strength of Vietnamese infantry, there are 2575 (ranked 10/137) on land combat vehicles including: main tanks, armored fighting vehicles, self-propelled artillery, towed artillery), including: vehicles armored fighting is 2,530 (ranked 28/137), self-propelled artillery 120 (ranked 32/137), towed artillery 350 (ranked 31/137). Regarding the navy, according to statistics from Global Firepower, Vietnam currently has 65 vehicles of all kinds including: destroyers–9, escort ships–14, submarines–6, patrol boats–26 in number. Vietnam's defence budget in 2019 was 3.365 billion (USD)[13].

The above figures show that Vietnam's defence potential is quite high compared to other countries in the region. In order to increase military potential, in recent years, Vietnam has focused on buying some modern weapons and equipment such as those of Su-30 generation fighters from Russia, or Vietnam bought 6 Chinese ships. Kilo class submarines of Russia's Project 636 Varshavyanka ("Kilo is a diesel-electric attack submarine, which is used for anti-ship and anti-submarine warfare. This is a third generation submarine (world's most advanced type), nearly 74 meters long, 10 meters wide, displacement 3,100 tons, speed 20 knots/hour (37 km/h), dive up to 300 meters deep, independent operation 45 days at night, with the crew of 52 people"[14]).

Besides, Vietnam also owns the S-300 defence system of Russia, which is one of the most modern missile defence systems in the world. According to the Stockholm International Peace Research Institute (SIPRI), Vietnam has bought two Russian S-300PMU[15] air defence missile complexes and Vietnam is currently negotiating to buy S-400 missile systems and the like. SU-35-class warplanes from Russia[16]. In addition, in recent years to increase its defence power, in addition to buying some modern weapons and equipment, Vietnam has also focused on cooperation. With traditional partners such as Russia, India it has undertaken initiatives to conduct research, improve and modernize existing weapons and equipment to improve the combat capability and combat effectiveness of Vietnam's defence forces. In particular, the current defence potential of Vietnam is also highly appreciated in the combat capabilities of military units, which are experiences accumulated over thousands of years of fighting against foreign invaders of the nation.

Current defence and security policy of Vietnam

The Party and State of Vietnam affirmed that, along with the process of building and developing along the socialist road, ensuring the defence and security tasks is an important task, often in the task of defending the Fatherland. Therefore, in recent years, Vietnam's policies and defence have been continuously supplemented and perfected through Party Congress, expressed in Resolutions, in Platforms, Defence Law, and in the National White Paper. In the case of Vietnam, these adjustments are necessary to match the development of the regional situation, the world and the revolutionary task of Vietnam in each specific historical period.

Over the past 30 years, though, Vietnam's defence and security policies have been adjusted to fit each specific historical period. But since the renovation to date (1986 up to now), Vietnam has consistently implemented the 3 defence policy guidelines: not joining forces, military alliances of one side against the other; not allow foreign countries to set up military bases or use Vietnamese territory to oppose other countries; and do not threaten or use force in international relations (Clause 3, Article 4, Vietnam Defence Law 2018).

In order to implement that policy, the Communist Party of Vietnam advocates to build a peaceful, self-defense, all-people, all-sided, independent, autonomous, self-reliant and increasingly modern defense. Vietnam National White Paper in 2009 determined: "The nature of Vietnam's defence is peace, self-defence... for the purpose of protecting national interests, protecting independence, autonomy and protecting the owner. Rights in all aspects and territorial integrity of the Socialist Republic of Vietnam. Vietnam advocates not to use force or threaten the use of force in international relations, resolving all disagreements and disputes with other countries by peaceful means", in principle: respect for poison establishment, sovereignty, unity, territorial integrity, non-interference in each other's internal affairs, equality and mutual benefit based on Vietnam's current laws and international treaties that Vietnam has signed and ratified.

Besides, the Communist Party of Vietnam determines that the task of defending the Fatherland is not the task of one or two individual individuals but the task of the entire people, of the entire political system. It is true that the

Vietnamese revolution has been mobilized in recent years, because the people are the main force doing revolution under the Party's leadership. Built on the great unity bloc of the entire nation, on the basis of promoting the potential and intellect of the people, the defence potential must constantly be strengthened, modernized and defended in national defence and security. Belonging to, not being dominated by any foreign forces to lose the revolutionary and progressive nature. In addition, Vietnam's current policies on national defence and security also emphasize the combination of national power, in which the Communist Party of Vietnam determines national power which is a decisive factor for the strength of Vietnam's national defence and security, of which the armed forces are the nucleus.

The purpose and mission throughout Vietnam's defence and security policy is to firmly defend the national independence, national sovereignty, territorial integrity, and protect the prosperous, free and happy life of the people. On the other hand, Vietnam's current national defence and security policies aim to increase the potential and strength of national defence and security to prevent, prevent, repel and defeat all anti-conspiracy plans. Sabotage and aggression by enemies cause political instability, social safety, contribute to the protection of peace in the region and in the world.

The salient feature of the Vietnam National Defence Strategy is to show a deep sense of the people, that is, of the people, by the people and for the people, as "national defence and defence of the country; hold the country early, from afar, since the country is not yet in danger, bringing peace, self-defense, with the combined strength of the whole nation combined with the power of the times; based on the Party's right political line - the decisive factor"[17]. Therefore, strong national defence and security strong enough to protect the country in all situations is an important condition and foundation to uphold political stability, ensuring a peaceful and stable environment for the development of the country. To carry out that task, in recent years, Vietnam's defence and security has been constantly renovated and modernized.

In the objective to build the country during the transition to socialism in 2011, the Communist Party of Vietnam affirmed: "The stability and sustainable development of all aspects of the socio-economic life are the foundation of national defence and security"[18]. The National Party of Vietnam is very focused on: building a posture of national defence associated with the posture of people's security, building a "posture of the people" to the foundation to promote the synergy of the entire nation; combining socio-economic with national defence and security; defence, security and foreign affairs; strengthen international cooperation on defense; regularly supplement and perfect the mechanism of the Party leadership, the State manages the cause of building and consolidating national defense. The combination of the above factors is the basis for building a strong national defence and security base in both politics, ideology and organization meeting the requirements and tasks of protecting the Socialist Republic of Vietnam. In addition, to ensure a strong national defence and security, the Communist Party of Vietnam emphasizes paying attention to increasing economic, political, and scientific-technological capacities and human resources for the field of national defence and security, and to improve the quality and efficiency of forecasting the future trends of the international and regional situation.

In summary, Vietnam's current defence and security policies clearly reflect the nature of peace, self-defence and revolution. The additions in Vietnam's current defence and security policy have no other purpose but to increase the strength to protect independence, autonomy and territorial integrity, smashing all plots and actions against the sabotage of hostile forces, and to protect the country from outside threats in the context of complicated international and regional situations. The Communist Party of Vietnam affirmed that although the current task of building and developing the country in the direction of socialist is central, the task of ensuring national security and defence must always be focused. It is a crucial and regular task not to be lax in spite of peace in the country, so that the country will not be surprised by any situation.

Review of Vietnam's Defence White Paper

White paper is a type of text that helps readers understand the nature and different aspects, expressing transparency and transparency in the guidelines and policies of a subject on a specific issue. According to the Vietnamese dictionary, the white paper is "a book published by the government or foreign ministry, in order to present to the international public opinion, systematically and with reference to a political, economic or literary issue requires important interactions"[19]. Therefore, the defence white paper is a document that represents the most basic contents of a country's defence policy in the world.

In Vietnam, the White Paper on National Defence was published by the Ministry of Defense, which clearly shows the content and nature of Vietnam's current defence policy, which is peace and self-defense. Vietnam National Defence White Paper is the realization of the Party's guidelines on defence and security over periods, in order to propagate Vietnam's defence viewpoints, guidelines and policies with the people and the international community. In addition to confirming the achievements that Vietnam has achieved after many years of revamp in the field of national defence and security, such as basically completing the border demarcation and maritime boundary demarcation with neighbouring countries, the delimitation of boundaries between South Vietnam and China in the Gulf of Tonkin have been completed to facilitate the development of maritime border areas between Vietnam and neighbouring countries. Vietnam's defence white paper also shows Vietnam's position in the South China Sea disputes, islands and some other issues such as the strategy of peaceful resolution of disputes even with hostile forces. These disputes and the sabotage activities of the hostile forces towards the current Vietnamese government have seriously affected the stability and sustainable development of Vietnam.

Few highlights of Vietnam's National Defence White Paper 2009 are discussed below which includes:

Firstly, awareness of the world and regional security situation of Vietnam: Vietnam's defence white paper appropriately reflects the happenings, the regional and international situation is evolving in a complicated and unpredictable direction with major countries adjusting their strategy. That, on the one hand, creates favourable conditions for Vietnam to develop, but on the other hand also has many potential risks of tensions and conflicts in some other areas in the world. However, peace and cooperation are still the prevailing trends in international relations today. For Vietnam, the white paper clearly reflects Vietnam's achievements and limitations after many years of renovation and the potential risks causing political instability for the country. Therefore, in order to protect the country, so that the country will not be surprised by any situation, Vietnam defines the defence and security task as a regular and important task.

Secondly, Vietnam's current defence policy: The Vietnam National Defence White Paper clearly shows the basic issues of Vietnam's defence policy, which attaches importance to peace and self-defense. Vietnam advocates not to use force in resolving disputes. In order to protect the country, to increase its defence potential and capacity, Vietnam advocates to expand international cooperation in the field of defence and security of Vietnam. In addition, Vietnam recognizes that international cooperation and dialogue is a channel to increase understanding among nations, thereby promoting peace, preventing conflicts, and wars in all its manifestations.

Thirdly, on the current construction of Vietnam's defence: Through Vietnam's defence white paper, one can easily see that Vietnam advocates building a national defense, attaching to people's security and building the posture. A full scale defence prepares every Vietnamese citizen as a soldier and in the task of economic development, Vietnam always pays attention to the arrangement of defensive positions in these key areas. Throughout the country, in order to firmly defend the independence, sovereignty, territorial integrity and ensure and maintain national security in all aspects. Vietnam's defence power is the power of the great national unity bloc, the entire political system, with absolute leadership of the Communist Party of Vietnam, unified under the management of the State.

In order to build a strong national defence and security, capable of defending the fatherland in every situation, Vietnam advocates to increase defence potential in the following aspects: political –psychological; economic potential; scientific and technological potentials; complemented with military strength. The increase in Vietnam's defence and security potential is necessary in the context of complicated international and regional situations. This increase in power is intended to deter, suppress and counter the activities of hostile forces that are taking advantage of the favourable international environment to conduct anti-sabotage activities that threaten security and politics of Vietnam.

Fourthly, on building Vietnam's defence forces, the Vietnam National Defence White Paper confirms that the people's army and the militia and self-defence force are the key forces of the people's armed forces for national defence in all situations. Therefore, Vietnam always focuses on training, fostering sustenance skills, operational skills and tactics for its force with professional training courses, for Army, Air Force, Navy. Throughout thousands of years of history of building and defending the country with many practical experiences in combat, building capable forces has been summarized by Vietnam, so that the national defence and security of a strong country. It must meet the mission requirements, besides the human factor, weapons, technical equipment, and logistical support are also important factors. Therefore, besides paying attention to research, development and improvement of weapons and equipment, Vietnam also recognizes the need for cooperation in research and development of modern weapons with the countries with the background. Defence development and research with Russia, and India are the works in progress.

In summary, the Vietnam White Paper is the official document of Vietnam to announce to the world about the most basic contents of defence policy, commitments on more transparency in defence modernization and at the same time, Vietnam National Defence White Paper also aims to propagate the views, military guidelines, and defence policies of the Party and State of Vietnam such as building a national defence in association with people's security. To raise awareness among people and the political system about the task of protecting the Socialist Republic of Vietnam in the contemporary period.

Strategic alliances and prospects for Vietnam in the future

Alliance is an important term in international relations that indicates the link between nations with a specific purpose, some forms of union such as: Economic, political, military or combination of fields like: Economic-Political, Political-Military. In history and at present, alliances among nations, for example: European Union (EU), the North Atlantic Treaty Organization (NATO), or the allied forces fighting against fascism during World War II, etc. Through the examples above, it can be seen that the Union is under obligation to ratify treaties and agreements. Countries join forces with each other to combine resources and power to solve specific problems, threats to security and stability of a country in certain historical periods (For example: Allied countries in the Second World War joined to fight and destroy fascism).

The defence and security alliance has many different levels, the lowest level of the alliance is usually activities such as joint drills, intelligence sharing, weapons transfer or mutual assistance through foreign affairs. The higher level coalition includes a number of commitments on joint defence, coordination and operational support as needed. However, at any level, when an alliance is formed, it will lead to a change in the balance of power at regional level and even globally.

In the context of many international changes since the end of the Cold War, countries have been seeking their own development directions to ensure independence, sovereignty and territorial integrity. There are many countries joining different alliances, but also many countries do not join any union to ensure independence in foreign policy. Vietnam is one of many countries not joining any coalition. Since its renewal until now, Vietnam has committed to implement the 3 no policy: "do not join forces, military alliances of one party against the other; do not allow foreign countries to set up military bases or use Vietnamese territory to oppose other countries" (Article 4, Vietnam Defence Law 2018).

This policy of the Party and the State of Vietnam is completely correct in the context of the international changes in the direction of complexity and unpredictability. More importantly Vietnam is a particularly important geostrategic country in Asia, located on one of the most important international maritime routes in the world. Therefore, Vietnam has become the target of aggression and territorial disputes by many world powers throughout its history up till now. With this policy, Vietnam has shown goodwill to integrate and expand cooperation with countries around the world for the sake of peace and prosperity, based on the principle of respect for independence, sovereignty and integrity.

In addition, Vietnam has expanded, established and re-established relationships with most countries and territories in the world. "To date, Vietnam has diplomatic relations with 188/193 UN member states, being active members of more than 70 international and regional organizations; establishing strategic partnerships with 16 countries, comprehensive partnerships with 11 countries"[20]. In particular, Vietnam has established a special strategic partnership with the three countries: the Federal Republic of Russia, the People's Republic of China and the Republic of India. The partners' understanding and trust between Vietnam and other countries has been increasing. Therefore, the prestige and influence of Vietnam on all political - economic - military - cultural aspects are increasing at the international arena.

However, in the context of increasingly complicated and unpredictable situations globally and regionally, Vietnam is also encountering too many risks and challenges. Moreover, sabotage of hostile forces with increasingly sophisticated schemes and tricks into Vietnam, through many different ways, even taking advantage of the development of social networks they may exist. In addition, from the beginning of the 21st century to the present, besides traditional security issues, the world has mentioned more non-traditional security issues such as food security, water security, security, maritime, terrorism, disease, sea level rise, etc. Therefore, Vietnam is in need of support and cooperation from the international community when facing with the emergence of more and more new security threats globally.

In the context of increasing global power competition, major powers are constantly seeking ways to expand their power and influence in all potential and important areas of the world. This has been a direct threat to the security and sovereignty of many countries around the world. Particularly, the East Sea of Vietnam (also known as South China Sea-SCS) is becoming a hot spot for power competition among major countries. The sovereignty disputes in the East Sea (SCS) are increasingly fierce, the disputes in the East Sea have become one of the most dangerous hot spots in the world, in which stands a risk of armed conflict. China's ambition to monopolize the South China Sea has been threatening the security, peace and stability of the region, seriously threats Vietnam's independence, sovereignty and territorial integrity.

From these issues, the need to improve Vietnam's capacity and defence and security strength has become more and more urgent because Vietnam's self-reliance is limited and Vietnam's participation in a loose alliance is fully capable to ensure national security and maintain the current political regime in Vietnam.

Some potential strategic alliances in the future that Vietnam can join:

First, the alliance with Laos and Cambodia: Vietnam - Laos - Cambodia are the three Southeast Asian countries located in the Indochinese peninsula that share many enduring relationships, especially the territorial border and in the historical struggle of the country. The history observed that when one country lost its independence, it also affected the remaining countries. Therefore, based on the special relationship between the three countries, an alliance between the three countries in the future is quite promising, to ensure security and stability for the development of Vietnam in particular as well as Laos and Cambodia in general.

Second, the alliance with India: Relations between Vietnam and India in last seven years (2009-2016) have made breakthrough developments, from strategic partnership to comprehensive strategic partnership. This shows that the political trust between the two countries is increasing. On that basis, the formation of a Vietnam and India military alliance is quite promising. On the other hand, the establishment of a military alliance between the two countries will bring a lot of benefits to both sides. Firstly, ensuring maritime security through the South China Sea facilitates the development stability of the two countries (about 50% of Indian goods go through the South China Sea). Secondly, establishing an alliance with India will help Vietnam take advantage of resources from India to develop the country, supports from India will help Vietnam improve its security and national defence capabilities. In contrast, establishing a military alliance with Vietnam helps India gradually penetrate deeply into ASEAN, to compete directly with other major countries in the region, and thereby enhance its position in Southeast Asia.

Within the framework of the "comprehensive strategic partnership" relationship, both Vietnam and India have identified defense-security cooperation as one of the main pillars in the relationship between the two countries. Therefore, in recent years, defence cooperation between Vietnam and India has been strengthened, for example, through joint exercises on Vietnam's waters in May 2018 and April 2019; through cooperation on training Indian officials and soldiers for Vietnam; cooperation on the navy and air force between the two countries has also been increasingly strengthened...

Third, alliance with Japan: In 1973, Vietnam and Japan officially established diplomatic relations. Since then, relations between the two countries have developed rapidly, deepened in all fields and the political belief has been constantly increased with the motto "reliable and stable partners for a long time" working towards sustainable development between the two countries. Japan is one of the few countries that always support Vietnam's restoration and international integration policies and helped Vietnam in its development (Japan is always one of the leading countries in the world providing capital for Vietnam). Meanwhile, with political trust in international forums, Vietnam always supports Japan to become a permanent member of the expanded UN Security Council. Like India, Japan shares many interests with Vietnam, especially the issue of maritime security in the South China Sea. Because most of Japan's economic activities go through the East Sea, if maritime security through the East Sea is not guaranteed, it will directly affect the stability and sustainable development of Japan. On that basis, sharing many benefits and with political belief, close cooperation between the two countries over the years. In the future, it is clear that an alliance between Vietnam and Japan is feasible and promising.

In addition to the three alliances that Vietnam can join as above, Vietnam can have military alliances with ASEAN countries, China and the United States, however, it takes time to resolve the obstacles in establishing Military alliances with these partners:

First, military alliances with ASEAN countries: Although ASEAN countries have been forming communities since 2016, there are many different views on some common issues. Differences between countries are caused by the interests of the countries that are not similar. For example, ASEAN could not make a joint statement when Cambodia failed to put maritime disputes in the East Sea between ASEAN countries and China in 2012.

Second, the military alliance with China: Although Vietnam and China are neighbour countries and share many common economic and political interests, the disputes on the sea and islands in the East Sea between Vietnam and China are very big and difficult barriers and cannot be overcome in a short time so that the two countries to establish alliances even though the two countries are comprehensive strategic partners.

Third, military alliance with the US: In 1995, Vietnam and the US officially normalized relations. Since then, the relationship between Vietnam and the United States has gradually made breakthroughs, mainly in terms of economy, trade and education. In 2016, before the good development of bilateral relations, the United States officially removed the arms embargo against Vietnam. This event marked an important turning point in defence relations between the two countries. The US and Vietnam defence exchanges have been more frequent. In 2018, the US aircraft carrier USS Carl Vinson visited Da Nang Vietnam or the visit of the USS Frank Cable submarine and the destroyer USS John S. McCain to Cam Ranh Bay in 2016. At the same time, in an effort to establish Establishing defence relations with Vietnam, the US has transferred a number of patrol boats to Vietnam to help Vietnam improve its maritime patrol capacity as a measure to ensure maritime security in the East Sea. Vietnam and the US relations in recent years have developed rapidly, but in the future, the relationship between the two countries cannot reach an alliance but can only be stopped at a comprehensive strategic partner. For that reason, both countries need time to get to know each other better.

In short, establishing military alliances is a form of linking nations together. In the history of human development, many alliances have been established, alliances between nations can be alliances between two countries or between groups of countries, alliances can be temporary or long period; length depends on the goal of that alliance. The alliances established are aimed at increasing resources and strength for the nation to ensure security, stability, sustainable development, independence and sovereignty of a nation. In Vietnam, from the reconstruction until now (1986 up to now), the Party and State of Vietnam have always implemented guidelines and policies of neutrality and peace. Vietnam advocates not to join any union, not allied with another country to oppose a third country. However, in recent years, the international and regional context has experienced many complicated developments, especially disputes over sovereignty over sea and islands in the East Sea and competition among major countries in the region has been increasingly taking place. Fierce maneuvers and drastic measures have seriously threatened Vietnam's security, sovereignty and territorial integrity. Recent regional and world developments require Vietnam to seriously assess the situation and identify partners and subjects to make appropriate policy adjustments.

Conclusion

Defence and security policy is one of the most important policies of a country to ensure security, independence, sovereignty, territorial integrity and sustainable development. Since *Doi Moi* up till now, the Party and State of Vietnam have always focused on national defence and security due to recognition of the importance of national defence and security to the cause of national construction and defense, which is based on inheriting experiences from previous generations and the reality of Vietnam's revolutionary history.

Vietnam's policies and policies on national defence and security have always been adjusted to suit the country's specific conditions and the regional and world situation. Vietnam's achievements in recent years are not separate from national defence and security policies. In order to protect the country from outside invasion risks and the sabotage of hostile forces, Vietnam always considers the defence and security upgradation as a regular and unending task.

With the nature of a national defence and security with self-defence and peace, Vietnam advocates building a national defense, attaching to the people's security and building a posture of national defense. At the same time, Vietnam advocates to strengthen cooperation and defence and security dialogues with countries around the world for the sake of peace and development to enhance national defence and security capacity. Along with increasing economic potential, Vietnam's defence potential has also been constantly strengthened and modernized to meet the task of protecting the Socialist Republic of Vietnam.

However, in an increasingly complex and complex international and regional context, the emergence of more and more new security challenges has seriously threatened security, independence, sovereignty and integrity of the territory of Vietnam. Additionally, certain limitations in national defence and security capabilities require Vietnam to make certain adjustments to national defence and security policies in order to increase defence capacity and strengthen the nation. While dealing with urgent demands for the task of defending the Fatherland, it is entirely possible that Vietnam joining a military alliance in the future.

Notes

1. Học viện Chính trị quốc gia Hồ Chí Minh (2018): Giáo trình Cao cấp Lý luận chính trị - Giáo dục quốc phòng và an ninh, Nxb. Lý luận chính trị, Hà Nội, tr.47
2. Terrence M. O'Sullivan and Jim Ramsay, "Defining and Distinguishing Homeland from National Security and Climate-Related Environmental Security, in Theory and Practice", Homeland Security & Emergency Management 12(1), 2015, page 50
3. Xem Học viện Chính trị quốc gia Hồ Chí Minh (2018): Giáo trình Cao cấp Lý luận chính trị - Giáo dục quốc phòng và an ninh, Nxb. Lý luận chính trị, Hà Nội, page 52-55
4. Hồ Chí Minh: Toàn tập - Tập 9, Nxb. Chính trị quốc gia, Hà Nội, 2011, page 59
5. Hồ Chí Minh: Toàn tập - Tập 8, Nxb. Chính trị quốc gia, Hà Nội, 2011, page 552
6. Hồ Chí Minh: Toàn tập - Tập 6, Nxb. Chính trị quốc gia, Hà Nội, 2011, page 5
7. Hồ Chí Minh: Toàn tập - Tập 4, Nxb. Chính trị quốc gia, Hà Nội, 2011, page 3
8. Đảng Cộng sản Việt Nam: Văn kiện Đảng toàn tập, Nxb. Chính trị quốc gia, Hà Nội, 2002, episode.21, page 535
9. Đảng Cộng sản Việt Nam: Văn kiện Đại hội đại biểu toàn quốc lần thứ VI, Nxb.Sự thật, Hà Nội, 1987, page 38-39
10. Đảng Cộng sản Việt Nam: Văn kiện Đảng toàn tập, Nxb. Chính trị quốc gia, Hà Nội, 2007, episode 51, page 142
11. Đảng Cộng sản Việt Nam: Văn kiện Đại hội đại biểu toàn quốc lần thứ VIII, Nxb. Nxb. Chính trị quốc gia, Hà Nội, 1996, page 39
12. Đảng Cộng sản Việt Nam: Văn kiện Đại hội đại biểu toàn quốc lần thứ XII, Nxb. Nxb. Chính trị quốc gia, Hà Nội, 2016, page 149
13. Xem https://www.globalfirepower.com/country-military-strength-detail.asp?country_id=vietnam, ngày 22/9/2019
14. Hợp đồng kỷ lục, Dẫn theo: https://vnexpress.net/interactive/2017/suc-manh-6-tau-ngam-kilo-viet-nam
15. Xem Bất ngờ: Việt Nam đã sản xuất được tên lửa S-300 nghi trang... y như thật, Dẫn theo: http://netnews.vn/Bat-ngo-Viet-Nam-da-san-xuat-duoc-ten-lua-S-300-nghi-trang-y-nhu-that-quan-su-150-0-1803780.html, ngày 23/9/2019
16. Xem Việt Nam đặt hàng vũ khí Nga: Sẽ có Su-35, S-400...?, Dẫn theo: https://thoidai.com.vn/viet-nam-dat-hang-vu-khi-nga-se-co-su-35-s-400-46518.html, ngày 22/9/2019
17. Đại tướng Ngô Xuân Lịch: Chiến lược quốc phòng, chiến lược quân sự Việt Nam - Sự kết tinh truyền thống dân tộc với ý Đảng, lòng dân, Dẫn theo: https://www.qdnd.vn/quoc-phong-an-ninh/xay-dung-quan-doi/chien-luoc-quoc-phong-chien-luoc-quan-su-viet-nam-su-ket-tinh-truyen-thong-dan-toc-voi-y-dang-

long-dan-537453, ngày 22/9/2019
18. Đảng Cộng sản Việt Nam: Văn kiện Đại hội đại biểu toàn quốc lần thứ XI, Nxb. Chính trị quốc gia – Sự Thật, 2011, tr.82
19. Từ điển Tiếng Việt, Nxb. Đà Nẵng, 2015, page 1105
20. Ngoại giao Việt Nam: Chủ động, sáng tạo và hiệu quả, nâng tầm vị thế đất nước, Dẫn theo: http://www.tapchicongsan.org.vn/Home/Doi-ngoai-va-hoi-nhap/2018/ 51858/ Ngoai-giao-Viet-Nam-Chu-dong-sang-tao-va-hieu-qua-nang.aspx, date 22/9/2019

References

Party Documents

1. Vietnam Defence Law (2018), Clause 3, Article 4, Lead by: https://luatvietnam.vn/an-ninh-quoc-gia/luat-quoc-phong-nam-2018-luat-so- 22-2018-qh14-164725-d1.html.
2. The Communist Party of Vietnam: Document of the Sixth National Congress, Publishing House, Truth, Hanoi, 1987.
3. Vietnam Communist Party: Document of the Eighth National Congress, Publishing House. Publisher. National politics, Hanoi, 1996.
4. The Communist Party of Vietnam: Complete Party Documents - Episode 21, Publisher. National politics, Hanoi, 2002.
5. Communist Party of Vietnam: Complete Party Document - Episode 51, Publisher. National politics, Hanoi, 2007.
6. The Communist Party of Vietnam: Document of the 11th National Congress, Publishing House. National politics - Truth, 2011.
7. The Communist Party of Vietnam: Document of the 12th National Congress, Publishing House. Publisher. National politics, Hanoi, 2016.
8. Ho Chi Minh National Academy of Politics (2018): Advanced Curriculum Political Theory - National Defence and Security Education, Publishing House. Political theory, Hanoi.
9. Ho Chi Minh: Complete episode - Episode 4, Publisher. National politics, Hanoi, 2011.
10. Ho Chi Minh: Complete episode - Episode 6, Publisher. National politics, Hanoi, 2011.
11. Ho Chi Minh: Complete episode - Episode 8, Publisher. National politics, Hanoi, 2011.
12. Ho Chi Minh: Complete episode - Episode 9, Publisher. National politics, Hanoi, 2011.
13. Record contract, Leaded by: https://vnexpress.net/interactive/2017/suc-manh-6-tau-ngam-kilo-viet-nam., September 19, 2019.
14. Vietnam National DefenceWhite Paper 2009.
15. Vietnamese dictionary, Publisher. Da Nang, 2015.
16. Vietnam People's Army Magazine: https://www.qdnd.vn.
17. The National DefenceJournal: https://www.qdnd.vn.
18. Communist Review: http://www.tapchicongsan.org.vn/.

Foreign Documents

1. Pankaj Kumar Jha: Vietnamese Defence White Paper 2009, Adapted from: https://idsa.in/idsacomments/VietnameseDefenceWhitePaper2009_pkjha_311209, September 22, 2019.
2. Terrence M. O Federalullivan and Jim Ramsay, "Defining and Distinguishing Homeland from National Security and Climate-Related Environmental Security, in Theory and Practice", Homeland Security & Emergency Management 12 (1), 2015.
3. David Hutt: EU, Vietnam to become brothers in arms, Led by: https://www.asiatimes.com/2019/08/article/eu-vietnam-to-become-brothers-in-arms/, 22nd/9/2019.
4. India, Vietnam to step up defencecooperation, oil exploration, Dothers-inhttps://economictimes.indiatimes.com/news/defence/india-vietnam-to-step-up-defence-cooperation-oil-exploration/articleshow/ 66732922.cms, September 23, 2019.
5. Vietnam and India agree to up trade, defencecooperation, Leading by: http://www.asahi.com/ajw/articles/AJ201811200042.html, September 23, 2019.
6. India, Vietnam to strengthen cooperation in atomic energy, defence and security, Leading by: https://www.thehindu.com/news/national/india-vietnam-to-streng then-cooperation-in-atomic-energy-defence-and-security/article27108387.ece, September 24, 2019.
7. Fact Sheet: India-Vietnam Defence Cooperation, at: https://currentaffairs.gktoday.in/fact-sheet-india-vietnam-defence-cooperation-12201863671.html, September 24, 2019.
8. Kyodo: Japan and Vietnam agree to Promote defence cooperation, Leading by: https://www.japantimes.co.jp/news/2019/05/05/national/politics-diplomacy/japan-vietnam-agree-promote-defense-cooperation/ #. XZSGDnM3vIU, September 24, 2019.
9. Japan and Vietnam Expand Defence Partnership, Led by: https://news.usni.org/2014/03/19/japan-vietnam-expand-defense-partnership, September 24, 2019.
10. Prashanth Parameswaran: Vietnam, Cambodia Boost DefenceTies The two sides are looking to expand their defencecooperation, Leaded by: https://thediplomat.com/2015/03/vietnam-cambodia-boost-defense-ties/, 26th/9/2019.
11. Vietnam-Cambodia Military Relations in Focus with Defence Minister Visit, Leaded by: https://thediplomat.com/2019/01/vietnam-cambodia-military-relations-in-focus -with-defense-minister-visit/, September 26, 2019.
12. Decades After War, What's Behind US-Vietnamese Military Cooperation, at: https://sputniknews.com/politics/201708101056360492-us-vietnam-china/, September 27, 2019.

7 Vietnam's Ties with Superpowers and the European Union

Thi-Hong-Hanh Nguyen

Vietnam-US Relations

Throughout its history, Vietnam has had long-standing allies and ties with many big countries in the region and in the world. However, the relationship between Vietnam and the US is still quite new because after the war, this relation took 20 years to heal a rift. In particular, on July 11, 1995, Former US President Bill Clinton and Former Prime Minister Vo Van Kiet officially signed a declaration to normalize US-Vietnam relations marking an important historical turning point in bilateral relations. Since then, the relationship between Vietnam and the United States has been continuously developing. On July 25, 2013 at the White House, Former President Truong Tan Sang and US President Barack Obama decided to establish *US-Vietnam comprehensive partnership*. In the current trend of global integration, the US and Vietnam have established many dialogues, especially in politics-security-defense, economy and development of Asia-Pacific region on the basis of the similarities of interests with the desire to increasingly strengthen close relations both in width and depth.

Vietnam-United States Economic Cooperation

Economic cooperation is a key area in the framework of bilateral cooperation between Vietnam and the United States after more than 24 years of normalizing relations and achieving new development through the signing of many important agreements. In July 2000, Vietnam and the United States officially signed the US-Vietnam Bilateral Trade Agreement (BTA) and took effect from March 26, 2001. This agreement is extremely important because it establishes a clear legal framework, creates a solid foundation and helps to further promote Vietnam-US trade relations. Besides, there are a number of other important agreements such as the Textile Agreement (effective since 2003), the Aviation Agreement (effective since January 2004). In November 2006, Vietnam officially joined the WTO and in the same year, the United States announced to grant Permanent Normal Trade Regulations for Vietnam (PNTR)[1].

An important milestone in the investment cooperation between Vietnam and the United States was the signing ceremony of the "Agreement on Trade and Investment Framework" (TIFA) on June 21, 2007, on the official visit of the former President Nguyen Minh Triet in Washington DC, USA. TIFA provides a base for the US and Vietnam to develop more extensive trade and investment relations through WTO and BTA, resolving bilateral trade disputes, especially on the implementation of commitments to protect the Intellectual property rights, expanding service markets, transparency in administration and law, thereby creating favourable conditions for US investors in Vietnam and promoting Vietnam-US trade. FDI inflows from the United States into Vietnam over the years have been quite large and focused primarily on the services, processing industry, light industry. In fact, since the BTA came into effect, exports of Vietnam to the US strongly increased: In 1995, the limit was only 169.7 million USD, in 2018 it increased to 47.53 billion USD. Goods exported to the US account for 20 per cent of the country's total export turnover. The US has become Vietnam's biggest export market and accounts for one fifth of the country's total export value[2].

Although Vietnam-US economic cooperation has achieved remarkable achievements, Vietnam is still facing many disagreements in economic cooperation with the United States, regarding the protection of a number of commodities. The fact that the United States has not yet recognized Vietnam as a market economy makes a lot of Vietnam's goods entangled in anti-dumping lawsuits, pressured and unable to penetrate deeper into the US market, typically, aquatic products (shrimp, Tra and Basa fish), textile and garment processing and footwear what are the key products of Vietnam exported to foreign countries. Vietnam also often faces strict technical barriers when exporting to the United States' market, mainly due to the huge disparity in economic and scientific potential of the two nations.

Vietnam-US security and defense cooperation

Vietnam-US security and defense cooperation has made rapid progress thanks to continuous efforts from both sides. In 1995, after Vietnam joined ASEAN and Vietnam- US diplomatic relations have established, the United States lifted economic sanctions on Vietnam but retained its sanctions related to defense. In December 2006, the ban on the sale of non-destructive military supplies to Vietnam was abolished; next, in October 2014, the United States lifted a part of its arms embargo on Vietnam, as long as those weapons and equipment were used for security and developing defence at sea. With a lot of efforts from both sides, in May 2016, President Obama announced a completely lifting of arms embargo against Vietnam. This eradicates the remnants of the War in Vietnam in the past, marking the military-mutual trust between the United States and Vietnam and promoting bilateral security-defense cooperation to a new stage.

In 2011, Vietnam and the United States achieved a "Memorandum of Understanding (MoU) on bilateral defense cooperation". MoU is a great important step in Security-defense relations between Vietnam and US. This is the first time, Vietnam and the United States formally formulate a clear cooperation framework. The MoU identifies 5 areas that promote defense cooperation, including: Maritime security cooperation; Cooperation in searching and rescuing; Peacekeeping activities; Humanitarian and disaster relief; Cooperation between defense universities and research institutes. In 2015, the MoU was officially upgraded to Vietnam – US Joint Vision Statement on defense relations. The newly-signed document aims to guide defense relations and cooperation which includes a range of areas, such as dealing with war legacy, delegation exchanges, experience sharing, maritime security, natural disaster relief, and support for Vietnam's participation in UN peacekeeping missions. The event that marks the turning point of defense cooperation between the two sides is the visit of the US aircraft carrier USS Carl Vinson to Da Nang (March 2018). This was the first time US aircraft carrier visited Vietnam since the war, so this event was considered that the two former enemies has gotten closer and strengthened the mutual defense trust between the two sides.

In the field of energy and nuclear, since 2001, Vietnam has sought to cooperate with the US in the field of civil nuclear. In October 2013, US Secretary of State John Kerry and Deputy Prime Minister Pham Binh Minh signed the US-Vietnam civil nuclear energy cooperation agreement. Under this agreement, the United States will share nuclear technology and nuclear fuel with Vietnam, deploy nuclear technology exchanges, cooperate in the field of nuclear security and storage, and at the same time give allowing US companies to export nuclear components and civil nuclear reactors to Vietnam. In May 2016, the United States and Vietnam signed an administrative agreement for this agreement, which includes building a mechanical ties, strengthening training and education, fostering effective supervisory agencies, strengthening export management, monitoring and ensuring security for radioactive nuclear and fuel, strengthening capacity to respond to events, increasing public-private cooperation and promoting civil nuclear trade between the two countries.

In addition, the two countries' military exchanges cooperation also included activities of humanitarian assistance, humanitarian relief, overcoming the consequences of wars, clearing of bombs and mines left by the war, installing prosthetic limbs for wounded soldiers and many other projects. The United States has also trained in peacekeeping and provided patrol boats, radars, and maritime surveillance aircraft... to the Vietnamese military.

Bilateral cooperation in the field of politics and diplomacy

In bilateral political-diplomatic cooperation, the greatest achievement is that the US and Vietnam have officially recognized each other's sovereignty, territorial integrity, national independence and have been increasingly developing equality cooperation and mutual benefit. Since the normalization of relations, the US and Vietnam have organized 6 high-level visits and many talks, contacts, and exchanges at many levels from high level to ministries, branches, businesses and people in order to gradually determine a framework for stable, long-term relations for the benefit of the people of each country and for peace, stability and development in the region and the world. The leaders of the two countries have met and supported each other at multilateral forums in the world.

In the current world context, international and regional issues have also become an important bridge in political-diplomatic dialogue between the US and Vietnam. In addition to cooperating together to solve issues related to climate change, disaster prevention and overcoming, global environmental and health issues, the United States and Vietnam work together in Anti-mass weapons or problems in the East Sea. China is an important factor influencing geopolitical trends in Asia and the US attitude towards Vietnam. Facing China's expanding ambitions, the United States has paid more and more attention to Vietnam because of its important geostrategic position in the "pivot to Asia" strategy and the "Free and Open Indo-Pacific" strategy (FOIP). The United States strengthens its participation in the Asia-Pacific region, especially in Southeast Asia. Competition between China and the United States is increasing, and ASEAN is an area where both superpowers want to increase their influence. This is the area of "soft power" competition between the US and China, when the long-standing US leadership is threatened by China, and cooperation with Vietnam and ASEAN countries can help the US curb China's ambitions in this region.

In recent years, the United States has many mechanisms to cooperate with ASEAN through multilateral conferences and forums, which is the basis for Vietnam-US political-diplomatic relations to further enhance and expand. As part of the US "Pivot to Asia" strategy, the Mekong River basin is a highlight of Asia's geopolitics, economy and culture. In July 2009, at the ASEAN Conference held in Phuket, Thailand, the United States announced the "Lower Mekong Initiative" (LMI), aiming to strengthen cooperation and enhance influence for the countries of Mekong river basin, including Vietnam. In addition, the United States also supports Vietnam's views about settlement of sovereignty disputes in the East Sea, respect for international law and the US made a declaration to help Vietnam deploy patrol naval activities with warships and B52 aircraft... to ensure international freedom of navigation in this area toward China's encroachment.

Citizen diplomacy (People's diplomacy) is also an important way that can unite the two countries in political-diplomatic relations. People's diplomacy means simply that a country (or a non-governmental organization) establishes a relationship with other non-governmental organizations of other nations. The Vietnam-US People's Diplomacy is expressed primarily through educational exchange activities. Vietnam and the United States have signed a "Memorandum of Understanding on setting up an Education Task Force". In the "Vietnam-US Joint Declaration" in 2017, the leaders of both sides highlighted the fact that Fulbright University officially came into operation in 2016, or grants worth $ 500,000 for the former students of Vietnam Education Foundation (VEF) and the first volunteers of Peace Programme were present in Vietnam. Such educational exchange programmes and photo galleries, art exhibitions, cultural fairs, etc. help people in both countries better understand each other's traditions and cultures, shorten the gap and the difference between people of the two countries and contribute to deepening bilateral political-diplomatic relations.

Through that visits, the people of the two countries have the opportunity to exchange information each other, especially Vietnamese is able to learn about US laws, the US market, mobilize the establishment of non-governmental organizations, humanitarian aid and health care funds. The cooperation between the US-Vietnam non-governmental organizations in efforts to tackle diseases, eliminate hunger and reduce poverty, and solve environmental pollution issues has witnessed remarkable development. Many projects and programmes on health and healthcare have been built and developed effectively, such as the 15 million USD HIV/AIDS prevention programme (2004)[3], SARS prevention cooperation, the project "Hygiene education and school nutrition"... After the "Joint Declaration on Health Cooperation between the two Ministry of Health" (December 1997), in 2004, President GW Bush declared Vietnam as one of the 15 countries to receive aid in The President's Emergency Plan For AIDS Relief (PEPFAR).

Besides, the two countries work together in resolving the humanitarian issues left behind by the war, especially the search for missing soldiers during the war. Vietnam began returning the remains of soldiers lost during the war (Missing in Action programme-MIA) to the United States in December 1975. As for POW, after the war, many American people believed that there were still prisoners detained in Vietnam, but after many investigations, the US Senate Committee in charge of POW/MIA issues gave the report concludes that there is no evidence of Americans living in Vietnam. As of April 2018, the two sides conducted 130 joint operations and 144 return visits with a total of 975 sets of remains, of which the US has identified nearly 720 cases. Besides, after Vietnam asked the United States to coordinate in dealing with the consequences of Agent Orange, in 2007, the US Congress approved the spending of 3 million USD with the purpose of supporting environmental protection and health care for Vietnamese people.

However, the bilateral political-diplomatic relationship between Vietnam and the United States still has many problems when the United States brings regularly democracy issues and human rights to put pressure. The two countries still have different political goals (one is the socialist system, the other is capitalist) and it has certain negative effects on the political-diplomatic cooperation between both sides. Therefore, Vietnam-US relations in the field politics always exist in the two sides of struggle and cooperation. Up to now, the two sides seem to be unable to have much cooperation in terms of theoretical dialogue and mechanism of Party channel dialogue due to ideological differences.

Vietnam-Russia Relations

In the 20s and 30s of the twentieth century, through revolutionary activities, leader Nguyen Ai Quoc (President Ho Chi Minh) laid the foundation for the friendship between Vietnam and the Soviet Union. In particular, on January 30, 1950, the Democratic Republic of Vietnam and the Soviet Union established officially diplomatic relations. The Soviet Union was one of the first countries in the world to recognize and formally establish diplomatic relations with Vietnam, marking a milestone for strong friendship and good cooperation between the two sides. In the most difficult years of the struggle for national independence, Vietnam always received valuable supports from the Soviet people.

In 1991, the model of Socialism in the Soviet Union and Eastern Europe collapsed. Vietnam lost its traditional friends and especially the disintegration of the Soviet Union, which made Vietnam lose a solid support in all aspects. Therefore, Vietnam is forced to adjust its foreign policy to adapt to the new context, especially the foreign policy with Russia Federation. The Russian Federation, as the successor of the Soviet Union–a traditional partner of Vietnam is still a country having great influence in the international arena. History shows that the relationship between Vietnam and the former Soviet Union and the Russian Federation today is always warm, overcoming the challenges of time.

Vietnam-Russia diplomatic relations

Vietnam-Russia relations were formally established in 1991 (after the Cold War) in the context of both nations have to adjust foreign policy. Under Foreign Minister Andrei Kozyrev (1992-1995), Russia implemented the Atlantic Policy and prioritized establishing relations with the United States in the hope of achieving the goal of transition to a free market economy integration with the world economy and the liberal democratic political system with major Western support. Therefore, Asia in general and Vietnam in particular were not in the priority policy of Russia. On the contrary, Vietnam did not give specific foreign policies to other countries but still prioritized big countries, including Russia. However, in the years 1991-1994, the relationship between Vietnam-Russia was "quiet", Russia was a "familiar and strange" partner of Vietnam. But since 1995, the relationship between the two countries has gradually been strengthened, developed and achieved good results.

Entering the twenty-first century, Russia has adjusted its foreign policy to Asia-Pacific, in which it placed a special priority on relations with Vietnam on the basis of respecting mutual benefits. Vietnam has become a leading interest partner of Russia in the region due to its geo-strategic location, an increasingly important role in Vietnam's Southeast Asia region and the traditional friendship of Vietnam–the Russian Federation. In strategic of returning to Southeast Asia, the Russian Federation has many advantages in Vietnam:

Firstly, Vietnam is a country in Southeast Asia where there have been dynamic developing for decades. Thanks to the "*Doi Moi*" process and active integration, Vietnam has achieved important achievements in the economics with a GDP growth of 6-8 per cent/year, a stable business investment environment, and a large purchasing power. Therefore, strengthening trade and economic relations with Vietnam will create opportunities to exploit crowded markets for Russian investment fields that have advantages such as oil, gas, energy and national defense military equipment, and aerospace. Through

Vietnam, Russia can gain conveniently access to ASEAN where considered quite new market. In contrast, ASEAN countries also see Vietnam as a channel through which to penetrate the vast markets of Russia and Community of Independent States (CIS).

Secondly, Vietnam has a key geostrategic position of Southeast Asia, from which Vietnam can control arterial maritime and air routes through the East Sea where related to strategic interests in security, economy and navigation of Russia. According to Vietnamese experts' opinion, Russia considers ASEAN a "nucleus of the Asia-Pacific regional integration process and strengthening cooperation with ASEAN is one of Russia's top missions". In particular, Russia considered Vietnam an important "link", a "catalyst" in the policy of spreading influence in Southeast Asia. At the first visit to Vietnam (February 28-March 2, 2001), President V. Putin affirmed: "Developing the relationship on all sides with Vietnam is considered one of the priority directions in foreign policy of the Russian Federation in Asia". In addition, Vietnam has resources that Russia can exploit such as oil and gas, rubber, vegetables, tropical agricultural products and tourism. Vietnam has an educated labour force and a part of this one has been trained in Russia, so they has an understanding of the situation of the two countries. The Vietnamese market is capable of consuming many Russian products, especially those heavy industry products.

For Vietnam, Russia is an external friendship power that Vietnam needs to continue to maintain and strengthen relations on all fields especially politics, economics, security and defense. Russia plays a "balancing" role for the relations of Vietnam with other powers and political-economic centers in the world. Moreover, the cooperation with Russia helps Vietnam take advantage of external resources for its socio-economic development, education, training, science and technology and technology transfer. Because Russia has rich and diverse resources, especially oil and gas, a large team of scientists and skilled workers, a similar socio-economic complete and modern infrastructure, a specific culture (Eurasian dual culture). Russia can provide Vietnam for machinery, weapons, raw materials and fuel, and import agricultural products, light industrial goods, and tropical products. Russia is able to participate in industrial projects, oil and gas exploitation, power industry development.

In June 1994, Vietnam and Russia signed the Treaty on the basic principles of friendly relations, as the basis for relations between the two countries. On that basis, in March 2001, the two sides signed the Joint Declaration on the *"Vietnam-Russia strategic partnership",* realizing the framework of bilateral relations in the 21st century. In particular, in May 5, 2012, Vietnam and the Russian agreed to upgrade bilateral relations to a new level–the relationship of *"Comprehensive strategic partnership";* and issued a *"Joint Statement on strengthening the comprehensive strategic partnership between the two countries".* This is a breakthrough development, opening an era of cooperation in both breadth and depth between Vietnam and the Russian. Besides, for the first time in its foreign doctrine, Russia mentioned the role of Vietnam: "Russia's foreign policy aims to enhance the dynamics of relations with nations in Southeast Asia, first of all, to develop strategic partnerships with Vietnam".

Russia's new foreign doctrine was approved by Putin on November 30, 2016, article 90 states: "Russia wishes to deepen its comprehensive strategic partnership with the Socialist Republic of Vietnam.... ". This clearly shows that Russia recognizes the importance of Vietnam in its foreign policy.

As one of the five countries of the Standing Committee of the United Nations Security Council, the Russian has always given Vietnam strong support for multilateral cooperation. The Russia is also one of the countries that actively support Vietnam as the only Asian candidate to join the seat of the UN Security Council Permanent Commissioner for the period 2008-2009 and 2020-2021. In addition to its active commitment to mutual support, Vietnam and the Russia also show many similar views on different fields within the scope of UN activities. This shows that Vietnam and Russia are still strengthening cooperation and mutual support, showing great responsibility in the goal of maintaining international peace and security, strengthening solidarity and friendship relations among peoples in the world.

Vietnam-Russia security and defense cooperation

The security-defense and military technology cooperation plays an important role in Vietnam-Russia relations. In the context that international relations continues to be complicated with many hotspots and tensions, especially relations between Russia and the United States and the EU continue to be difficult in international and regional affairs, such as strategic arms control, Syria, Ukraine; Vietnam and Russia need to cooperate closely in this field, making practical contributions to maintaining a peaceful and stable environment, economic development in each countries, strongly promoting the Vietnam-Russia comprehensive strategic partnership.

Asia-Pacific is a strategic priority area of major countries as the strategic competition between China and the United States tends to increase. Vietnam has identified Russia as one of the "most reliable and promising partners in military cooperation". Through high-level visits, the Ministry of Defense of the two countries signed many cooperation agreements. Russia has become a reliable partner in providing modern military-technical facilities, including ships underground for Vietnam. And Russia is willing to cooperate in new science and technology fields what are essential for the security of Vietnam. Vietnam is currently Russia's third largest arms import market after India and China. Specific defense cooperation programmes between Vietnam and Russia such as: Russia sold Gepard-class corvettes, Kilo-class submarines, T-90S/SK battle tanks, Sukhoi-class fighters... to Vietnam; Russia and Vietnam cooperate to build rocket ships; Russia helps Vietnam build a submarine base and modern naval infrastructure, train technical staff.

Vietnam-Russia economic cooperation and other fields

Since 1991, Russia has been struggling with an unprecedented severe economic crisis and at the same time struggling with dangerous separatism. The traditional relationship under the Agreement was broken, leading to a sharp decline in the Vietnam-Russia economic and trade relationship, but Vietnam always identified the Russia as the leading important economic partner. Vietnam always pays special attention to the issue of cooperative development in the fields of economics, trade and investment, because the Russian market is the largest consumer market in the world, and this is a traditional partner of Vietnam. Russia is also considered a "gateway" for Vietnamese goods to enter the market of CIS countries.

Since 1994, Vietnam-Russia economic relations have been prospering when the two sides have actively improved the legal basis of bilateral cooperation, focused on key areas in Vietnam such as oil and gas.... Up to now, this economic relation has been strongly promoted, focusing on the development of economic –trade and investment. Currently, in the field of investment, in 2018, Russia ranked 24th out of 129 countries and territories investing in Vietnam, with 123 projects and a total registered capital of $932 million. On the contrary, Vietnam has also had 22 investment projects in Russia with a total of new capital and increased capital of nearly $3 billion[4]. Cooperation in the field of exploration and sounding out oil and gas is a highlight in the high-level talks between Vietnam and Russia. Vietnam is Russia's major trading partner in Asia and the second in the ASEAN Community. By 2018, bilateral trade turn-over will reach 5 billion USD and strive to reach 10 billion USD by 2020[5]. At the Vietnam-Russia Joint Statement 2017, the Heads of the two countries emphasized the need to find "motivation of new growth" to ensure the dynamic development of economic and trade cooperation, the urgency of the tasks of increasing two-way trade turnover and perfecting the bilateral trade structure.

However, the economic cooperation between Vietnam and Russia has not exploited its full potentials. Specifically: The development of commercial economics is not commensurate to its traditions, potentials and strategic partnerships of the two sides. Two-way trade turnover between Vietnam and Russia only accounts for about 1per cent of the total trade turnover of Vietnam and the world. In this context of the world and the regions having a lot of fluctuations that both opportunities and challenges intertwined, promoting a strong relationship towards total trade turnover of 10 billion USD by 2020 is a rather modest target, however, without synchronous solutions from both sides, it is difficult to achieve.

On the Asia-Pacific Economic Cooperation (APEC), Vietnam and the Russian Federation emphasized the increasing importance of the Asia-Pacific Economic Cooperation Forum as an effective linkage mechanism, towards the joint efforts of member economies in order to further improve the environment of trade and investment cooperation, ensuring sustainable development and regional security. Joining the APEC has helped Russia actively integrate into the economic development process of the Asia-Pacific region. For Vietnam, joining APEC is an important basis to integrate rapidly and successfully into global economic institutions. Both sides' participation in APEC has not only promoted cooperation in all fields of economic, defence and diplomacy, but also is an effective channel to help Vietnam promote and deepen bilateral relations with the Russia Federation.

Cooperation on Culture, education, science and technology

Cultural, educational, scientific and technological cooperation between Vietnam and Russia continues to act as a bridge connecting the two nations. In order to realize the goals of industrialization and modernization and early become an industrialized country, Vietnam actively cooperates in education-training, science and technology with modern and advanced education including the Russian Federation. With the advantages of basic sciences, aerospace and military sciences, Russia has provided great assistance to Vietnam in training high qualified scientific and technical staves. Besides, a series of key projects in Vietnam were built thanks to the financial and technical assistance of the Soviet Union in the past when Vietnam had just experienced a devastating war, surrounded by embargoes. These are constructions of vital significance to Vietnam.

In a nutshell, Vietnam-Russia relation is a traditional friendship which is constantly strengthened and developed in the present time stemming from the close interests of each country. It can be said that, during nearly seven decades, since establishing diplomatic relations in 1950, becoming a strategic partner in 2001 and upgrading the relationship to the Comprehensive Strategic Partner in July 2012, the relationship between Vietnam and the Russian Federation has been tested over time and has become a valuable asset of the peoples of the two countries, developing strongly both in breadth and depth with great achievements in all fields.

Vietnam-Japan Relations

Vietnam and Japan are two Asian neighbouring countries with striking similarities. They are cultural intimacy, respect and trust each other that are tested over time, similarities in many strategic interests in a range of key areas such as economics, politics, and security, culture, society, and people. After more than 45 years of official establishment of diplomatic relations, the relationship is like the "brothers of the co-culture, co-race, co-continent" between Vietnam and Japan have developed rapidly, comprehensively, and demonstrated in deep cooperation in all aspects.

Vietnam-Japan diplomatic relations

The diplomatic relationship between Vietnam and Japan originated at the end of the sixteenth century when Japanese merchants came to Vietnam for business. On September 21, 1973, Vietnam and Japan officially established diplomatic relations. By 2006, both sides affirmed the Japan-Vietnam Joint Statement "Toward a Strategic Partnership for Peace and Prosperity in Asia" and was officially established in April 2009, bringing bilateral relations to a strategic partnership. Since then, this relationship has been constantly nurtured by the governments and people of the two countries.

In 2010, the two countries continued to issue the "Vietnam-Japan Joint Declaration on the comprehensive development of strategic partnership for Peace and Prosperity in Asia" (officially signed in 2014). In 2011, Vietnam and Japan issued "Joint Declaration" to implement action within the framework of "strategic partnership for peace and prosperity in Asia"... In January 2013, the two governments agreed to bring Vietnam-Japan strategic cooperation to a new level with the organization of "Vietnam-Japan Friendship Year" on the 40th anniversary of establishing diplomatic relations (1973-2013). In order to deepen the extensive strategic partnership between Vietnam and Japan, in September 2015, General Secretary Nguyen Phu Trong and Japanese Prime Minister Shinzo Abe approved the "Declaration on the Joint Vision of Vietnam-Japan Relations". In 2017, for the first time, Emperor Akihito and Empress Michiko have paid an official visit to Vietnam, marking an important historical milestone in the bilateral relationship between the two countries. On May 31, 2018, Former President Tran Dai Quang and Prime Minister Sindo Abe held a high level talks and declared to further promote the deep strategic partnership for peace and prosperity in Asia. The two countries also supported each other at multilateral forums, such as the United Nations, ASEAN, APEC, ASEM... Vietnam supported Japan to be a non-permanent member of the United Nations Security Council for the 2016-2017 term... Thus, after 45 years of establishing diplomatic relations (1973-2018), 10 years of establishing strategic partnerships for Asian peace and prosperity (2009-2019), relations between Vietnam and Japan booming in all fields, becoming a "bright spot" in bilateral relations in Asia-Pacific.

For Vietnam, Japan is the most important strategic partner in the future. Japan supports Vietnam to grow its role in regional affairs and Vietnam supports Japan's strong involvement with ASEAN and the Mekong sub-region, as well as its efforts to become a permanent member of the United Nations Security Council. Vietnam has an important position and plays strategic role in Southeast Asia, serving as a maritime gateway and a bridge between Southeast Asia and Northeast Asia. Regarding foreign affairs, Vietnam plays the role as a middle strategic power in regional issues. Vietnam needs to develop multilateral relations well to balance big countries, ensure multilateral foreign policy and prevent the possibility of being pulled into orbit by one of the major powers. Vietnam is a peaceful country with stable politics and no territorial conflicts with Japan, and Vietnam is willing to share its views and support Japan on many bilateral and multilateral issues.

Vietnam-Japan economic cooperation

The Vietnam-Japan bilateral economic relationship has been expanded and strongly developed in three main economic aspects as Japan's provision of ODA to Vietnam, investment and trade. Since reopening official development assistance (ODA) to Vietnam in 1992, Japan has now become the largest donor, accounting for more than a third of total ODA to Vietnam with committed capital about 2,800 billion Yen what was effectively used in the fields of infrastructure construction, industrial development, agriculture, energy, environmental protection, climate change response, poverty reduction ... Many projects implemented by Japanese ODA loans have become a symbol of the friendship and cooperation between the two countries, such as: International Terminals of Tan Son Nhat Airport, Noi Bai Airport, Nhat Tan Bridge, Can Tho Bridge, Hai Van Tunnel, Hai Phong Port, Bach Mai Hospital and Cho Ray Hospital, urban railways in Ho Chi Minh City and Ha Noi city, electric factories throughout Vietnam.

The types of cooperation of Japanese ODA not only provide financial support, technical cooperation also contributes significantly to the sustainable development of Vietnam. Japan has sent experts to ministries, agencies and sectors of Vietnam to advise on policy, transfer technology through projects in the fields of agricultural development and health care, support appropriate cooperation activities of NGOs, universities, local governances in the fields of economic cooperation at grassroots level of Japan. In contrast, large projects in Vietnam funded by Japanese ODA help increase exports of Japan to Vietnam and bring business opportunities to Japanese contractors. Japan's investment adjustments in policy to Vietnam from 2000 are most evident in Japan's commitments in the *Vietnam-Japan Joint Initiative to improve the investment environment and enhance the competitiveness of Vietnam*. This initiative is designed to enhance Vietnam's economic competitiveness through promoting foreign direct investment, in particular sharing and applying special policies, measures and priorities with the motto of fully promoting the active participation and commitment of both Governments. As of June 30, 2019, Japan has had 4,190 investment projects in Vietnam with total registered capital of 57,9 billion USD, the second largest investor among countries and territories investing in Vietnam according to a report by Ministry and Trade[6].

Vietnam is a middle income country (MIC), so Vietnam shifted from the recipient country to the development partnership. This means that financially, new ODA loans will be more difficult for Vietnam, especially the interest rate will be higher and the loan term will be shorter. Therefore, Vietnam and Japan promote the development of stronger trade relations instead of focusing on ODA support. Japan is one of the largest markets in the world and an important commercial market of Vietnam. The trade relationship between Vietnam and Japan is an import and export structure with clear complementarity, basically not competing directly with each other, so the trade balance between Vietnam and Japan is always in relative equilibrium. The two countries have signed and implemented three free trade agreements, including AJCEP, VJEPA and CPTPP, opening a big door for Vietnam's exports to the Japanese market. Japan is an important consumer market for Vietnam's key products, such as textiles, seafood, fruit and vegetables, timber and wood products, fertilizers, chemicals... In contrast, Vietnam imports Japan's raw materials for production, of which a significant portion is used for enterprises producing goods for export from Vietnam. In 2018 alone, Japan became the fourth largest partner of Vietnam with a two-way trade turnover of US $ 37.86 billion (up 11.9per cent), of which Vietnam exported US $ 18.85 billion, importing export 19.01 billion USD[7].

Despite achieving many results, the trade size is still relatively small compared to the economic potentials between the two countries. Vietnam mainly exports to Japan the labour-intensive goods and natural resources but imports the goods that contain a high content of gray matter. Especially with signed trade agreements, which require stricter requirements on hygiene, product quarantine, product quality as well as other non-tariff barriers will be challenges for Vietnamese products to penetrate into Japan.

Vietnam-Japan defense and security cooperation

On August 2, 2016, of Japan's Ministry of Defense published a Defense White Paper in 2016 with the title Defense of Japan 2016, including the following: An overview of the security environment around Japan, in which mainly mentions to challenges coming from North Korea and China; National security strategy, Defense policies and Japan-US alliance. Japan's defense and security Initiatives are aimed at protecting the lives and property of the peoples, as well as protecting Japan's territory, airspace, and waters. One of the three main pillars of Japanese defense policy is strengthening ties with neighbouring countries, especially those that share a common challenges to counter China in the East Sea issues.

Vietnam and Japan established a strategic partnership in 2009, but defense cooperation was limited to military delegation exchanges and visits of Japanese naval ship to Vietnamese ports. In the period of 2009-2018, defense and security links were quickly strengthened and diversified through six times of Vietnam-Japan Strategic Partnership Dialogue on diplomacy, security-defense at level of Deputy Minister of Foreign Affairs (since 2010), 6 times of Vietnam-Japan defense policy dialogue at Deputy Minister level (since 2012), 6 times of Deputy Security Dialogue at Minister-level (since 2013). In the *Joint Statement on Strategic partners for Peace and Prosperity in Asia in 2009*, the two sides agreed to set up military attaches at each country's embassy, exchanging information on defense relations and starting building trust. The meetings of military officers of two sides, high-ranking officers meetings of of Vietnam's Ministry of Defense and the Japanese Defense Department are held periodically, followed by the periodical meetings of Vietnam's Minister of Defense and the Director of the Japanese Defense Bureau, have gradually increased the level of meetings between Vietnam and Japan. The issue of most concern is the coastal defense against China's violation of Japan's sovereignty over the Senkaku Islands of Japan and sovereignty over the East Sea over Vietnam.

The bilateral relations between Vietnam and Japan are developing in a good way with a strong economic foundation, high level of mutual trust and great similarity of strategic benefits, especially Japan-Vietnam agrees on issues related to China. In defence-security cooperation, Japan always supports Vietnam to strengthen its power to maintain balance of power in the region. More importantly, Japan is a permanent power in East Asia and has a troubled relationship with China for a long time. This makes naturally Japan become a security partner of Vietnam and Japan's security commitments more credible. Vietnam's desires are also in line with Japan's intention and Shinzo Abe's security and defense policy, which aspires to "normalize" Japan's defense position and reduce risks from security subordination to the United States. This momentum will continue to become stronger in the coming years due to uncertainties in US policy towards the region.

However, the two sides faced many obstacles such as the restriction of the principle of pacifism in the Japanese Constitution. On the other side, Japan could not provide patrol boats to Vietnam due to the principle of Japan's ODA Charter. Joint military drills are planned with a range of technical issues such as the language, cryptographic rules, etc. In addition to the achieved results, the cooperation to resolve national security issues between Vietnam and Japan has still faced many difficulties because the Japanese Constitution does not allow to declare war, own an army or fight abroad. Vietnam and Japan cannot form a real military alliance, both can only deal with and solve problems that have arisen through joint statements, dialogues or calling for collective efforts. In the context of China is a sensitive, mutually beneficial element with Vietnam and incessantly conflict with Japan.

One problem that both Japan and Vietnam cannot ignore is the reaction from China. Vietnam-China relations always present delicate and complex issues, not to mention the Comprehensive strategic partnership agreement. On the other side, Vietnam is also the gateway of the east-west economic corridor and the southern economic corridor, and a strategic partner of Japan, so it is easy for Vietnam to share its views on the Indo-Pacific strategy. On the Japanese side, the Abe government is ready to cooperate with any country that endorses the Indo-Pacific strategy, of which Vietnam is the key. Japan and the United States work together to accomplish three goals like: compete with China, expect ASEAN countries to be aware of this strategy, and call for cooperation with India and Australia. In fact, over the past years, Vietnam has called on Japan to help improve the capacity of law enforcement at sea according to the Abe doctrine, hoping to strengthen Japan's defense cooperation to improve maritime security, on this base to deal with China's expansion in the East Sea and along with ASEAN members to ensure that open and free seas are governed by laws and regulations, not by force.

It can be said that, based on the harmony of traditional culture with many similarities such as belonging to the wet rice civilization, the polytheism of ancestor worship and Buddhism, Vietnam has become an extremely important partner that shares many of strategic interests with Japan. With a strategic geopolitical position, tough stance against China's extravagant actions and certain importance on the presence of the US, Vietnam has received special attention from Japan in supporting the sustainable development and build links in the spirit of extensive strategic partners. Vietnam-Japan relations are gradually becoming friendly and cooperative relationships in the direction of stability, long-term and mutual trust. This is a very important political policy in long-term directions for the development of bilateral relations, and at the same time meet the strategic interests of each party in the 21st century.

Vietnam-European Union (EU) Relations

It can be said that the European Union (EU) is an international subject playing a very important role on the world political chessboard as well as a strong pillar of the world economy. In the process of formation, development, integration and deep linking, the EU has achieved many successes in the general policies of institutions, making an important contribution to the development of the world, such as peace, stability, foreign politics, development cooperation, economics and trade, investment, finance, social development, human rights, education and training... With 28 member countries, the total population is more than 500 million people, the European Union is now an economic entity with the largest total commercial value in the world, and its economic competitiveness on par with the US superpower, so EU has become a model playing greater and greater in the international arena.

The world is witnessing the trend of globalization, trade liberalization, bilateral and multilateral cooperation in all fields. EU has found that Asia-Pacific is a dynamic developing region with many countries and subjects with important influence, making great contributions to the overall development of the world, such as China, Japan, India, Korea, ASEAN... Asia-Pacific also is receiving special attention of the world as the major powers are gradually implementing specific strategies to increase their influence in this region. A notable strategic adjustment came from the United States- the most important strategic partner of EU. In early 2011 US announced its shift of global strategic focus to Asia-Pacific and Free and Open Indo-Pacific strategy (FOIP) today. In 2013, China launched the strategic Initiative "Belt and Road Initiative (BRI)" to implement the "Chinese Dream". In this context, through specific steps in the fields of politics, democracy, economics, investment, trade, development cooperation, the EU has also built a strategy to strengthen the cooperative relations with the Asia-Pacific region to gain more presence in the region and promote deeper relations with regional countries in which Vietnam is receiving special important attention. Therefore, Vietnam always attaches great importance to diplomatic relations with the EU as a top objective in formulating and implementing foreign policies with countries and entities around the world.

Vietnam–EU relations on politics and diplomacy

Vietnam and the EU have established traditional development cooperation relations both at the union level as well as with EU member countries. On November 28, 1990, the European community (EC) and Vietnam established diplomatic relations. In the 1991-1995 period, cooperation between EU with Vietnam mainly focused on seven main activities: Humanitarian aid and implementation of the EC's international programme for the reintegration of

Vietnamese refugees returned from the first residence countries. Funding activities related to the management and conservation of natural resources through the greenery and nature conservation programme in Nghe An. Implementing a technical programme for transition to a market economy in the fields of accounting and auditing, domestic investment insurance, standards and quality, intellectual property, economic planning and information. Supporting non-governmental organizations (NGOs) in implementing projects to develop urban and rural, supporting independent activities in different areas in plan of the EC investment partners (ECIP). Implementation of joint research projects under science and technology Development (STD) for developing countries and International Scientific Cooperation (ISC). Food and provisions aid.

In 1995, the Framework Agreement on cooperation between Vietnam and the European Community (the precursor of the European Union)–referred to as the 1995 Framework Agreement, was signed and marked a new development milestone when establishing an exchange forum on the situation of the implementation of cooperation programmes between Vietnam and the EU in the field of trade economy. The agreement covers a rich and diverse content of cooperation, from the two sides' commitment to giving each other Most Favoured Nation Status in trade to promoting investment, expanding cooperation on economics and science, intellectual property rights, cooperation on environmental protection, information and communication, drug abuse control.

After establishing diplomatic relations, the leaders of Vietnam and the EU constantly organized high-level visits to promote and strengthen this cooperative relationship. The first was the visit of the French President F. Mitterrand in February 1993, the first Western head of state to Vietnam since 1975. After that, a series of visits from the EU leaders: President of the Republic of Austria, Prime Minister of Sweden, Prime Minister of the Netherlands. On the Vietnamese side, prominent in this period was the trip of President Le Duc Anh to the 50th anniversary of victory over fascism in France in 1995, followed by a visit of Prime Minister Vo Van Kiet to a series of EU member states and the European Commission. When welcoming the Vietnam's Prime Minister, Mr. J. Delors-President of the European Commission continued to emphasize that considering Vietnam as a country must receive the "necessary assistance and cooperation". More important is the meeting of President Tran Duc Luong and the President of France, who headed the ASEAN and EU blocs as the two Presidents. This special meeting promoted the relationship not only for Vietnam and the EU, but also cooperation between two of the largest regional institutions in the world increasing.

Over the past years, Vietnam-EU relations have seen positive and comprehensive development, especially, the official signing of the Partnership and Cooperation Agreement (PCA) and kicked off negotiations on a free trade agreement (FTA) in June 2012. These are important development steps, creating a solid basis for promoting strong and profound and practical relations between Vietnam and EU. The exchange of high-ranking leadership delegations has been ongoing in recent years, and political consultations at the level of Deputy Minister of Vietnam-EU have played an important role in the political-democracy relationship of the two sides, provides a forum for bilateral and multilateral issues that EU and Vietnam have common concerns such as human rights, sustainable development, climate change, regional and international security. It can be said that the EU is the first partner of Vietnam to have an overall strategy for cooperation and Vietnam is also the first country in Southeast Asia to come up with a comprehensive cooperation strategy with the EU.

Vietnam–EU relations in economics, trade, investment

The EU is a reliable partner playing an important role in supporting Vietnam's integration process into the global economy. The support from the EU has greatly contributed to the successful implementation of market-oriented reform policies, helping Vietnam to make great economic developing progress, contributing to empowering the position and role of Vietnam in the region and the world. The EU is one of the major donors to Vietnam with the EU's Official Development Assistance (ODA) for Vietnam increasing from 140 million Euro (1996-2001) to 162 million Euro (2002-2006) and 304 million Euro (2007-2013). In particular, in the period 2014-2020, the EU committed to provide Vietnam with 400 million Euro of assistance, focusing on two areas: sustainable energy and institutions. Specifically in the field of energy, the EU pays special attention to sustainable energy, rural energy, efficiency to use energy, in parallel with the implementation of the "Programme of supporting energy development policy and strengthening access to sustainable energy to rural, mountainous and island areas". The EU also helps Vietnam implement projects to upgrade public governance and laws, such as the Justice Partnership Programme (JPP), Justice Initiatives Facilitation Fund (JIFF), the EU Justice and Legal Empowerment programme in Vietnam (EU JULE), and The EU Public Finance Modernization Project (EU-PFMO).

The most remarkable milestone in the trade and investment relations between Vietnam and the EU is the successful signing of the EU-Vietnam Free Trade Agreement EVFTA (2019). This is one of the most ambitious and comprehensive trade and investment agreements that the EU has ever signed with a developing country; At the same time, it is the second important agreement in the ASEAN region after Singapore. EVFTA will eliminate over 99per cent of tariff lines on goods imported from Vietnam to the EU, because of Vietnam is a developing country, so 65 per cent of the value of EU exports to Vietnam will be free which accounts for about half of the total tariff lines at the time of effective and the remaining tariff lines will be abolished within the next ten years. This is the fastest ever elimination of tariffs for a country like Vietnam. This has proved the goal of integration and deeper trade relations between Vietnam and the EU. In ASEAN region, Vietnam is the leading country in exporting goods to the EU, and the Agreement will also facilitate EU investment in Vietnam. As of March 2019, 24/28 EU countries have invested in

Vietnam with 2,235 projects with total registered capital of 24.64 billion USD, ranked 5th among the largest investors in Vietnam (after Korea, Japan, Singapore, Taiwan). Bilateral relations between Vietnam and EU member countries have also gained new achievements. For example, German economic cooperation is a bright spot in bilateral relations. Germany has always maintained the position of Vietnam's largest trading partner in the EU. Two-way trade turnover in 2018 reached over 10 billion USD. Germany's investment in Vietnam reached USD 1.9 billion, continues to maintain the EU's fourth position in investment in Vietnam and is a major and effective partner of Vietnam in scientific-technological cooperation.

The cooperation between Vietnam and the EU at multilateral forums and international organizations is always highly appreciated by the cohesion, consensus and support, especially in the framework of ASEAN-EU cooperation, ASEM and United Nations. Under the framework of ASEAN-EU cooperation, Vietnam and the EU jointly promote partnership between the two regions through key mechanisms such as the Trans-Regional EU-ASEAN Trade Initiative (TREATI), the Regional EU-ASEAN Dialogue Instrument (READI). The two sides also work closely in addressing global issues such as climate change (together committed to implementing the Paris Agreement on climate change, sustainable development), energy security, counter-terrorism, anti-proliferation, and illegal migration. Especially, on the issue of the East Sea, the EU has shown a strong interest in respecting the international law, upholding law in international relations, advocating the settlement of disputes through peaceful measures on base of international law, UNCLOS 1982 as well as concerning about the security and freedom of navigation and overflight in the East Sea.

In October 2017, the European Parliament adopted a Resolution on EU – ASEAN relations, including the East Sea issues. The resolution is a call for the EU to respect and further promote compliance with UNCLOS, call for China to accept the court ruling, support ASEAN's efforts toward a swift conclusion of negotiations on the Code of Conduct in the East Sea (COC). The resolution also calls for member states to seriously implement the Europe Code on arms exports and underlines the importance of non-proliferation of weapons of mass destruction. On this side, Vietnam also appreciated highly the EU's role in international security and peace issues as well as the EU's position on maintaining stability and ensuring respect for international law in the region and the East Sea; especially in the context of unilateral actions has increased tensions, eroded trust and violated the interests and sovereignty of countries, causing great concern to regional and international public opinion.

Conclusion

In the construction and development process, from being surrounded and embargoed, Vietnam has established diplomatic relations with other countries and territories in the world, in which it is noteworthy to build and develop diplomatic relations with many world superpowers, such as the United States,

Russia, Japan and EU countries... So that, Vietnam has achieved important successes, contributing to the successful implementation of the country's renovation. As a result, from a poor, backward country after the war, mainly having relations with countries in the socialist system, Vietnam has expanded its rich and diverse cooperation relations with Capitalist countries with great results. Through diplomatic relations established in all fields with powers and the EU, Vietnam's position is increasingly asserted in international relations and becoming an important and indispensable partner in the cooperation relations system in Asia-Pacific. As such, Vietnam's influence and attractiveness in international relations is constantly increased and emphasized. This has contributed to affirming that Vietnam has achieved the criteria of a new middle power in East Asia.

Notes

1. https://2001-2009.state.gov/p/eap/rls/rm/68939.htm
2. Vietnam at https://ustr.gov/countries-regions/southeast-asia-pacific/vietnam
3. Decision No. 36/2004/QD-TTg of March 17, 2004, approving the national strategy on HIV/AIDS prevention and control in Vietnam till 2010 with a vision to 2020
4. https://www.vcsc.com.vn/tin-chi-tiet/vn-russia-to-boost-trade-cooperation/290277
5. https://bizlive.vn/biznews/vietnam-russia-work-to-bring-bilateral-trade-to-10-billion-usd-in-2020-3469522.html
6. https://gbs.com.vn/gbs.vn/japanese-investors-registered-capital-of-us57-9-billion-into-vietnam/
7. http://vietnamexport.com/tinh-hinh-xuat-nhap-khau-viet-nam-nhat-ban-12-thang-2018/vn2530168.html

References

1. Diệu An, *"Việt Nam hoan nghênh lập trường của EU về Biển Đông"*, Tuổi trẻ online, truy cập ngày 5/8/2019
2. Lê Hoàng Anh, "Điểm lại chính sách ngoại giao của Nhật Bản đối với khu vực Đông Nam Á qua các đời thủ tướng", Tạp chí Nghiên cứu Đông Bắc Á số tháng 8/2014.
3. Báo quốc tế, "45 năm quan hệ ngoại giao Việt Nam-Nhật Bản: Thời gian ngắn cho bước tiến dài", 09/9/2018.
4. Báo Vietnamnet, "Toàn văn Tuyên bố chung Việt Nam-Hoa Kỳ", ngày 12/11/2017.
5. Vũ Thị Hồng Chuyên, "Chính sách của Việt Nam đối với Liên bang Nga (1991-2017)- Một số đặc điểm chủ yếu", 10/5/2018
6. Việt Cường, "Tuyên bố chung Việt Nam-Liên bang Nga", Báo Điện tử của Đài tiếng nói Việt Nam-VOV, 30/6/2017
7. PGS.TS. Vũ Văn Hà-PGS.TS. Phạm Thị Thanh Bình, "Vai trò của Việt Nam trong khu vực Châu Á-Thái Bình Dương", trích Kỷ yếu hội thảo quốc tế Vai trò của Việt Nam trong khu vực Châu Á - Thái Bình Dương, Nxb. Thế giới, 2011.
8. Lê Hồng Hiệp, "Việt - Mỹ cần tận dụng lực đẩy từ chuyến thăm của tàu USS Carl Vinson", Báo Nghiên cứu quốc tế, ngày 5/3/2018.
9. Lưu Thúy Hồng, "Những biến động trong chính sách hướng Đông của Liên bang Nga", Học viện Báo chí Tuyên truyền, 15/12/2017.
10. Phạm Bình Minh, "Quan hệ đối tác chiến lược toàn diện Việt - Nga 65 năm - Một

chặng đường", Bộ Ngoại giao Việt Nam, truy cập ngày 10/12/2017, http://www.mofahcm.gov.vn/en/mofa/nr040807104143/nr040807105001/ns150129140300.

11. Trần Quang Minh, "Điều chỉnh chính sách của Nhật Bản đối với Việt Nam trong lĩnh vực hợp tác về thương mại, đầu tư và ODA từ năm 2000 đến nay", Nghiên cứu Đông Bắc Á - số 3, 3/2013.
12. Vũ Bình Minh, "Chính sách đối ngoại của Liên minh châu Âu đối với khu vực Châu Á - Thái Bình Dương trong bối cảnh mới", Luận văn Thạc sĩ Châu Âu học, 2018.
13. Nghiên cứu quốc tế, số 75,"Quan hệ Việt - Mỹ những năm đầu thế kỷ XXI: Một vài nhận xét về thực trạng và dự báo triển vọng".
14. PGS, TS Nguyễn Thị Quế - ThS Nguyễn Thị Thúy, "Chiến lược xoay trục, tái cân bằng của Mỹ đối với châu Á - Thái Bình Dương", Tạp chí Lý luận Chính trị, 20/1/2016.
15. TS. Trần Việt Thái, "Về sách trắng quốc phòng Nhật Bản năm 2016", Tạp chí Nghiên cứu Đông Bắc Á số tháng 3/2017.
16. Trần Thị Mai Thành - Đồng Bích Ngọc, "Quan hệ Thương mại Việt Nam - Nhật Bản: Thực trạng, vấn đề và giải pháp", Nghiên cứu Đông Bắc Á - số 5, 5/2017.
17. TS. Nguyễn Thị Thanh Thuỷ, "Ngoại giao nhân dân trong quan hệ Việt Nam - Hoa Kỳ", Trường Đại học Khoa học Xã hội và Nhân văn, Đại học Quốc gia Hà Nội, 2018.
18. Lê Thanh Vạn, "Quan hệ Việt - Nga những chặng đường lịch sử đáng nhớ", Tạp chí Lịch sử Đảng, 7/2017.
19. Trần Thị Vinh, "Việt Nam trong chiến lược của Hoa Kỳ ở khu vực Châu Á - Thái Bình Dương: Luận giải từ lịch sử và hiện tại", Báo cáo Hội thảo Khoa học tại VAS, Hà Nội, tháng 9/2013.
20. GS. Toshiharu Tsuboi, "Khả năng và những vấn đề trong hợp tác phòng vệ Việt Nam - Nhật Bản", Tạp chí Nghiên cứu Đông Bắc Á số tháng 3/2014.
21. The Constitution of Japan, Chapter II, Article 9: https://japan.kantei.go.jp/constitution_and_government_of_japan/constitution_e.html.
    https://vn.usembassy.gov/20160523joint-statement-us-vietnam/
    https://vn.usembassy.gov/20160523joint-statement-us-vietnam/
22. "Khái niệm mới về chính sách đối ngoại của Liên bang Nga", Toàn văn Phát biểu của Tổng thống Nga Vladimir, 30/11/2016;
23. "Quan hệ Việt Nam- Nga dưới thời tổng thống Vladimir Putin (2012- nay)", Nguyễn Thị Thanh Hồng, tr. 51;
24. Asia Times, 2017;
25. Báo cáo của Ban Chấp hành Trung ương Đảng khóa X, tháng 01 năm 2011;
26. Báo Thế giới và Việt Nam, "Minh chứng cho truyền thống hòa hiếu và bao dung của Việt Nam", ngày 27/4/2018;
27. Bộ Ngoại giao, "Tài liệu cơ bản Quan hệ Việt Nam – Liên minh Châu Âu (EU)", Cập nhật đến tháng 6/2019;
28. Diệu An, "Việt Nam hoan nghênh lập trường của EU về Biển Đông", Tuổi trẻ online, 5/8/2019;
29. Đại Sứ Quán Liên Bang Nga Tại Cộng Hòa Xã Hội Chủ Nghĩa Việt Nam, Khái niệm về chính sách đối ngoại của Liên Bang Nga Phê Duyệt theo Sắc lệnh của Tổng thống Liên Bang Nga ngày 30/11/2016 № 640;
30. Đinh Công Tuấn, "Hơn 20 năm quan hệ hợp tác Việt Nam – Liên minh châu Âu", Tạp chí Cộng sản, 11/3/2011;
31. GS. TS Vũ Dương Huân, "60 năm quan hệ Việt – Nga", 18/4/2010;
32. Hải quan Việt Nam,"Xuất nhập khẩu giữa Việt Nam và Hoa Kỳ: Diễn biến giai đoạn 2010-2018 và cập nhật tháng 1/2019", ngày 28/2/2019;
33. Hồ sơ Thị trường Nhật Bản, Ban Quan hệ Quốc tế - VCCI, 6/2018; Nghiên cứu

quốc tế, số 75,"Quan hệ Việt – Mỹ những năm đầu thế kỷ 21: Một vài nhận xét về thực trạng và dự báo triển vọng."

34. Phạm Bình Minh, "Quan hệ đối tác chiến lược toàn diện Việt - Nga 65 năm - Một chặng đường", Bộ Ngoai giao Việt Nam, truy cập ngày 10/12/2017, http://www.mofahcm.gov.vn/en/mofa/nr040807104143/nr040807105001/ns150129140300;
35. Sách trắng các vấn đề Thương mại & Đầu tư và Kiến nghị 2018, Eurocham, Ấn bản lần thứ 10;
36. Sách xanh Ngoại giao 2018, Bộ Ngoại giao;
37. Tổng hợp từ "Tài liệu cơ bản Quan hệ Việt Nam – Liên minh châu Âu (EU)" của Bộ Ngoại giao;
38. The Constitution of Japan, Chapter II, Article 9: https://japan.kantei.go.jp/constitution_and_government_of_japan/constitution_e.html;
39. (Trần Quang Minh, "Điều chỉnh chính sách của Nhật Bản đối với Việt Nam trong lĩnh vực hợp tác về Thương mại, Đầu tư và ODA từ năm 2000 đến nay", Nghiên cứu Đông Bắc Á – số 3, 3/2013)

8 Comprehensive Strategic Partnership between Vietnam and India

Van-Son Nguyen

Vietnam-India Politics and Diplomacy Relations

History has shown that Vietnam and India have established an extremely cordial relationship and Vietnam has become one of the international partners with a special position for India. Over nearly 50 years of diplomatic relations, with great efforts by the governments and people of the two countries, the relationship between Vietnam and India has overcome many difficulties, challenges and gained great large achievements, becoming an "important factor to ensure regional peace and security".

The Vietnam-India relationship has come from similarities of culture and history and is fostered by the Parties, Governments and people of the two countries. The connectivity is vividly shown when the Indian people always supported and helped the Vietnamese people during the war of independence and reunification, many Indian people sacrificed their lives for supporting Vietnam. Despite being a country with an extremely big population, the Government and the people of India have still provided assistance to the Vietnamese people on food and financial loans at preferential interest rates, contributing to help the Government of Vietnam overcome the socio-economic crisis when Vietnam was under severe siege by international hostile forces during the 1970s and 1980s. When Vietnam was in the situation of being attacked and isolated by hostile forces because our army helped the revolution of this country to overthrow the Pol Pot regime, India was the first and only country not in the socialist system recognizes the Government of the People's Republic of Cambodia, supports Vietnam's viewpoint on the Cambodian issue and considers the actions conducted by the Vietnamese army in Cambodia in the 1980s to be righteous meaning[1].

With the efforts by the Governments of the two countries, India-Vietnam relations have been developing well in recent years. The two countries regularly perform high-level exchanges and contact to enhance mutual understanding and create an important basis for increasing and strengthening political trust between the two countries. There were a lot of high-level visits paid between the two sides before establishing a strategic partnership in 2007 such as: Visits paid by Vietnamese side, Prime Minister Pham Van Dong visited India in 1978 and 1980, General Secretary Le Duan (1984), General Secretary Nguyen Van Linh (1989), General Secretary Do Muoi (1992), President of the National Assembly of Vietnam, Nong Duc Manh (1994), Prime Minister Vo Van Kiet (1997), President Tran Duc Luong (1999), General Secretary Nong Duc Manh (2003)—during this visit, Vietnam and India issued a joint statement on comprehensive cooperation between the two countries in the 21st century. Visits paid by Indian side: Prime Minister Rajiv Gandhi (1985 and 1988), President R. Venkatraman (1991), Vice President K.R. Narayanan (1993), Prime Minister P.V. Narasimha Rao (1994), Prime Minister A.B. Vajpayee (January 2001), National Assembly Chairman Somnath Chatterjee (March 2007)[2]. After 35 years of establishing diplomatic relations with remarkable efforts, the two countries officially issued a Joint Statement on the establishment of a "strategic partnership" in 2007. This is an important milestone in the history of political and diplomatic relations between Vietnam and India as well as an important basis to upgrade bilateral relations to a new height based on the principle of respect for independence, sovereignty, territorial integrity and mutual benefit.

The world is facing many dramatic changes, particularly the global economic crisis in 2008 which has an enormous impact on international politics and nations all over the world. Regarding the South East Asia region, on 7th May 2009, China submitted a claim of illegal sovereignty over the East Sea to United Nations, after Vietnam and Malaysia submitted to the United Nations' Commission on the Limits of the Continental Shelf (referred to as CLCS) their reports on expanded continental shelf[3] (6th May 2007). This claim has faced fierce opposition from many countries in the region and around the world, creating a tense atmosphere, even a risk of conflicts among the nations having maritime disputes with China including Vietnam. These tensions tend to escalate as China performs increasingly aggressive actions in the East Sea. Besides, big countries have more and more strong presence in the East Sea area through patrol activities to demonstrate their support for maritime freedom in the Sea and to restrain China's ambitions.

These above-mentioned issues exert dramatic impact on the relationship, the process of association and cooperation among the countries in the region who have shared benefits, including the relationship between Vietnam and India. After setting up a "strategic partnership", the two countries, with desire to develop their relationship to be more intensive and practical, continue organizing high-level visits. In which, some remarkable visits were made, including the visits to India paid by former President Truong Tan Sang in 2011, General Secretary Nguyen Phu Trong in 2013, former Prime Minister Nguyen Tan Dung in 2014 and the visit to Vietnam paid by India's President Pranab Mukherjee in 2014"[4]. In September 2016, India's Prime Minister Mr. Narendra Modi paid an official visit to Vietnam. In this visit, the two sides officially upgraded their relations to a "comprehensive strategic partnership", demonstrating the high level of political trust between the two countries. At the same time, conditions are created to "promote Vietnam-India relationship to develop more intensively and stably in accordance with the aspirations of the two countries' Party, Government and people, meeting their requirements on national security, integration and development in the new situation.

Particularly, within 3 years of 2016-2019, Vietnam and India organized five high-level working visits. This is "a rare occurrence in bilateral relationship not only between Vietnam and India but also among other countries[5]". India's working visits to Vietnam were paid by its Prime Minister Mr. Modi (September 2016) and its President Mr. Ram Nath Kovind (November 2018). Vietnam's visits to India were paid by its National Assembly Chairwoman Nguyen Thi Kim Ngan (December 2016), Prime Minister Nguyen Xuan Phuc (January 2018) and the late President Tran Dai Quang (3/2018).

In order to realize the political commitments between Vietnam and India, in July 2017, during his working visit to India, Deputy Prime Minister and Foreign Minister Pham Binh Minh, on behalf of Vietnam Government, signed "The Plan of Action to implement the Comprehensive Strategic Partnership for the period 2017-2020". "This Plan is an important framework to guide the comprehensive cooperation areas of bilateral relationship, including politics, national defence-security, economics, energy, connectivity, science and technique, information technology, education-training-research, culture-tourism, people-to-people exchanges, law and justice, health-agriculture-fisheries and breeding, finance and credit, and cooperation in regional and international forums[6]".

On regional and international forums, the two countries always share similar opinions and support other's political stance, namely: Regarding sovereignty disputes in the East Sea, both sides affirm that all the disputes need to be settled through negotiation and peace solutions pursuant to international laws in order to maintain peace, prosperity and ensure maritime security and safety across the East Sea; Vietnam affirmed it would be a bridge to promote connections and cooperation between India and ASEAN countries; Vietnam supports India's greater presence in the region through its implementation of "Look East Policy" previously and "Act East Policy" currently. Vietnam and India always agree to support others in multilateral mechanisms, particularly at the United Nations, the two countries agree to support others to be candidates for the position of a non-permanent member of UN Security Council, Vietnam for the 2020-2021 term, India for the 2021-2022 term. Vietnam also affirms its consistent opinion of supporting India to become a permanent member of the United Nations Security Council upon the extension of this Council[7]. Besides, the two countries also perform close coordination and support others in multilateral forums such as, Association of Southeast Asian Nations (ASEAN), ASEAN regional Forum (ARF), ASEAN Defence Ministers Meeting Plus (ADMM +), etc.

Thus, the outstanding development of Vietnam-India relationship also gains great results from the friendly, long-standing and traditional relations between the two peoples over the history of thousands of years through cultural exchanges and acculturation, particularly through the spreading of Buddhism into Vietnam. In the recent years, the relationship between Vietnam and India has become increasingly strong as a result of efforts made by both sides on the basis of mutual understanding and high political trust. The two sides agree to further develop their bilateral relationship intensively, being appropriate to the two countries' potential and advantages in order to enhance their position and role in the region and in the world.

Vietnam-India's relationship in Economics and Commerce

Vietnam and India's economic-commercial relationship is one of the two main pillars of their comprehensive strategic partnership for the purpose of bringing prosperity to the two countries. In recent years, the economic and commercial relationship between Vietnam and India have developed rapidly and made many achievements. *Vietnam–India's commercial relationship* have been continuously developing since India started strongly implementing its Look East Policy in 1992, whereby the bilateral commercial turnover has been raised rapidly from USD 50.9 million in 1991-1992 into over USD 1.5 billion in 2007[8]. In the period of 2007-2009, though the economies of Vietnam and India suffered many negative impacts caused by the 2008 world economic crisis, but their two-way trade in 2009 reached USD 2 billion anyway[9]. Particularly, the official effectiveness of ASEAN- India Free Trade Agreement in 2010 created favourable conditions for Vietnam and India's economies to perform more exchanges. In 2010, the two-way trade between the two countries was estimated at over 2.7 billion USD[10], an impressive figure indicating the rapid development of their economic and commercial relations.

However, that figure is still not commensurate with the two countries' potentials and friendly relationship in the current period. Compared to that of other countries in the region, in the 2011-2012 fiscal year, Vietnam's two-way trade with India (3.9 billion USD[11]) was ranked 5th among ASEAN countries, "lower than that of Singapore (USD 26.445 billion), Indonesia (USD21.31 billion), Malaysia (USD 13.538 billion), Thailand (USD 8.3344 billion), followed by that of Myanmar (USD 1,870 billion), Brunei (USD 1,647 billion), the Philippines (USD 1,448 billion), Cambodia (USD 107 million), and Laos (USD 104 million)[12]". That has set up the requirements and tasks for Vietnam and India to find ways to promote developing their economic-commercial relations, so that it really becomes one of the main pillars in "Vietnam–India's strategic partnership" and commensurate with their potentials, advantages and the political determination of the two sides' leaders. India's main products exported to Vietnam include iron and steel products, leather products, agrochemicals, plastics, power supply and software. Vietnam's products exported to India include crude oil, coal, natural rubber, pepper, tea, computer parts, electronic products, cinnamon, spices, and textiles, etc.

In order to promote trade and investment, Vietnam and India have established Vietnam-India Entrepreneurship Development Center (2006), Vietnam-India Business Forum. Vietnam-India Business Forum, with the participation of leading enterprises in Vietnam, was organized by the Confederation of Indian Industry (CII), Federation of Indian Chambers of Commerce & Industry (FICCI), Indian Merchants Chamber Association (IMC) in combination with Vietnam Chamber of Commerce and Industry (VCCI).[13]

In the 2015-2016 period, the two-way trade between the two countries increased into USD 7.8 billion and in the 2017-2018 period this figure was USD12.8 billion. The two countries are aiming to reach their target of USD 15 billion by 2020. India is being one of Vietnam's 10 largest trading partners[14], while Vietnam becomes India's 28th largest trading partner[15]. According to the Joint Subcommittee on Trade at deputy-minister level, currently, the areas prioritized by Vietnam and India in their cooperation include: textiles, leather, pharmaceuticals, agriculture, engineering, agriculture and tourism.

Regarding investment, the investment cooperation between Vietnam and India has also developed rapidly and made many significant achievements. According to statistics, by the end of September 2018, the total registered investment capital of Indian enterprises and investors in Vietnam reached USD 877 million, with 201 investment projects, this figure is ranked at 29/129 nations and territories investing in Vietnam. Most Indian investors and enterprises' projects focus on fields such as: processing, manufacturing, telecommunications, information technology and mining. Currently, many large Indian groups such as TATA, ONGC, Essar, etc. have been performing successful investments in Vietnam. In the other side, currently, Vietnam has 8 investment projects in India with a total registered capital of USD 6.16 million, mainly in the field of distributing animal feed products, construction materials, exported cosmetic products and computing products[16].

Thus, the economic and commercial relationship between Vietnam and India in recent years have been developing rapidly and have prospects of better cooperation in the future. However, to make the two countries' economic and commercial relationship commensurate with their potential and comprehensive partnership, more efforts need to be made, particularly the regular attention and guidance of two countries' leaders.

Vietnam-India's relationship in National defence amd security

After nearly 50 years, from 1972 up to now, since the establishment of the two countries' diplomatic relation, their bilateral relationship has developed rapidly in many fields. It is affirmed that besides economic-commercial cooperation, national defence-security cooperation is a key field in the comprehensive strategic partnership between Vietnam and India.

Vietnam and India have started their cooperation in national defence-security since the early 1990s of the twentieth century. So far, Vietnam and India have agreed to identify national defence-security cooperation as an important factor to promote the peace, cooperation, stability and development of South East Asia in the context that the countries in this region are facing China's aggressive actions in the East Sea. Nations having sovereign claimant with China are seeking to develop their defence power and call for support from the international community and countries having shared benefit with them to protect their legitimate benefits. Both India and Vietnam have legitimate benefits for maintaining and stabilizing peace in the Indo-Pacific region generally and the East Sea particularly since the East Sea plays an important role in the economic development strategy and national defence-security of both Vietnam and India. The East Sea has not only provided food for residents living on coastal areas for thousands of years, but also is an entrance for Vietnam's commercial exchanges with regional and international markets. The East Sea creates conditions for Vietnam to develop key economic sectors such as fisheries, oil and gas, maritime transportation, ship building, tourism, etc. The natural conditions of Vietnam's coast have created extremely huge potentials for Vietnam's maritime transportation industry. Along Vietnam' coast, there are ten locations with appropriate conditions to construct deep-water ports and many locations to locate normal ports with a total cargo volume of 50 million tons/year[17]. In addition, in Vietnam's strategy of national defence and security, the East Sea is considered as a frontier to protect Vietnam afar.

For India, the East Sea, where over 55% of its commercial activities are performed[18], is one of its lifeblood trade links closely connecting its economy with partners around the world. In addition, according to military experts, the East Sea is a buffer zone and a shield to the East helping India "prevent attacks from outside area performed by big countries, an important stepping platform to expand its strategic influence into Western Pacific[19]", equalizing its power with that of big nations inside and outside the region in the context of increasingly higher competition among big countries in the region and greater presence of China in Indian Ocean.

In 1994, Vietnam and India signed a memorandum of defence cooperation. This is an important milestone in the national defence and security cooperation between the two countries. Since then, Vietnam and India's national defence cooperation has been constantly developing and becoming increasingly practical. The most obvious change was the official visit paid by India's National Defence Minister George Fernandes to Vietnam in March 2000. During this visit, many cooperation agreements on national defence and security were signed by the two sides, in which one of the most important documents is the new Protocol on national defence cooperation between Vietnam and India. This Protocol opened up the opportunity to share information on intelligence activities and organize joint training courses for the two countries' coast guard forces for preventing pirates. In particular, India also provides support to Vietnam in training pilots (Su-30), submariners[20], etc. and in producing a number of small and medium-sized weapons. Since 2003, the two sides have started conducting deputy-minister level defence dialogues, many cooperation and exchange programmes between their national defence forces have been implemented ever since.

In high-level talks between the Vietnam and India, their leaders always pay close attention to the relationship in security and national defence between the two countries. In October 2014, in the visit to India paid by Vietnam's Prime Minister Nguyen Tan Dung, his Indian counterpart Mr. Modi also affirmed that "The national defence cooperation between India and Vietnam is one of our most important relationships. India is about to continues committing to modernizing Vietnam's national defence and security forces. This includes the expansion of our diverse training programmes, joint exercises, and cooperation in providing defence equipment[21].

In addition, many dialogues on national defence and security between Vietnam and India have been conducted. "One of the remarkable dialogues is the 8th Vietnam-India national defence strategy dialogue held in Ho Chi Minh City (November 8th, 2013). The two sides have strengthened high-level meetings between their National Defence Ministries, cooperation in training cadres, particularly naval cooperation, expanded air force cooperation and promoted cooperation in developing military industry"[22]. On 4-7/12/2016, Minister Ngo Xuan Lich also paid an official visit to India, the two sides agreed to continue promoting their defence cooperation into new level of development and many joint coordination programmes between the two countries has been signed, particularly programmes on air defence and air force. Particularly, in September 2016, during an official visit to Vietnam, India's Prime Minister Narendra Modi granted a 500 USD million line credit to Vietnam to purchase defence equipment in order to enhance its defence capacity. In the context of untoward happenings in the region, Vietnam, in its policy and stance, always considers India as an important partner. "Vietnam advocates the policy on balancing the relations among big countries. Vietnam considers India as an important factor in its policy of balancing its forces and determine to strengthen its relations with India[23]", developing the strategic partnership between the two countries into a new level on the basis of mutual benefit, similar opinions on issues of mutual concern.

In November 2018, India's President Mr. R. Kovind paid a working visit to Vietnam at the invitation of Vietnam's General Secretary and President Mr. Nguyen Phu Trong. In this meeting, the two leaders continued affirming that the two countries' relationship has been increasingly developing intensively in all fields and national defence and security continues to be the main pillar in the "comprehensive strategic partnership" between Vietnam and India. "Both leaders consider their cooperation on national defence and security as a strategic, effective, practical one and agreed to promote their cooperation, supporting human resource training and implementing the cooperation between the two countries' army forces. India expressed its willingness to share its experience on organizing and training the United Nations' peacekeepers and provide support to Vietnam in overcoming war consequences[24]". Regarding security cooperation, the two countries have strengthened their cooperation in crime prevention and criminal science; Drug prevention and terrorism avoidance. However, both leaders affirmed that Vietnam and India still have big potentials for national defence and security cooperation in the coming time.

In addition to promoting bilateral cooperation in national defence and security, Vietnam and India also promote their cooperation in multilateral regional defence and security forums to share their common views on solving security challenges in the region, particularly at the ASEAN Defence Ministers Meeting (ADMM+), ASEAN Regional Forum (ARF), Asia's Premier defence Summit (Shangri-La Dialogue-SLD), etc. For example, "Both India and Vietnam participated in the ADMM+'s Expert Group on humanitarian mine actions to promote removing unexploded ordnance left over after wars[25]".

The joint announcements of Vietnam and India show that their cooperation on national defence-security will continue to be the main pillar in their bilateral relationship. In the coming time, Vietnam – India's national defence cooperation will open up many good prospects. The followings are prospects for national defence cooperation between Vietnam and India in the coming time:

Firstly, both Vietnam and India use many weapons with origin from the former Soviet Union and Russia today, so the two countries can perform transferring advanced technologies and upgrade weapon equipment to extend the life span and enhance the capacity and effectiveness in combat of the equipment. In addition, cooperating with India, who is ranked at 4th in the world and 2nd in Asia in terms of military strength, will help Vietnam develop its military industry; accelerate researches and technology transfer for some India's modern equipment and weapons to Vietnam, bringing opportunities to Vietnam for receiving some modern military equipment and weapons from India.

Secondly, India is a leading nation in naval power in Asia. While Vietnam's naval power and coastal protection forces are limited in facilities, equipment and manpower, Indian Navy's greater presence in the East Sea will help Vietnam prevent pirates to ensure maritime security and safety in the East Sea and perform rescue missions. Also, India Navy's greater presence in the East Sea will help Vietnam protect and ensure its security to the East.

Thirdly, with the policy of developing a revolutionary, regular, elite People's Army, gradually performing modernization and proactively integrating into the world and developing its defence sector in the new situation, the need for training Vietnam's human resources and defence officers is so immense. India definitely can help Vietnam in this issue. Currently, India has been helping to train hundreds of military officers and granting scholarships to 50 Vietnamese officers each year under technical cooperation programmes. Therefore, for becoming comprehensive strategic partners and striving to further develop the two countries' bilateral relationship, in the coming time, India can continue helping Vietnam train its defence officers and grant more scholarships to Vietnamese officers. Besides, Vietnam needs to promote experience exchanges with India to improve the combat capability of its coast guard forces.

Fourthly, India also has a great potential for atomic energy and space science, while it is the weakness of Vietnam. Therefore, the potential in cooperation between Vietnam and India in atomic energy and space science is enormous.

Fifthly, the Communist Party of Vietnam's 12th National Delegation defined the task for Vietnam's Military industry with the content of "gradually forming military industrial complexes. This is the first time in its history of military industry, the Communist Party of Vietnam set up a policy to develop military industrial complexes. Meanwhile India is one of a few countries in the world successfully forming and developing military industrial complexes[26]". Therefore, the cooperation potential in developing military industrial complexes between Vietnam and India is very great, this is definitely founded as Vietnam and India have become "comprehensive strategic partners" since 2016.

Over the past years, Vietnam and India relations have developed rapidly in all fields, of which national defence-security cooperation is considered as one of the main pillars of the two countries' comprehensive. India has a great potential for military strength, on the basis of comprehensive strategic relationship, over the past time, India has been providing great support to Vietnam in strengthening its defence capabilities. Although many achievements in national defence and security cooperation have been achieved, those results are still small compared to expected targets of the two countries.

Vietnam-India's relationship in Culture and Education

Culture

Vietnamese and Indian have had an intensive cultural connectivity through the penetration of Indian Buddhism into Vietnam. Although Buddhism originated in India but after penetrating into Vietnam, this religion, with its good philosophy and values, quickly has harmonized with Vietnamese culture and folk beliefs and became an important part of Vietnamese culture and beliefs to this day. Therefore, the culture of the two countries shares similarities and that is an important basis for increasingly greater connection and exchange between the two countries. Exchange activities have become one of the important contents in their bilateral relationship so far and India's implementation of its "Act East Policy" have created favourable conditions to strongly promote its bilateral cultural cooperation with Vietnam in both width and depth.

In 1976, Vietnam and India signed a bilateral agreement on cultural cooperation, this is an important milestone in the two countries's cultural relationship. Since then, they have annually held many rallies, photo galleries, exchanged art delegations, organized film festivals, etc., on the occasion of the two countries' establishment of relations, to introduce the beauty, country and people of Vietnam and India to the people of the two countries. In March 2015, the Indian festival in Vietnam was successfully organized with many programmes such as folk dances, food festivals, Buddhist festivals, etc., making a great contribution to helping the Vietnamese people gain more in-depth knowledge on Indian culture and people. In 2017, on the occasion of 10th anniversary of the two countries' strategic partnership establishment, The Vietnamese Ambassy in India hosted many Vietnamese cultural events in India. In particular, on the occasion of the 45th anniversary of Vietnam and India's diplomatic relationship establishment, on April 20, 2017, the Indian Embassy in Vietnam launched the Indian Cultural Center in Hanoi. The establishment of this Center is about to bring to Vietnamese people opportunities to learn more about Indian culture and people. In addition, in 2014, India's Ministry of Culture, Vietnam's Ministry of Culture, Sports and Tourism, Indian Embassy in Vietnam and Vietnam Buddhist Sangha jointly organized the Indian Buddhist Festival at Phat Tich temple (Tien Du District, Bac Ninh Province, Vietnam). These practical activities have made significant contribution to promoting the understanding and political trust between the two countries, and culture has become a strong tie to connect Vietnam and India in the current period.

Education and Training

India has a fairly developed education-training system, in which many institutions are highly ranked in Asia. India's development of education and training in recent years have provided a great amount of high-quality human resources for India's development needs. "Since 1999, Vietnam has paid attention to researching India's education system and conducted many bilateral discussions to propose measures to enhance its cooperation with India in education and training between. In recent years, India has always granted many scholarships for Vietnamese students to come to India to study, research and improve their professional skills". India has many reputable universities and research institutes with disciplines to develop high-quality human resources in the fields of Engineering and Technology, Computer Science, Information Technology and Biologic Technology, Medicine and Pharmacy, Agriculture, etc., meanwhile in Vietnam these sectors are still limited. Currently, "India is provide support to Vietnam in training high-quality human resources in many fields such as information technology, economics, law, English, etc." through many short-term and long-term scholarships.

Currently, Vietnam is one of the countries receiving many scholarships from India within the framework of the India Technical and Economic Cooperation (ITEC) programme, annually ITEC grants 150 scholarships, and 16 scholarships under General Cultural Scholarship programme (GCSS), 14 ones under Education Exchange programme (EEP), etc. In particular, the India Government has supported Vietnam's Ministry of Education of Vietnam with the supercomputer PARAM project (under the project of "Support to improve the capacity of high-performance computing in Vietnam"). Therefore, education-training has a great potential for cooperation between Vietnam and India in the current period.

In addition to cooperation in key areas, Vietnam and India also expanded their cooperation in energy and science – technology, etc. within the framework of "Comprehensive Strategic Partnership". These are important fields that the two countries paid great attention development. Ensuring food security and energy security are important factors for a country to develop stably and sustainably in the current period and future. Particularly, in the context of the scientific and technological revolution growing and penetrating more and more deeply into all areas of societies and people's living, researching and having advanced technologies to apply them to production and living activities shortening their development gap with advanced countries in the world.

Conclusion

In recent years, the bilateral relationship between Vietnam and India has made a breakthrough development in many aspects from politics-, economics-commerce, national defence-security, etc. The rapid development of the two countries's relationship in recent years is the most obvious evidence of their friendship and cordiality between Vietnam and India, which has been cultivated over thousand years of history and continuously developed by generation of the two countries's leaders on the basis of high political trust and sharing many similar benefits.

The relationship between the Vietnam and India has made most rapid progresses ever in the history of the two countries's diplomatic relations. However, the development is still not commensurate with the potentials and expectations of the two governments' leaders. Vietnam and India have many potential areas for their future cooperation such as agriculture development, energy and science-technology, etc. The "comprehensive strategic partnership" between the two countries will be an important premise to help them further develop their bilateral relations into reality, deeper growth in the future, based on the principle of respecting independence, sovereignty, territorial integrity and mutual benefit.

Notes

1. Nguyen Canh Hue: Reviewing the Recognition by India on the Cambodian Government, History Study Magazine, *No. 1/2002.*
2. Refer to Basic information about India and Vietnam – India Relationship, Link: http://www.mofahcm.gov.vn/vi/mofa/cn_vakv/ca_tbd/nr040819102240/ns070731083003, ngày 16/10/2019.
3. Refer to China's "Nine-Dash Line" claim on East Sea and legal arguments. Link: http://tiasang.com.vn/-dien-dan/yeu-sach-duong-luoi-bo-cua-trung-quoc-tren-bien-dong-va-cac-luan-diem-phap-ly-5062, dated 10/10/2019.
4. Viet Cuong, Vietnam – India relationship developing more and more intensively and practically, Link: https://vov.vn/chinh-tri/quan-he-viet-naman-do-ngay-cang-sau-rong-di-vao-thuc-chat-734741.vov, dated 19/10/2019.
5. Khanh Lan, Vietnam and India's relationship gaining increasingly intensive and practical development. Link http://dangcongsan.vn/chao-xuan-ky-hoi-2019/xuan-que-huong/quan-he-viet-nam-an-do-ngay-cang-phat-trien-sau-rong-va-thuc-chat-512209.html, dated 19/10/2019.
6. Refer to Deputy Prime minister and Foreign Minister paying official visit to India, link: https://vnembassy-newdelhi.mofa.gov.vn/vi-vn/News/EmbassyNews/Trang/Ph%C3%B3-Th%E1%BB%A7-.
7. Refer to Thanh Ha: Vietnam – India's joint statement on the visits to Vietnam paid by President Ram Nath Kovind, Link: https://laodong.vn/thoi-su/toan-van-tuyen-bo-chung-viet-nam-an-do-nhan-chuyen-tham-cua-tong-thong-ram-nath-kovind-642420.ldo, dated 18/10/2019.
8. Refer to Associate Prof. and Dr. Do Duc Thinh: India's Economic cooperation with ASEAN and with Vietnam (Part 1). Link: http://cis.org.vn/article/3688/hop-tac-kinh-te-giua-an-do-voi-asean-va-viet-nam-phan-1.html, dated 20/10/2019.
9. Refer to Associate Prof. and Dr. Le Van Toan: Vietnam–India relationship in economics, trade and energy. Information and Communications Publishing House, Hanoi, 2017, page 9-10.
10. Refer to Associate Prof. and Dr. Le Van Toan: Vietnam–India relationship in economics, trade and energy. Information and Communications Publishing House, Hanoi, 2017, page 229.
11. Refer to Associate Prof. and Dr. Le Van Toan: Vietnam–India relationship in economics, trade and energy. Information and Communications Publishing House,

Hanoi, 2019, page 9-10.

12. Associate Prof. and Dr. Do Duc Thinh: India's Economic cooperation with ASEAN and with Vietnam (Part 1). Link: http://cis.org.vn/article/3688/hop-tac-kinh-te-giua-an-do-voi-asean-va-viet-nam-phan-1.html, dated 20/10/2019.
13. Vu Luyen, Indian President paying visit to Vietnam from 18 to 20/11. Link: http://thoibaotaichinhvietnam.vn/pages/thoi-su/2018-11-15/tong-thong-an-do-ram-nath-kovind-tham-viet-nam-tu-18-den-20-11-64364.aspx, dated 20/10/2019.
14. Vu Luyen, Indian President paying a working visit to Vietnam from 18 to 20/11. Link: http://thoibaotaichinhvietnam.vn/pages/thoi-su/2018-11-15/tong-thong-an-do-ram-nath-kovind-tham-viet-nam-tu-18-den-20-11-64364.aspx, dated 20/10/2019.
15. Refer to Associate Prof. and Dr. Le Van Toan: Vietnam – India relationship in economics, trade and energy. Information and Communications Publishing House, Hanoi, 2019, page 81.
16. Refer to Nguyen Huong: Vietnam – India: more new fields for cooperation. Link: http://kinhtevn.com.vn/viet-nam-an-do-them-nhieu-linh-vuc-hop-tac-moi-36528.html, dated 21/10/2019.
17. Refer to Vietnam's Sea and Islands: Potentials and advantages. Link: https://sonoivu.hanoi.gov.vn/thong-tin-tuyen-truyen/-/view_content/2386499-bien-dao-viet-nam-tiem-nang-va-loi-the.html, dated 22/9/201.
18. Refer to: India–Malaysia: Naval exercise. Enhancing combat capacity on South China Sea, Link: https://www.biendong.net/bien-dong/30501-an-do-malaysia-dien-tap-hang-hai-tang-cuong-nang-luc-tac-chien-tren-bien-dong.html, dated 20/9/2019.
19. Cooperation for development between Vietnam and India in economics, national defense and security in the context of free and expanded Indian Ocean-Pacific Ocean, National Political Publishing House, page 91.
20. Refer to: India providing Su-30 pilot training to Vietnam, Link: https://vietnamnet.vn/vn/thoi-su/an-do-dao-tao-phi-cong-vn-lai-tiem-kich-su-30-211836.html, dated 25/9/2019.
21. Associate Prof. and Dr. Nguyen Van Lan: Vietnam–India relationship: From strategic partners to comprehensive strategic partners. Link: http://www.tapchicongsan.org.vn/Home/Doi-ngoai-va-hoi-nhap/2018/53393/Quan-he-Viet-Nam-An-Do-Tu-Doi-tac-chien-luoc.aspx, dated 21/8/2019.
22. Associate Prof. and Dr. Nguyen Van Lan: Vietnam–India relationship: From strategic partners to comprehensive strategic partners. Link: http://www.tapchicongsan.org.vn/Home/Doi-ngoai-va-hoi-nhap/2018/53393/Quan-he-Viet-Nam-An-Do-Tu-Doi-tac-chien-luoc.aspx, dated 21/8/2019.
23. Cooperation for development between Vietnam and India in economics, national defense and security in the context of free and expanded Indian Ocean-Pacific Ocean, National Political Publishing House (2018), page 88.
24. General Secretary and President receiving and participating in talks with; Prime Minister and National Assembly's Chairwoman meeting with India's President, Link: https://nhandan.com.vn/chinhtri/item/38305402-tong-bi-thu-chu-tich-nuoc-don-hoi-dam-thu-tuong-chinh-phu-chu-tich-quoc-hoi-hoi-kien-tong-thong-an-do-r-kovind.html, dated 22/8/2019.
25. Associate Prof. and Dr. Le Van Toan: Vietnam–India: 45 years of diplomatic relation and 10 years of strategic partnership, Hanoi, 2017, National Political Publishing House, page 414.
26. Cooperation for development between Vietnam and India in economics, national defence and security in the context of free and expanded Indian Ocean-Pacific Ocean (2018), National Political Publishing House, page 225.

References

Vietnamese

1. Viet Cuong: *Vietnam-India relationship developing more and more intensively and practically*, Link: https://vov.vn/chinh-tri/quan-he-viet-naman-do-ngay-cang-sau-rong-di-vao-thuc-chat-734741.vov, dated 19/10/2019.
2. Khanh Lan: *Vietnam and India's relationship gaining increasingly intensive and practical development*, Link: http://dangcongsan.vn/chao-xuan-ky-hoi-2019/xuan-que-huong/quan-he-viet-nam-an-do-ngay-cang-phat-trien-sau-rong-va-thuc-chat-512209.html, dated 19/10/2019.
3. Thanh Ha: *Vietnam – India's joint statement on the visits to Vietnam paid by President Ram Nath Kovind*, Link: https://laodong.vn/thoi-su/toan-van-tuyen-bo-chung-viet-nam-an-do-nhan-chuyen-tham-cua-tong-thong-ram-nath-kovind-642420.ldo, dated 18/10/2019.
4. Associate Prof. and Dr. Do Duc Thinh: *India's Economic cooperation with ASEAN and with Vietnam (Part 1)*, Link: http://cis.org.vn/article/3688/hop-tac-kinh-te-giua-an-do-voi-asean-va-viet-nam-phan-1.html, dated 20/10/2019.
5. Refer to Associate Prof. and Dr. Le Van Toan: *Vietnam–India relationship in economics, trade and energy*, Communications Publishing House, Hanoi, 2017, page 9-10.
6. Refer to Associate Prof. and Dr. Le Van Toan: *Vietnam – India, new context and new vision*, Communications Publishing House, Hanoi, 2017, page 9-10.
7. Cooperation for development between Vietnam and India in economics, national defence and security in the context of free and expanded Indian Ocean-Pacific Ocean (2018), Publishing House of Political Theory, page 91.
8. Refer to Father promoting Vietnam–India's strategic partnership, Link: http://www.cpv.org.vn/chinh-tri/thuc-day-manh-me-hon-nua-quan-he-doi-tac-chien-luoc-viet-nam-an-do-336537.html, dated 22/10/2019.

English

1. A new chapter in Vietnam-India relations, Link: http://tgvn.com.vn/a-new-chapter-in-vietnam-india-relations-67106.html, dated 20/10/2019.
2. Prashanth Parameswaran: What's Next for Vietnam-India Defence Relations?, Link: https://thediplomat.com/2018/08/whats-next-for-vietnam-india-Defence-relations/, dated 18/10/2019.
3. Sanghamitra Sarma: India-Vietnam Relations After Modi's Visit, Link: https://thediplomat.com/2016/09/india-vietnam-relations-after-modis-visit/, dated 18/10/2019.
4. Sumit Kumar: India-Vietnam Relations Elevated to Comprehensive Strategic Partnership, Link: http://www.indiandefencereview.com/spotlights/india-vietnam-relations-elevated-to-comprehensive-strategic-partnership/, dated 19/10/2019.
5. Vietnam-India Relations: Past, Present, and Future, Link: http://www.ipcs.org/comm_select.php?articleNo=5491, dated 18/10/2019.

9 Vietnam-China Neighbourhood Relations: From Past to the Present

Thu-Ha Nguyen

Throughout history, the relations between Vietnam and China have always experienced certain vicissitudes. However, the significant changes in international political relations since 1991 have had the direct influence on Vietnam-China relations. Since the normalization of Vietnam-China relationship, the bilateral relations have developed comprehensively in many fields. The relations with China play the key role in Vietnam's foreign policy as China has certain advantages such as large geographical area and international clout, vast neighbourhood, traditional friendship and similar political institutions"[1].

Historically, the direct rule of Chinese feudalism been imposed upon Vietnam for more than 1,000 years of Northern domination (179 BC-938). For more than 10 centuries, the Vietnamese people tenaciously fought against the domination of foreign invaders, and won great victories, especially the event when Ngo Quyen defeated the Tang army and proclaimed himself king (938) to terminate more than 1,000 years of Northern domination. Since then, Vietnam had been no longer a district of China, but an independent country. During this period, Vietnam adopted the flexible foreign policies of tribute regime, sending diplomatic missions to China for conferred titles and maintaining independence[2]. The period witnessed the frequent armed conflicts between the two countries due to China's invasion of Vietnam and assimilation toward the Vietnamese people. Therefore, Vietnam adopted few aspects of Chinese culture such as Buddhism, Confucianism[3], painting, architecture, sculpture and achievements in natural sciences (such as Vietnamese lunar calendar, treatment by acupuncture methods). However, Vietnam has localized it to build up its own culture imbued with Vietnam's national identity.

After the Treaty of Tientsin (1885), France declared an end to the Franco-Chinese War, forcing the Qing army to withdraw from the north of Vietnam and acknowledging French protection for Vietnam. Under the French colonial rule, the life of the Vietnamese people was extremely miserable, social contradictions were fierce, many fighting movements broke out, and many revolutionists led to fight against the French, typically, Phan Boi Chau, Phan Chau Trinh, Nguyen Thai Hoc, etc. In the context of severe persecution by the French colonialists, the domestic revolutionary zones suffered many losses; many Vietnamese people went to China to continue their revolutionary activities, especially to learn about the Xinhai Revolution 1911, at the same time, to seek to connect the activities in Vietnam to push up revolutionary movements with the new victories. Particularly, the revolutionary activities of leader Nguyen Ai Quoc - Ho Chi Minh in China have received the support and assistance of the Chinese. Since then, the Vietnam-China relations converged with the point of view: *"The great majority of Vietnamese people strongly agree with the Chinese resistance"*[4] and together with an affirmation—a call: *"Vietnam-China relationship is as close as lips and teeth. Open lips cannot keep teeth warm"*[5].

Vietnam and China have been close neighbours. The people of the two countries always attached deeply, mutually helped and supported one another in the struggles against imperialism and for the sake of the people's revolution of each country. The Vietnamese politically and spiritually supported the Chinese, sometimes coordinated with the Chinese in struggling to serve the cause of national liberation. The Chinese, despite many difficulties, especially in the early years of the People's Republic of China, provided immense assistance to the Vietnamese people in the two wars of resistance against the French colonialists and American imperialists (1945-1975). China was the first to establish diplomatic relations with Vietnam (1950). With the communist brotherhood, China provided its aid of food, fuel, infantry, artillery and ammunition for Vietnam's revolution during the 1950-1954 period, and became a transshipment station of weapons, ammunition and goods aided from other countries to support Vietnam, etc. During the 1965-1975 period, China sent many military units to Vietnam for supportively upgrading and repairing the roads along the Vietnam and China border. It also constructed the railway and motorway transportation from the border to other provinces and cities, contributed to boosting the goods transportation to the Vietnam southern battlefield. The material and spiritual assistance of China in the two wars was considered the noble symbol of international proletarian solidarity, making an important contribution to the victorious cause of national liberation of Vietnam. The victory of the Vietnam's revolution not only contributed significantly to the peace and stability of Southeast Asia and had the great influence in the world, but also opened up the prospective cooperation between the people of the two countries[6].

Suffering rift and tension (1976-1989), Vietnam-China relations deteriorated when China believed that Vietnam's actions in Cambodia in the 1970s were aiming at "proclamation dream" in Southeast Asia, and there was accusation that the Chinese living in Vietnam faced persecution. In addition, the close relationship between Vietnam and the Soviet Union became deeper at that time when the Soviet Union was expanding its influence on Southeast Asia and it snubbed China. Vietnam and China have experienced serious disputes when China continuously engaged in aggressive actions against Vietnam, such as occupying the Paracel Islands of Vietnam (1974) causing war at the Northern border of Vietnam (1979), sending troops to occupy seven islands in the Spratly Islands of Vietnam (1988)[7]. The actions adversely affected the bilateral relations.

After the Cold War (1991), the bipolar world was shattered with the collapse of socialist model in the Soviet Union and Eastern European countries. Therefore, all of them needed to normalize their relations. In November 1991, during the visit to Beijing by General Secretary Do Muoi and Prime Minister Vo Van Kiet, the leaders of Vietnam and China announced the normalization of bilateral relations. The two nations made the joint announcement stating that friendship and good neighbourliness should be developed. Since then, generally, the relations between Vietnam and China, in spite of the existing difficulties, have developed extensively in all aspects. Recognizing the importance of the stable and friendly relations between the two neighbouring countries pursuing socialism, the high-level leaders of the two nations have regularly communicated and exchanged views with each other, and continuously strengthened the framework of bilateral relations. Since 2008, Vietnam-China relations have improved into "comprehensive strategic cooperative partnership", constantly expanded, deepened in all fields and brought the practical benefits to the people of two countries.

The two nations have regularly paid the mutual visits to meet high-level leaders, reinforcing the foundation for the fellow feeling by the two countries as well as the two Parties, thereby gradually closing the gaps in the bilateral relations. During the meetings, the two nations have agreed on the friendly and neighbourly cooperation in the relations, based on the five principles of peaceful coexistence and dispute resolution through amicable negotiation, and set neither target at any third country nor influence on its relations with others[8].

Vietnam and China both pursued communism and aimed at building their own institution under the one-party communism, so the two parties had the close and deep relations. The two Parties promoted and maintained cooperation between themselves based on the active annual exchange of delegations and well-established in-depth, practical and effective mechanism of exchange between the Party Committees, contributing to improving the joint awareness to control and address the questions and problems between the two administrations[9]. In particular, the State operation of the China's Communist Party considered as the perfect model pursued by the Communist Party of Vietnam. In 1993, in China, the Party and State positions unified, so General Secretary Jiang Zemin had been elected as the State President of China; the unification was at pinnacle in the period of Xi Jinping[10]. In Vietnam, historically, Ho Chi Minh held both positions of State President and Party's Chairman. In 2018, when President Tran Dai Quang suddenly died of a serious illness, this position was vacant, which needed to be filled immediately. On 23 October 2018, at the 6th session of the XIV National Assembly, 99.79 per cent of National Assembly deputies voted to elect General Secretary Nguyen Phu Trong as the President of the Socialist Republic of Vietnam for the 2016-2021 term.

Besides the procedural similarities, the strict management measures acquired by the Communist Party of Vietnam from China taken up judicially to solve the corruption problems in the administration. In general, the Communist Party of Vietnam's policy is relatively more democratic than that of

China, which stems from Vietnam's principle of consensus-based leadership under which the intra-party democracy and civil society were considered as less repressive[11]. In recent years, both the countries, in international forums, conferences and meetings, have expressed their appreciation for the bilateral relations, agreed to maintain high-level visits and communication, intensified strategic exchange, consolidated political trust, deepened the cooperation for mutual benefits and promoted important mechanisms of cooperation. Based on "16 gold words" and "four good things", at the meetings and exchange sessions, the two sides have emphasized the similarities in the bilateral relations, controlled and handled satisfactorily the existing disagreements and the followed issues, and promoted the continuous development of Vietnam-China comprehensive strategic cooperative partnership[12]. The Vietnamese always appreciate, preserve and nurture the everlasting friendship between the two nations.

On Economic-trade Cooperation and Investment

In recent years, the trade-economic cooperation between Vietnam and China have been enhanced affecting in many aspects of socio-economic development of both countries. Since the normalization of relations, Vietnam-China trade turnover has increased by approximately 3,000 folds, from USD 32 million (1991) to nearly USD 106.7 billion (2018)[13]. Since 2004, China has been Vietnam's largest trading partner. China is the most important trading partner and the largest import market for Vietnam; at the same time, the second largest export market of Vietnam, ranked behind the United States[14]. In 2018, Vietnam surpassed Malaysia to become China's No. 1 partner in ASEAN, and became the eighth largest trading partner, the fifth largest export market and the ninth largest supply market of China in the world. This shows the great potential and mutual supportiveness in trade between the two countries[15].

In addition to the advantages of cultural similarity and consumer habits, the Vietnam-China bilateral trade relation is increasingly thriving thanks to the geographical advantages. It is witnessed that border trade is a key part of the trade relation between the two countries. The joint land border of about 1,400 km[16] with 21 border gates including 4 international border gates, 7 main border gates, 10 minor border gates, 56 trails, and 13 border markets[17], has created extremely favourable conditions for the trade development and exchange between Vietnam and China in general and border trade in particular. The imported and exported goods through the border gates are diverse and rich in term of types. The exported commodities from Vietnam usually include minerals, agricultural products and handicrafts, while those transferred from China are mainly simple machinery and equipment for a number of agricultural and industrial production industries[18].

However, due to the relatively loose trade policies and state management, there is still an unhealthy competition between businesses of both countries. At the same time, the import ease of the Chinese market for raw agricultural products has sometimes caused Vietnamese farmers to produce low-quality, unsafe and risky products, which are even refused by Chinese businesses. A prominent feature of the trade relation between Vietnam and China is Vietnam's trade deficit. In addition to the rapid increase of two-way trade turnover, the difference in the rate of Vietnam-China import and export is disadvantageous for Vietnam. Currently, Vietnam suffers from trade deficit of USD 24.2 billion with China[19]. The reason for the trade deficit is that Vietnam's supporting industries have the need for production materials imported from China but meeting the following criteria of affordable price, short geographical distance and satisfied quality and diverse goods. Particularly, in the context that the US-China trade war shows no little sign of ending soon, Vietnam is facing the risk of Chinese commodities' domination in Vietnam's domestic market to affect consumption patterns. The commodities can be labeled with other origins, namely "Made in Vietnam" to avoid the tax imposition by US, which not only makes the trade deficit with China much more serious but also puts Vietnam at the high risk of trade sanctions imposed upon by the US.

In terms of investment cooperation China have paid the special attention to promoting the implementation of the "Belt and Road Initiative" (BRI) in neighbouring areas, targeting at continuously promoting and developing economic cooperation between China and neighbouring countries, and stimulating the dependence of neighbouring countries on China through investment, not with the exception of Vietnam. China is currently implementing 6,175 projects with the total registered investment of about USD 65 billion; in the first half of 2019 alone, China is the largest investor in Vietnam with nearly USD 1.79 billion for 364 projects[20]. This stems from the fact that Chinese enterprises transfer their investment to Vietnam to evade taxes, "hide" origin, and export goods to the US when US is imposing the high tax rates on many items of Chinese goods. Chinese projects are located in almost all localities of Vietnam, mainly in big cities, key economic zones, coastal provinces and border, and in many different fields[21]. China's investment in Vietnam is relatively special, which is mainly in the form of EPC contractor[22], but not just FDI or ODA[23]. According to research by Vietnam Institute for Economic and Policy Research (VEPR) under University of Economics and Business, Vietnam National University, Hanoi, this form of investment makes China's investment capital into Vietnam less outstanding than that of other countries that have invested for a long time in Vietnam. Because this source of capital is business-oriented and calculated very carefully with the focus on only infrastructure development but no strong investment like that of Japan and South Korea in the fields of energy, petroleum and gas and electronics. In addition, loans and projects implemented in the form of EPC result in the negative issues in Vietnam, such as corruption, social impact, financial dependence, environmental issues, economic effectiveness, and delay in implementation; therefore, not all China's investment plans are accepted by Vietnam.

On National Security and Defense

The Vietnam-China relations are neighbourly with the long history but bears many sensitive issues. With regard to national security and defense, China imposes its policies for big countries upon its neighbours, including Vietnam. For the centuries-long history, China has always desired to occupy Vietnam as a province of its territory. China's strategy imposed upon Vietnam is consistent, including two key points: Firstly, encroachment and invasion of land, rivers and sea, and secondly, diffusion of its influence and soft power/soft borders[24]. This leads to many difficulties and challenges in the border demarcation on land and at sea, and became a sensitive issue in the diplomatic relationship between the two nations.

Vietnam-China land border was first legalized by the Treaty of Tianjin 1885, and the two Qing-French Conventions 1887 and 1895, with the length of over 1,400 km, adjoining seven provinces of Vietnam. Dien Bien and Lai Chau, Lao Cai, Ha Giang, Cao Bang, Lang Son and Quang Ninh provinces were contiguous to Yunnan province and Zhuang Autonomous Region in Guangxi Province (China). From Vietnam's regaining of independence in 1945 to the 1970s, the Sino-Vietnamese border, as agreed upon by France and the Qing Dynasty, was relatively peaceful. However, after 1970, China changed its perspective to resolve the border issue in its own favour. As a result, the relationship between Vietnam and China became worse because the intervention in territorial disputes between both and armed actions in the Paracel and Spratly Islands caused Sino-Vietnamese War. Earlier also China incited the Pol Pot's forces to invade Vietnam on the southwest border, and directly invaded Vietnam on the northern border, killed the Vietnamese people and seriously destroyed the Vietnam's economic and cultural bases in war zones.

In the 1980s, after the Sino-Vietnamese War of 1979, the tensions on the borders of the two countries subsided. Vietnam and China reached the 1993 Agreement on Basic Principles for the Settlement of Border Territory Issues, and negotiated in term of three issues: land border, Delimitation of the Tonkin Gulf and the Eastern Vietnam Sea (SCS) issue[25]. After many years of perseverance and effortful negotiation, on December 30, 1999, in Hanoi, Vietnam and China signed the Land Border Treaty. On December 31, 2008, the two nations completed the demarcation and marker planting throughout the land borderline. This is a historic event, opening a new page in the history of Vietnam-China relations. The two countries have had, for the first time, a complete land border, shown clearly in the legal documents. This benefitted the two countries and laid the foundation for building up a border of long-term peace, friendship and stability to enhance the development of economic-trade cooperation. The documents on Vietnam-China land border management completed in July 2010, including the Demarcation Protocol, the Agreement on Border Management Regulations and the Agreement on Border Gates and Regulations on Land Border Gate, and have officially taken effect since that time.

Up till 2019, the two nations have been negotiating to sign the Agreement regarding free navigation at the Bac Luan river mouth and the Agreement of cooperation in protecting and exploiting the tourism resources of the Ban Gioc Waterfall. Regarding the Tonkin Gulf, the two signed the Agreement on the Delimitation of the Tonkin Gulf (2000), the Tonkin Gulf Fisheries Cooperation Agreement (2000) and the Tonkin Gulf Fisheries Cooperation Protocol (2004). These documents implemented smoothly; the management of fishing and protection of resources has gradually been put in proper order and minimized conflicts that may arise. The two sides also performed effectively the two navies' joint inspection and investigation of fishery resources in the joint fishing and patrol areas in the Tonkin Gulf. The completion of two out of the three historic issues has contributed to increasing the trust between the two, creating a driving force to promote the "comprehensive strategic cooperative partnership". At the same time, these milestones marked the determination of the two parties, the States and the people of Vietnam-China in resolving all the territorial border issues by amicable negotiation through bilateral mechanism. Particularly, in the international and regional aspects, the completed demarcation and marker planting of Vietnam-China land borders make the concrete contributions to peace, stability and development in the region, and affirmed the set general principles of international law: resolving territorial border issues by peaceful means; non-use of force or threat of force in resolving international disputes[26].

Referring to the territorial border issue between Vietnam and China, the settlement of order in the East Sea (South China Sea), namely the sovereignty over the Paracel Islands and the Spratly Islands, are the "primer" for all disagreements between the two countries. This conflict stems from the long history. At the end of the 17th century, the Nguyen Dynasty of Vietnam sent a group of fishermen, named Hoang Sa (Paracel), to seize the island and harvest bird's nests and seafood to bring to their Lord. That front-line anglers of King Nguyen gave the island the Vietnamese name, Hoang Sa island. In 1816, King Gia Long officially merged and established sovereignty over Hoang Sa Island. However, China claimed their sovereignty over these islands, which have existed for thousands of years. According to the Ministry of Foreign Affairs of China in 2014, "Chinese activities in the Eastern Sea date back over 2000 years ago. China calls this island Xisha". History has also witnessed a conflict in sovereignty of Spratly Islands when Vietnam believes that the claim of sovereignty over the Spratly Islands should be based on the arguments of actual possession and continuous management and peace in the Spratly Island's placed under feudal dynasties. From viewpoint of China, it is called Nansha Islands and affirms that this Island is a part all-encompassed by the southern part of the nine-dash line – the name referring to the maritime boundary of the Eastern Sea subject to People's Republic of China (China)'s advocate and unilateral claim of sovereignty[27].

Talking about the present time, after many years of negotiation and agreement, the East Sea (SCS) dispute between Vietnam and China has achieved positive results. Both sides have signed an "Agreement on the basic principles for resolving maritime issues between Vietnam and China" (2011) as a basis for resolving the East Sea disputes. Accordingly, both sides agreed to maintain a peaceful settlement for the East Sea dispute based on respect for international law, the 1982 United Nations Convention on the Law of the Sea and the spirit of the DOC. Based on this Agreement, both sides established a specialist-level negotiation mechanism to address the issues of the Tonkin Gulf and a specialist-level negotiation mechanism for cooperation in less sensitive areas at East Sea. So far, after the negotiations, both sides have achieved some results, such as agreeing to set up a Technical Expert Group to conduct joint surveys for delimitation and cooperation for mutual development in the areas outside of the Tonkin Gulf; select 03 projects in less sensitive fields for research and pilot testing (the Cooperation Project in researching the management method for the sea and island environment in the areas outside of the Tonkin Gulf between Vietnam and China, the Research Project in holocenne sediment comparison between Red River Delta and Truong Giang River Delta and the Cooperation Project on the method for search and rescue at the sea areas between Vietnam and China). In order to find the basic, long-term and beneficial solutions for both sides on maritime issues, Vietnam and China have established a Working Group to discuss our cooperation on the mutual development in sea areas during the Government Negotiation Visit on the territorial border of Vietnam-China (2013).

However, in recent years, the relationship between Vietnam and China has entered a period of crisis when China has expanded their border blatantly in the East Sea. Their actions may stem from the goal to achieve the great revival of China, realizing the Chinese dream. In 2013, China has made an illegal exploration by constructing a drilling rig in the Paracel Sea, which was located 17 nautical miles from Vietnam 's Tri Ton Island and 80 nautical miles deep in the continental shelf and exclusive economic zone of Vietnam. Not only did they prohibit unrelated vessels from approaching the areas of operation of the rig, China also initially mobilized about 80 ships, then regularly maintained over 100 ships of all kinds including missile boats, submarine patrol boats, and maritime vessels with full of intimidating and aggressive weapons.

This action has been part of a series of tensions that China has been involved with to create disputes and threaten the peace and stability in the East Sea since 2009, but it is also not a simple nature, with a higher level of danger. Not only did they bring drilling rig deep into the continental shelf of Vietnam, China also brought both civilian and military forces with the intention of provoking and proactively causing collisions to bring the situation closer to conflict, blatantly challenging Vietnam's and international responses while overlooking Vietnam's efforts to maintain the peace in the region. This action means China is willing to unilaterally change the status quo in the disputed areas of East Sea. Proactively conducting natural resource exploitation is actually an act of deliberate appropriation to other countries, a continuation of their nine-dash line claim to the countries involved in this disputed area. The 981 rig is considered a tool to mark the great leap of China's economic measures in the East Sea with the purpose of changing the situation of oil and gas exploitation in this disputed area[28].

However, by proactively pushing the relationship with Vietnam to right beside "the crater of war," China, of course, does not just stop with a goal of economic and resource exploitation in the East Sea. The fact that China has brought their most advanced drilling rig to Vietnam's exclusive economic zone and continental shelf includes both political and military goals, either immediate and long-term with a message not only for Vietnam. This is considered a decisive action in China's process of monopolizing the East Sea, following their declaration of the nine-dash line claim by using force on the islands in the East Sea to build military bases and logistics facilities to strengthen their navy. This was the message of China to other great powers in the world, especially the US, to declare the new order of the Pacific region at that time. It is not exaggeration to say that the event of Hai Duong 981 rig was a crisis in the relationship between Vietnam and China in the recent period[29].

With a purpose to demonstrating their growing strength and readiness to prevent legitimate maritime economic activities of other countries in the East Sea, as well as to participate in illegal natural resource exploration on the continental shelf of neighbouring coastal countries, China has conducted a confrontation with Vietnam at Vanguard Bank. Despite the repeated protests from Vietnam and international pressure, China continues to conduct their operation of Haiyang Dizhi 8 survey ship and its accompanying vessels in the exclusive economic zone (EEZ) and the continental shelf of Vietnam. In response to this incident, Vietnam implemented a policy of "strategic patience", using diplomatic channels to express a strong opposition stance to China's actions.

In the context of China's aggressive actions in the East Sea, there are also reactions from other countries in the region with common interests at sea, including big countries such as US, Japan and India as well as the world community. Vietnam has enlisted the support of partners and friends around the world. Through his speech, Vietnam Foreign Minister Pham Binh Minh condemned China's actions at the 52nd ASEAN Foreign Ministers Meeting (AMM) in Thailand[30]. Within the multilateral framework, ASEAN (including Vietnam) and China have signed the Declaration on the Conduct of Parties in the East Sea (DOC), the Guidelines for Implementation of DOC and the ASEAN-China Joint Declaration on the occasion of the 10th anniversary of DOC. ASEAN is now ready and actively negotiating with China on the development of the Code of Conduct in the East Sea (COC).

The United States has always considered the East Sea as an extremely important area. At present, their actions to assert US's position in the East Sea and surrounding areas mainly include the campaign named "freedom of navigation and passage through the Taiwan Strait". In response to China's actions in the East Sea, the United States has strengthened their presence of military power in the East Sea through regular patrol operations by aircraft and warship on the harbours of the US Coast Guard (USCGC). Facing the serious instability of the current dispute in the East Sea. Now, Vietnam understands that diplomacy is the first and last line of defence that will help Vietnam to focus on a long-term benefit from maintaining a stable and peaceful relationship with China instead of a short-term benefit from chasing Chinese ships out of its waters.

Vietnam and China relations have now entered a new phase after two terms of National Congress in both countries, with many profound changes in the country's foreign policy orientation. For Vietnam, the 12th National Conference of Representatives held in January 2016 have marked the first time that foreign affairs were included in the topic of the Congress. It declared "making a clean and strong Party; promoting the strength of the entire nation and socialist democracy; comprehensively and synchronously promoting the renovation process; firmly defending the Fatherland, maintaining a peaceful and stable environment; building a foundation to quickly turn Vietnam into an industrialized country towards modernization"[31].

Compared to the 11th National Congress, the 12th National Congress has added the theme "firmly defending the Fatherland, maintaining a peaceful and stable environment" to emphasize the importance of foreign affairs in the overall development of the country and at the same time, clearly highlighting the two most important tasks of foreign affairs, which is to firmly defend the Fatherland and maintain a peaceful and stable environment to implement the tasks of national construction in the next 5 years and afterwards. The Vietnamese Communist Party affirms three things: *Firstly*, the national interests and the state interests are identical. *Secondly*, Vietnam's national-state interests are determined based on the basic principles of international law with equality and mutual benefit, not including selfish and narrow mindsets. *Thirdly*, ensuring the national-state interests must be the supreme principle of all foreign affairs, and the nation-state interests must be the ultimate requirement and the first norm to evaluate the effectiveness of all foreign affairs[32].

On the China side, the 19th Chinese Communist Party National Representatives Congress was held in October 2017 with the theme "Do not forget the initial heart and determination, bear in mind the mission, raise the great banner of socialism with Chinese characteristics, determined to comprehensively build up a Xiaokang Society, achieving a great victory of socialism with Chinese characteristics in the new era, striving tirelessly for the dream of reviving the great Chinese nation"[33]. At this Congress, the "Xi Jinping Thought" was formally put into charter, with the main theme being the "Xi Jinping Thought on Socialism with Chinese Characteristics in a New era". Since the time of Mao Zedong, the founder of modern China, this is the first time an incumbent ideological leader has been recorded and formally named in party regulations. With the results achieved in orienting Chinese foreign policy, since the 19th National Congress, China has seen an increasingly assertive image in regional and international affairs to the world, which was gradually transitioning from "hiding in concealment" to "rising in strong pace ". China has actively built relations with big countries by proposing a new model of big-country relations with the United States, increasing geopolitical influence through the strategic initiative "Belt and Road"; challenging the role and influence of traditional financial institutions through the establishment of many new international financial institutions such as Asia Infrastructure Investment Bank and New Development Bank; proactively scrambling and expanding influence by associating neighbouring foreign policies with "big-country diplomacy", "energy diplomacy", "sea strategy", which are most evident by their competition for natural resources and energy in Central Asia, South Asia and Southeast Asia. China's ultimate goal is to gain recognition from the international community as one of the global leaders with an equal position with the US[34]. With many profound changes in the foreign policy of both countries, Vietnam-China relations are expected to overcome the great challenges ahead. By taking advantage of the common ideology and close geopolitical relations, both countries can maintain, consolidate and develop an increasingly strong comprehensive strategic cooperation relationship.

Conclusion

From the past to the present, Vietnam and China have had neighbourhood relations with thousands of years of history with rich, diverse and very complex multidimensional relations in terms of economy, politics, culture, national defense and security, etc. During the period of national liberation struggle and the resistance war against France and the United States, Vietnam has received great support and assistance from China; At the same time, Vietnam also paid the same deeds to the Chinese Revolution. But after Vietnam successfully unified the country, the relationship between Vietnam and China became complicated because China always tries to put Vietnam in a dependent position on all aspects. Under these conditions, Vietnam has proactively set up a subtle as well as flexible foreign policies on the principle of maintaining independence, sovereignty and territorial integrity of the country.

Since the two countries normalized relations (1991-2019), Vietnam and China have regularly paid annual visits and conducted high-level meetings to gradually improve relations between the two countries. Particularly, in 2008, Vietnam and China have officially upgraded their relations to "comprehensive strategic partnership and cooperation" based on respecting *the 16 golden words of "Láng giềng hữu nghị, hợp tác toàn diện, ổn định lâu dài, hướng tới tương lai (Neighbourly friendship, comprehensive cooperation, long-term stability, future orientation)".* Since 2008 until now, although there are some disagreements, especially in the East Sea disputes, the achievements in diplomatic relations between the two countries in the fields of politics - diplomacy, economics - trade, national security - defense, etc., are a testament to the development of diplomatic relations between the two countries. As for Vietnam, being a neighbour of a big country with relentless efforts to subdue the Vietnamese people like China, the fact that Vietnam can maintain our independence, sovereignty and territorial integrity through a peaceful and flexible foreign policy based on respect for international laws has proved the bravery and vigor of the Vietnamese nation. Accordingly, Vietnam's position in the international arena enhanced with great influence in the Asia-Pacific region, becoming an important connectivity in regional and international relations. This, once again, has contributed to affirming that Vietnam has meet the criteria of a new medium-rank power in East Asia.

Notes

1. *Vietnam-China relation: Situation and problems raised*, Publishing House of Political Theory, 2016, page 5.
2. Tran Nam Tien, "Vietnam's behavioural culture in relation with China during the Middle Ages - From the viewpoint of "honouring - tribute", VNU University of Social Sciences and Humanities, 2012
3. Mai Ly Quang, "Glimpses of Vietnam", The gioi Publishers, 2004.
4. Ho Chi Minh, "Full episode", Volume 3, page 186
5. Ho Chi Minh, "Full episode", Volume 5, page 187
6. Assoc. Prof. Dr. Ho Khang, "China helped Vietnam in Military aspects 1950-1954 period", Vietnamese Institute of Military History, Ministry of National Defense, 2014
7. Robert S. Ross, "The Indochina Tangle: China's Vietnam Policy", 1975–1979 (New York: Columbia University Press, 1988), p. 253
8. China: Characteristics of foreign relation policy in Asia, Special reference dated 23 July 2001
9. According to Vietnam's Diplomatic Bluebook 2018
10. Nguyen Khac Giang, *"Is Vietnam Going the Way of China?"*, The Diplomat, 22/02/2018
11. Le Tuan Thanh, *"Political relationship between Vietnam and China since normalization of relation"*, Vietnam Institute for Northeast Asian Studies, No. 2 (84) 2-2008
12. According to Vietnam's Diplomatic Bluebook 2018
13. Bao
14. *Ibid.*
15. Journal of Industry and Trade, June 2019
16. Statement by Spokesperson of Ministry of Foreign Affairs of China on 15 January 2019: "two countries' 1,450-kilometer long land border become the link for bilateral cooperation and relations."
17. *Ibid.*
18. Le Dang Minh, "Vietnam-China Trade Relation: Situation, problems and solutions", Van Hien University, 30 August 2016
19. *Ibid.*
20. According to data from the Foreign Investment Agency, Ministry of Planning and Investment, and Complaints, as of the end of June 2019
21. Ngoc Linh, China's FDI into Vietnam: increased amount with increased shortcomings, Tien Phong Newspaper, July 22, 2019
22. EPC contract (standing for Engineering Procurement and Construction), is a type of construction contract of which the Contractor performs all work from technical design or construction drawing design and supply of materials and equipment to the construction of works, works items and test run and hand over of the works to the Owner.
23. *"Some comments on China's investment in Vietnam"*, Vietnam Institute for Economic and Policy Research (VEPR), July 2019

24. *Vietnam-China border issue,* Truth Publishing House, 1979
25. Basic document on China and Vietnam-China relations,
26. *Vietnam's land border,* Ministry of Foreign Affairs, National Border Committee of the Ministry of Foreign Affairs, 2010
27. Appendix of News A on September 03, 2019
28. Trần Quang, *Trung Quốc đã sẵn sàng sử dụng sức mạnh cứng,* Nghiên cứu Biển Đông, 2014
29. Phuong Nguyen, "From the rig event, looking back on China and Vietnam-China relations", China Studies No. 6 (154) - 2014
30. Le Hong Hiep, "Vietnam's dilemma when confronting China at Vanguard Bank", International Studies, 2019
31. According to the documentary content of 12th National Congress of CPV
32. Ibid.
33. "Full text of Xi Jinping's report at the 12th National Congress of the Chinese Communist Party," Xinhua News Agency, 2017
34. Dr. Nguyen Phu Tan Huong, "Vietnam foreign policy with some key partners after the Cold War - Part I", Diplomatic Academy, 2017

References

1. *"Some comments on Chinese investment in Vietnam",* Vietnam Economic and Policy Research (VEPR), July 2019.
2. "Full text of Xi Jinping's report at the 12th National Congress of the Chinese Communist Party," Xinhua News Agency, 2017.
3. *"China: Foreign Policy Characteristics in Asian",* Special reference document, July 23, 2001.
4. *Import and Export Report 2018,* Ministry of Industry and Trade.
5. *Vietnam's land border,* Ministry of Foreign Affairs - Committee of National Border, 2010.
6. "Ha Thu, A breakthrough in customs clearance of Vietnam-China border," Border Newspaper, 16 December 2018.
7. "Compelete works by Ho Chi Minh", Vol. 3, Vol. 5.
8. Insun Yu, "History of Vietnam-China relations in the 19th century, tributary institutions, real and unreal", Journal of Historical Studies, No. 9-2009.
9. Le Dang Minh, "Vietnam-China Trade Relation: Situation, Problems and Solutions", Van Hien University, 30 August 2016.
10. Le Hong Hiep, "Vietnam's dilemma when confronting China at Vanguard Bank", International Studies, 2019.
11. Le Tuan Thanh, "Political Relations between Vietnam-China since normalizing relations until now", Northeast Asian Studies, No. 2 (84) 2-2008.
12. Mai Ly Quang: *Glimpses of Vietnam*", World Publishing House, 2004.
13. Ngoc Linh, "Chinese FDI into Vietnam: increasing but with many shortcomings," Tien Phong Newspaper, 22 July 2019.
14. Nguyen Khac Giang, *"Is Vietnam Following the Way of China?",* The Diplomat, 22 February 2018.
15. Nguyen Duc Su, *"Position and role of Confucianism in Vietnamese society",* Nghe An Cultural Magazine, 19 January 2011.
16. Assoc. Prof. Ho Khang, *"China's military assistance to Vietnam in the years of 1950-1954",* Vietnam Military History Institute, Ministry of Defense, 2014.

17. News Appendix A, 3 September 2019.
18. Phuong Nguyen, "From the rig event, looking back on China and Vietnam-China relations", China Studies No. 6 (154) - 2014.
19. Robert S. Ross, *"The Indochina Tangle: China's Vietnam Policy",* 1975-1979 (New York: Columbia University Press, 1988), p. 253.
20. Vietnam Diplomatic Green Book 2018.
21. Susan L. Shrink, "China: Fragile Superpower"; 2007.
22. Dr. Nguyen Phu Tan Huong, "Vietnam foreign policy with some key partners after the Cold War - Part I", Diplomatic Academy, 2017.
23. Basic documents on China and Vietnam-China relations, Ministry of Foreign Affairs.
24. Journal of Industry and Trade, June 2019.
25. Dr. Dinh Thi Hien Luong, *"China's Perception on National Power",* Diplomatic Academy, National Political Publishing House – the Truth.
26. *Statement by Chinese Foreign Ministry Spokeswoman* on 15 January 2019*:* "1450 km of land border between the two countries become a bridge of cooperation and friendship".
27. *According to data of Foreign Investment Agency,* Ministry of Planning and Investment, as of the end of June 2019.
28. Tran Nam Tien, "Vietnam's behavioural culture in relations with China during the Middle Ages - From the perspective of "ordination – tributary"", University of Social Sciences and Humanities, 2012.
29. Tran Quang, *"China is ready to use hard power",* East Sea Study, 2014.
30. Border issues between Vietnam and China, National Political Publishing House of Vietnam, 1979.

10 Vietnam's Relations with Laos, Cambodia and Thailand

Thi-Hong-Mai Nguyen

VIETNAM-LAOS-CAMBODIA AND THAILAND IN THE FRAMEWORK OF COOPERATION

Vietnam-Laos Relations

Vietnam-Laos relations in the field of politics-diplomacy, security-defense

In the context of the collapse of socialism in the Soviet Union and Eastern Europe, the two countries continued to advance rapidly on the path of innovation, maintaining political orientation, stabilizing national security and expanding foreign relations towards diversification and multilateralization.

Political relations continue to be respected by the two sides. During the official visit to Laos by General Secretary and President Nguyen Phu Trong (February 2, 2019), the two sides agreed to upgrade from the relationship "traditional friendship" to the "great friendship". This is considered an important historical milestone creating a breakthrough in cooperative relations between the two countries in the coming time. The two sides have strengthened cooperation in the field of politics that continues while organizing annual meetings between the two Politburos of the two Parties; promoting negotiation and exchanging of delegations between leaders of the Parties, the State, ministries, departments, branches, mass and friendship organizations and localities, especially localities sharing common borders. To enhance comprehensive cooperation and bring the special relations between Vietnam and Laos to a new height, the two sides should continue to supplement and complete procedures and policies as well as effectively implement the set of strategic agreements and targets with a broader, more comprehensive and long-term vision to constantly consolidate, strengthen and further develop the special comprehensive cooperation and relations. "Despite hardships faced, Vietnam wish to preserve and protect the Vietnam-Laos relationship, so that the relationship between Vietnam and Laos will stand forever as do mountains and rivers".

The cooperation on security, defense and foreign affairs has achieved many important results that contribute to firmly protecting the political-social stability and security of each country, enhancing the both countries' position, influence of and reputation in the region and in the world.

Vietnam-Laos cooperation in foreign affairs has been promoted in three aspects: Party's foreign relations, State diplomacy and People's diplomacy. In order to create a favourable environment for protecting and building the country along the socialist orientation, the two countries have clearly defined the multilateralization and diversification in international relations, and expansion of foreign affairs relations with countries in the region and the world.

In security and defense cooperation, with the motto "helping a friend is to help yourself", "your security is also ourselves security", both of Governments and the Ministry of Public Security have signed agreements and decrees on cooperation and mutual assistance in security. The two sides attached great importance to the exchange of information and experiences in building forces, combating intrusions, combating riot and neutralizing the "peaceful evolution" activities of hostile forces. Vietnam helps Laos to consolidate and build a high-quality security force to meet the requirements of the new situation. The Ministry of Defense of Vietnam helps Laos to develop a long-term defense strategy, build a comprehensive and national defense strategy in each period to suit the situation. Security and defense cooperation between the two countries has been constantly strengthened in all areas, especially in training and practicing. The two sides have coordinated to implement security and defense cooperation agreements; signing the A Protocol on the Vietnam-Laos boundary and national border markers; the Agreement on Vietnam -Laos border and border checkpoint management regulations, implementing the Agreement between the two Governments on resolving the issue of free migrants and unmarried marriage in the Vietnam-Laos border region.

Vietnam-Laos economic relations

In the field of trade: Vietnam and Laos want to further expand trade relations on the basis of equality and mutual benefits, respect for the traditional cooperation and international trade. Many trade agreements were signed between the two countries: Vietnam - Laos Trade Agreement; Vietnam - Laos Border Trade Agreement; Agreement on transit of goods; promulgating Lao regulations on goods transiting the Vietnamese territory. Besides, both side have formulated a plan to implement the Agreement amending the Agreement between the two Governments on cooperation in the development of electric power and mines projects...; promoting trade in small-scale trade, building some free trade zones at border gates... Many supermarkets and centers to introduce Vietnamese goods have been built in localities of Laos.

Trading exchange plays an important role in bilateral relations. Vietnam is one of the major trading partners of Laos. In the 2001-2004 period, the two-way trade turnover between Vietnam and Laos reached about 687.8 million USD, an average of 137.5 million USD/year, but in the 2011-2019 period, this two-way trade turnover increased sharply that has exceeded the targets setting by the two governments. Specifically, 734 million USD in 2011; in 2015 reached 890 million USD; in 2016 reached 823.4 million USD; in 2018, it reached 1 billion USD[1]. According to data of the General Department of Vietnam Customs, in 2018, Vietnam's exports to Laos reached 595 million USD, imports from Laos reached 437 million USD. By the end of July 2019, the trade turnover between Vietnam and Laos reached 663.8 million USD, up 13.1 per cent over the same period in 2018. Vietnam's exports to Laos reached 404.7 million USD, up 18, 8 per cent. Vietnam's imports from Laos reached 259 million USD, up 5.2 per cent[2]. The governments of the two countries set a target to increase bilateral trade turnover by 10 per cent or more, striving to reach the target of Vietnam - Laos two-way trade of 4 billion USD by 2020.

The key export items of Laos are: Wood and mineral products (copper ore, copper and copper products), video equipment components, garments, agricultural products such as coffee, corn, cassava, rice and cattle. The main export markets are Thailand, China and Vietnam. Meanwhile, Laos' import items focus on major groups such as petroleum, iron and steel, transportation vehicles, electrical equipment, machinery, steel, iron and steel products, and auto parts. Vietnam's import products from Laos are mainly rubber, fertilizer, ore and minerals. In 2018, Vietnam is still the third trading partner of Laos, after Thailand and China.

In the field of investment, jointing and cooperation: Vietnam has been one of the leading countries in Laos' large investment. By 2018, Vietnamese investors has invested in more than 400 projects with a total registered capital of more than 4.1 billion USD, of which implemented capital was 1.4 billion USD[3] and was the 3rd investor investing in Laos. Some typical projects of Vietnamese enterprises may be mentioned to: Xekamanı and Xekamanxanxay hydroelectric projects have generated electricity sold to Vietnam, bringing a large source to Laos' budget. Cooperation between the two countries in the Vung Ang ports and agreement of purchasing electricity. Many projects were effective that has been contributing positively to the development economics of the two countries as well as creating jobs, social welfare... This has helped Laos to well implement the poverty reduction policy, so Vietnam have been recognized and high appreciated by the Laos government.

In the field of non-refundable aid, in the 1996-2000 period, Vietnam provided nearly VND 350 trillion (approximately USD 26.6 million) to Laos, in the 2001-2005 period, it was VND 560 billion, equivalent to USD 37 million; helping Laos to complete 8 investment projects, 19 planning programmes and preparing investment, and 15 support programmes for industries and localities in Laos. The implementation of projects using aid capital also achieved good results. In 2018, 12 projects were completed, handed over and put into use. The non-refundable aid capital and the assistance of ministries, branches and localities of Vietnam in recent years has contributed positively to capacity building, facilities improvement, and solutions to deal difficulties for many ministries, branches and localities of Laos, especially localities with revolutionary traditions in deep-lying and remote areas. Many constructions and projects have marked and are highly appreciated by Laos. Vietnam's assistance to Laos has contributed to strengthening and promoting the traditional friendship, special solidarity and comprehensive cooperation between the two countries.

Vietnam-Laos relations in some other fields

Cooperation in the fields of culture, education and training continues to achieve positive results. The two sides have been collabourating to prepare to announce the project: *"History of special relations of Vietnam - Laos, Laos - Vietnam (1930-2007)"* and use it to teach in schools of the two countries, contributing to propaganda and education on traditions, strategic meanings and the special importance of Vietnam-Laos relations. Vietnam continues to offer Laos many scholarships annually at all levels of education (college, university, postgraduate); effectively implement the instructions of the two Prime Ministers on reorganizing and improving the quality of cooperation in education and training. Many activities has organized to attract Lao students to study at Vietnamese universities on their own. The training of staff and human resources for Laos has been increasingly strengthened in both quantity and quality. As of 2018, the number of Lao international students studying in Vietnam is more than 14,000, including an agreement of over 3,400 people[4].

The cultural relationship between Vietnam and Laos was formed very early in history and increasingly strengthened, expanded and developed. This cooperation is carried out in many fields such as conservation, museum, performing arts, cinema, information and press publishing, international cooperation, staff training, etc. cooperation documents, cooperation strategy agreements, cooperation agreements have been signed by the two parties over the years and the implementation process, the results achieved in the implementation of such cooperation agreements and agreements. Besides, traveling Laos–Viet is developing. The number of tourists traveling between Vietnam and Laos is increasing. In 2015, the number of Laos visitors to Vietnam reached 113,992 people, the number of Vietnamese tourists to Laos was more than 950 thousand people[5]. The two countries also collabourated with Thailand to build a road trip tour between the three countries.

Health cooperation between Vietnam and Laos has been increasingly strengthened and developing, especially among border provinces. Agreements on health cooperation are also signed annually. Vietnam is committed to strengthening cooperation, helping Laos to build and develop a health network from the central to grassroots levels. Vietnam is willing to exchange and transfer experience on disease prevention and control; implementation of social programmes, such as malaria prevention and control, goiter, expanded immunization, traditional medicine, prevention of infectious diseases. In addition, Vietnam also helps Laos in training and improving the qualifications of Lao health workers under the general programme. Vietnam has helped Laos build two new friendship hospitals like in the province Hunan worth about 20 million USD and in Xieng Khouang province worth 17.6 million USD[6].

Regarding transport, the two countries have accelerated the implementation of transport connecting projects in the framework of bilateral and sub-regional cooperation; study and expand the "one-stop-one-stop" inspection model to other pairs of international border gates between the two countries. The two sides implemented effectively the Memorandum of Cooperation Strategy in the field of transportation; projects of the Hanoi-Vientiane highway, the Vientiane-Vung Ang railway and the Nongkhang international airport in Hunan province and the construction of other important roads linking the two countries.

Regarding the post and telecommunications, Vietnam and Laos have cooperated to build an optical cable line along the 8th road connecting the two countries. Vietnam actively supports Laos' proposal to be connected to Vietnam's undersea optical cable for international communication.

Vietnam-Cambodia Relations

Relations Vietnam-Cambodia in the field of politics and diplomacy, security defense

With the motto "good neighbours, traditional friendship, comprehensive cooperation, long-term sustainability", Vietnam - Cambodia relations constantly develop in all areas. The two sides have been maintaining the exchange delegations at all levels, especially senior leaders of the two countries. Exchanges between ministries, sectors, localities and people-to-people were strengthened. The localities of the two countries have also established close relationships, especially with the border provinces, contributing to consolidating and enhancing mutual trust and understanding between leaders and people of the two countries.

Security-defense cooperation between Vietnam and Cambodia continues to enhance to meet task of protection accompanying the national building of both countries. The Vietnamese and Cambodian army often exchange high-level military delegations, signing many cooperation documents. Cambodia has committed to continuing cooperation, especially in resolving border issues between the two countries. Up to now, the two sides have completed more than 84 per cent of the demarcation and landmark planting and both sides determind to complete this work early to make the two countries' borders a border of peace, friendship, cooperation and development sustainably for the mutual benefit of two countries' peoples.

Vietnam-Cambodia relations in the economic field

In the field of trade: Governments of Vietnam and Cambodia have effectively implemented the mechanism of bilateral economic trade cooperation, and coordination in multilateral mechanisms; building and perfecting important legal bases in trade development, promoting bilateral trade between Vietnam and Cambodia. Vietnam is currently the third largest trading partner of Cambodia among more than 140 countries and territories. In the 1997-1999 period, two-way trade turnover reached about 130-150 million USD/year, by 2001 increased to 169 million USD, in 2010 reached 2.83 billion USD. In particular, in 2018, the trade turnover between the two countries reached 4 billion 704 million USD. It is expected that by the end of 2019, the trade turnover of the two countries will reach 5 billion USD[7] as committed by the leaders of the two countries.

Cambodia is a good market consuming many strong products of Vietnam, such as petroleum, steel, textiles, textile materials, plastic products, machinery, equipment and spare parts, many kinds of fertilizers. In 2019, iron and steel continued to be the main export items to the Cambodian market, accounting for 25.1 per cent of the proportion, equivalent to 95.13 million USD, up 56.48 per cent in volume and 47.69 per cent in value compared to with January 2018. The second is textile and garment, reaching 55.89 million USD, up 46.59 per cent; petroleum increased by 53.26 per cent in volume and 42.64 per cent in value, the average export price of 563.46 USD/tonne, down 6.93 per cent[8]. This is also one of the markets supplying raw products and raw materials, which are inputs for consumption, domestic production and export of Vietnam, such as raw agricultural goods, raw forestry, raw seafood and mineral products. The main products that Vietnam imports from Cambodia include: rubber, cashew nuts, wood, corn, tobacco materials and steel scrap... Over the past years, Vietnam has effectively cooperated with Cambodia in bilateral economic and trade cooperation mechanisms and combination in multilateral mechanisms; building and perfecting important legal bases in trade development, such as Vietnam-Cambodia bilateral trade promotion agreement...

In the field of investment, joint ventures and associates: As of 2019, Vietnam is one of five countries with the most foreign direct investment (FDI) in Cambodia (after China, Thailand, Japan and South Korea). Investment activities of Vietnam in Cambodia have rapidly increased in recent years and are present in 18/24 regions, provinces and cities of Cambodia, mainly concentrated in Phnom Penh capital and the provinces bordering Vietnam like Kratie, Mondukiri, Svay Rieng. FDI has been used to invest in most important industries and fields of Cambodia, most concentrated in the field of agriculture and forestry (accounting for nearly 70 per cent of the total registered capital); finance - banking - insurance (accounting for 9.4 per cent of the total registered capital); tele-communications (accounting for 7.5 per cent of the total registered capital); the rest projects are in the fields of aviation, minerals, manufacturing and processing industry, warehousing, import and export trade, healthcare, construction, tourism - hotel, real estate and other services. Many projects have been put into operation, bringing good results and creating stable jobs for thousands of Cambodian labourers. Vietnam's agricultural and industrial tree planting projects have contributed to socio-economic development of Cambodia, improved the lives of the local people, improved the environment, and changed people's habits, especially nomadic practice of Cambodian people. Many investment projects of Vietnam have strong brands in Cambodia such as Viettel's telecom Metfone; Cambodian national airline Angkor Air is controlled by Vietnam Airline; The Bank for Investment and

Development of Cambodia, Cambodia - Vietnam Insurance Company (CVI); many Cambodian agricultural products invested by Vietnamese enterprises, exported to European, Japanese and Korean markets... Investment activities of Vietnamese enterprises have contributed practically to the economic development and social security of Cambodia. In 2019, Cambodia has 19 investment projects in Vietnam with a total capital of 63.42 million USD, ranking 49th out of 103 countries and territories having investment activities in Vietnam and focusing mainly on agriculture, forestry, fisheries, and commercial business[9].

Vietnam-Cambodia relations in some other areas

- *Education:* The two countries have strengthened cooperation in the field of training and development human resource for the sustainable development of the two countries, including the promotion of setting up a Vietnam Learning Center at Royal University of Phnom Penh. Every year, the number of Cambodian students studying in Vietnam and Vietnamese students going to Cambodia to study are increasing in both quantity and quality. Now, there are about 4,000 Cambodian international students studying in Vietnam, of which 800 are granted scholarships. Every year, the Cambodian Government grants 15 scholarships to Vietnamese cadres and students studying in Cambodian universities. In addition, each year Cambodia also grants Vietnam 20 short-term scholarships to study Khmer language within 2 years in Cambodia. Currently, about 200 Vietnamese students are studying in Cambodia, including scholarships and self-sufficiency. Particularly in 2019, the Cambodian Government has provided 35 scholarships for Vietnamese students to study in Cambodia[10].
- *Tourism:* The Vietnam Airlines and the Cambodia's Ministry of Tourism have signed a cooperation agreement on tourism development in 2019-2021 in Cambodia in order to connect tourism between the two countries. And this agreement makes an important contribution to developing the tourism field of "Golden land - Southeast Asia". Vietnam is continuously ranked the second country (after China) in the number of tourists to Cambodia. In 2018, there were about 900,000 Vietnamese tourists coming to Cambodia. In the opposite direction, in 2017, 222,000 Cambodian visitors came to Vietnam[11].
- *Transportation:* With the policy of "Open sky" in order to promote socio-economic cooperation, trade, tourism and connect the two economies, Vietnam and Cambodia have conducted negotiations towards increase the quota of vehicles crossing the border between the two countries; deploy projects on traffic. There have been many transportation cooperation projects which have been put into effectively use: Long Binh border bridge (An Giang)-Chrey Thom (Kandal); Ho Chi Minh City-Phnom Penh Expressway and transport traffic at Le Thanh (Gia Lai)-Odaao (Rattanakiri) border gates. The two countries signed a Memorandum of Understanding on Transport Cooperation Strategy 2018- 2025, vision to 2030.

- *Post and Telecommunication:* Vietnam and Cambodia have signed a lots of important cooperation documents on post and telecommunications, such as: Cooperation plan between Ministry of Information and Communications of Vietnam and Ministry of Post and Telecommunications of Cambodia; The cooperation agreement between the Department of Information Security (Vietnam) and the General Department of ICT (Cambodia); The digital signature cooperation agreement between BKAV Group and the Ministry of Post and telecommunications of Cambodia. Vietnam have also helped to develop services in the Cambodian Post industry, as well as support the construction of anti-network infrastructure on a national scale[12]. Vietnam offers 3 full scholarships for Cambodian students at Posts and Telecommunications Institute of Technology of Vietnam under an ICT training programme in 100 per cent English (Viettel's scholarship, worth 27,000 USD/person/course)[13].

Vietnam-Thailand Relations

Vietnam-Thailand relations on politics-diplomacy, security-defense

On August 6, 1976, Vietnam and Thailand established diplomatic relations, creating a new turning point, opening the direction of development in bilateral relations. In the 1979-1991 period, Vietnam and Thailand relations almost leveled off because of many factors. Since 1992, relations between the two countries have been constantly strengthened and increasingly improved and developed, especially after Vietnam officially joined ASEAN (1995). In recent years, this bilateral relationship has been active and has many positive changes. In June 2013, Vietnam and Thailand upgraded their relations to "strategic partners" and became the first two ASEAN countries to establish strategic partnerships with each other. Next, the two sides signed the Action Plan to implement Vietnam-Thailand Strategic Partnership for the period 2014-2018. The two countries have also strengthened people-to-people exchanges. Up to now, 16 provinces and cities of Vietnam have built a cooperative relationship with cities and provinces in the Northeast of Thailand.

Vietnam-Thailand security-defense relation is constantly promoted, based on the principles of respect for each other's independence, sovereignty and territorial integrity; resolving all disputes by peace; not threaten force or use force, not interfere with each other's internal affairs; cooperation in the exchange of experience, joint patrol on the sea, the mutual visits of military and security delegations of the two countries took place regularly and became increasingly effective. A series of important cooperation agreements were signed, creating a basis for relations between the two countries to continue developing, especially the Agreement on delimitation of maritime boundaries on August 9, 1997, considered as a model for settlement regional and international disputes[14].

Vietnam-Thailand relations in the economic field

In the field of trade, economic and trade cooperation between the two countries has made great progress. Thailand is currently Vietnam's largest trading partner in ASEAN. Vietnam is Thailand's second largest export partner in ASEAN and the 7th in the world. Two-way trade turnover from nearly 5.8 billion USD (2009) increased to 9.41 billion USD (2013), reaching 11.5 billion USD (2015), 12.5 billion USD (2016) and reaching 17.2 billion USD (2018). The two countries set goals to strive for two-way trade turnover to reach 20 billion USD by 2020[15].

In the field of investment, Thailand is now the 9th largest investor among 126 countries and territories investing in Vietnam with 521 valid investment projects worth 10.38 billion USD of registered capital[16]. In particular, investment projects focus on areas such as infrastructure development, energy, processing industry and service sectors. Thailand's investment projects are present in 41/63 provinces and cities of Vietnam. Vietnamese businesses currently invest in Thailand about 18 projects with registered capital of about 28.8 million USD.

Vietnam-Thailand relations in a number of other areas

- *Regarding education:* Two Ministries of Education of Vietnam and Thailand have signed a Memorandum of Understanding on educational cooperation (2004), promoting cooperation programmes to build common education through exhibitions and strengthening cooperation between universities, developing educational institution, exchanging teacher and student. The Thailand Government annually grants about 100 university and master scholarships to Vietnamese students, supports a number of Vietnamese universities to teach Thai language, and organizes Vietnamese teaching at many Thai educational institutions. In addition, the two sides also exchanged training activities, youth exchanges and exchanges in the field of information and communication.
- *Regarding tourism:* Thailand is an important partner for the development of Vietnam's tourism industry. Every year, the number of other tourist of Thailand is constantly increasing. In 2017, the number of Thailand and Vietnamese tourists visiting each other reached over 1 million visitors. In 2018, there were more than 300,000 Thai visitors to Vietnam, an increase of 14.3 per cent compared to 2017, ranked second in the Southeast Asian group to Vietnam and more than 1 million Vietnamese visitors to Thailand, up 9.46 per cent compared to 2017 and ranked 3rd in the group of Southeast Asian visitors to Thailand[17]. The increasing number of Thai tourists traveling to Vietnam has brought many benefits to Vietnam's tourism industry, especially to help promote Vietnam's image to the world.

VIETNAM WITH LAOS-CAMBODIA AND THAILAND IN REGIONAL AND INTERNATIONAL COOPERATION

Cambodia-Laos-Vietnam Development Triangle (CLV)

The CLV development triangle relations has been established in 1999 playing important role in the cooperation between Vietnam, Laos and Cambodia. The three countries focused on development cooperation in 13 provinces in three countries. These are 5 Central Highlands provinces of Vietnam (Kon Tum, Gia Lai, Dak Lak, Dak Nong, and Binh Phuoc), 4 provinces in Southern Laos (Attapu, Saravan, Champasac and Sekong) and 4 provinces of Northeastern Cambodia (Modunkiri, Strung Treng, Rattanakiri, and Kratie). This cooperation has contributed to further improving economy of 13 provinces in the triangle in particular and economic cooperation between the three countries in general.

Located on the Indochinese peninsula, the three countries all have their own advantages and complement each other for development. With the implementation of the visa waiver policy, people in the Indochina peninsula are free to move. And also thanks to the connection policy, the three countries have an open border. The Vietnam-Laos border has been completed with 8 international border gates and 17 national border gates. Vietnam's border with Cambodia is still in the process of delimitation. However, among 10 international and 65 national border gates, the secondary border gate is open for trade and people-to-people exchanges. The roads system of the three countries are also connected to each other. Vietnam's economic centers are connected with the major cities of Laos and Cambodia, and bridges are built to connect traffic between Cambodia and Laos, between Cambodia and Vietnam, facilitating road traffic between the three developed countries.

In addition, CLV cooperation in the field of banking, education, health achieved many results. Vietnam's education and healthcare system for the Central Highlands region and the communes along the border also partly help the people of the two neighbouring countries to share. CLV cooperation has created comprehensive connectivity, leading to the economic development of the Triangle and towards the goal of improving the lives of people in the Development Triangle. In 2016, GDP of the Development Triangle Area reached 9-10 per cent, higher than the average growth rate of all three countries. Thus, the CLV cooperation mechanism has affirmed the important indispensable role not only for the Development Triangle area but has been expanded to the entire territory of the three countries of Laos, Cambodia and Vietnam[18].

Besides the bilateral cooperation between Vietnam - Laos, Vietnam - Cambodia and the Triangle relationship, the three countries have also promoted tripartite cooperation within regional and international frameworks such as the Association of Southeast Asian Nations. - ASEAN, Mekong River Commission (MRC), Greater Mekong Subregion (GMS), Ayeyawad - Chao Praya - Mekong three-river economic cooperation strategy (ACMECS), The Cambodia – Laos – Myanmar – Vietnam (CLMV) cooperation helps fuel socio-economic development in these countries, and narrow development gap between Vietnam and other ASEAN nations.

Cooperation within ASEAN

Four countries of Vietnam, Laos, Cambodia and Thailand are member countries of ASEAN, in which Vietnam have joined ASEAN in July 1995, Thailand in August 1967, Laos in July 1997 and Cambodia in April 1999. Vietnam, Laos and Cambodia and Thailand always support each other at international and regional forums. The four countries have participated in effective mechanisms and solutions to prevent conflicts, create favourable conditions to build a peaceful, friendly and cooperative environment with ASEAN member countries, consolidate independence and sovereignty of nation and promote regional linkages on all of areas. Countries have been effectively implementing many agreements, such as: "Treaty of Amity and Cooperation in Southeast Asia – TAC", "Declaration of ASEAN harmony" (1976), "Declaration on the East Sea"(1992); "ASEAN Regional Forum – ARF"(1993), "The Southeast Asian Nuclear-Weapon-Free Zone Treaty (SEANWFZ)" 1996, "ARF Vision 2020", "The Declaration on the Conduct of Parties in the East Sea (DOC)" (2002) and ASEAN Declaration II (2003) with" Roadmap for building the ASEAN Community in 2015", including the initiative to build the ASEAN Security Community (ASC)[19], the Declaration of the ASEAN's six-point principle on the East Sea 2012.... August 2017, Vietnam, Cambodia and other countries related to the East Sea signed an agreement to sign a code of conduct (COC) to contribute on maintaining peace and stability in the region. On November 18, 2012, in Phnom Penh (Cambodia), Vietnam - Laos, Cambodia and ASEAN countries signed the "ASEAN Human Rights Declaration – AHRD". This is an important political document of ASEAN to create framework for strengthening cooperation and promoting and protecting human rights in the region.

Political-security cooperation efforts of the four countries and the ASEAN are focused to address the main aspects: Resolving sovereignty disputes in the East Sea; consolidating ARF into an effective tool to ensure regional security; perfecting the mechanism of dispute settlement among member countries; amending TAC, trying to integrate major countries into the regional framework; preventing and combating drug trafficking across the borders, realizing the goal of a drug-free ASEAN, consistently orienting the vision to build the ASEAN Community without drugs; Vietnam-Laos-Cambodia together with ASEAN countries build the ASEAN Political-Security Community (APSC) with the main goal of promoting ASEAN security and political cooperation to a new height, contributing to bringing ASEAN from an Association to a close intergovernmental cooperation organization with a higher level of alignment on legal grounds of the Charter.

Special politics-security relations between Vietnam-Laos-Cambodia is important in strengthening friendship solidarity and strengthening cooperation among ASEAN member countries, contributing to strengthening the basic principles that guide the relationship between ASEAN countries for the cause of peace and prosperous development of Southeast Asia and Asia-Pacific.

ASEAN member countries have also proposed many measures to further promote ASEAN's existing economic integration programmes, such as: ASEAN Free Trade Area (AFTA), ASEAN Industrial Cooperation programme (AICO), Agreement ASEAN Investment (ACIA), ASEAN Trade in Goods Agreement (ATIGA), ASEAN Framework Agreement on Services (AFAS), ASEAN Electronic Framework Agreement (E-ASEAN).... ASEAN member countries want ASEAN become a competitive economic region, promote sustainable equilibrium development and narrow the development gap... Vietnam-Laos-Cambodia and ASEAN member countries have decided to build the ASEAN Economic Community (AEC) (2015) to make ASEAN a single market with a unified production base and free circulation of goods and services, investment, capital, talents and skilled workers. Accordingly, three governments and ASEAN member countries are continuing to take the necessary policy measures in order to take full advantage of the opportunities and potentials of the AEC and the frameworks. Regional economic links to develop on all fields.

Greater Mekong Sub region Cooperation (GMS)

GMS was started in 1992 between six countries sharing the Mekong River, namely China, Myanmar, Laos, Thailand, Cambodia and Vietnam. The Asian Development Bank (ADB) also participates in GMS as the adviser, sponsorship and closing partner to support development[20]. Up to now, GMS Cooperation is increasingly proving to be an effective model of cooperation between ASEAN countries and external partners, making the Mekong Sub-region a bridge to two emerging economies in Asia as China and India. GMS cooperation is truly a forum of friendship, cooperation that benefits all participants. In the early years of the 21st century, GMS cooperation has expanded into a new development period with many positive changes. The First Greater Mekong Sub-region Summit (GMS-1, Phnom Penh, 2002) and the Second High-Level Summit (GMS-2, Kunming, 2005) outlined the principles of cooperation, placing foundations for the vision of an integrated sub-region, harmony and prosperity. The 3rd Summit (GMS-3, Vientiane, 2008) with the theme *"Enhancing competition through deeper connectivity"*, on the basis of assessing the progress in cooperation to implement *"GMS development action plan for the period 2008-2012"*.

The Greater Mekong Sub-region Cooperation has given top priority to develop transport infrastructure and it has up to now achieved the most outstanding results, focusing on three main economic corridors: (1) East-West Economic Corridor (EWEC), 1450 km long, starting from the port city of Mawlamyine (Myanmar) running through Thailand and Savanakhet (Laos), Quang Tri, Thua Thien - Hue, Da Nang (Vietnam) provinces. EWEC has become the first operational corridor in the Mekong sub-region since 2007. The East-West Corridor connecting the Pacific and Indian Oceans across the four countries in the Mekong Sub-region is really taking effectively to promote

ASEAN linking cooperation. (2) North-South Economic Corridor (NSEC) includes 3 routes along the North-South axis is Kunming-Chieng Rai-Bangkok, Kunming-Hanoi-Hai Phong and Nanning-Hanoi. (3) Southern Economic Corridor (SEC) consists of 3 routes connecting southern Thailand through Cambodia with Vietnam. The development corridors are considered as a solution to take advantage of and promote the factors of position-strategy, geography-economy, geography-politics, and geography-security and international relations to connect the three regions of Southeast Asia-Northeast Asia-South Asia

The basic priority directions in the Greater Mekong Sub-region cooperation include: cooperation to promote in drug prevention in Southeast Asia; protecting environment and using sustainably Mekong water; cooperation in tourism development... The Greater Mekong Sub-region Cooperation process contributes to promoting the integration of ASEAN, especially among countries and territories with adjacent borders, attracting investment in socio-economic development, narrowing the gap of development between new members and ASEAN 6 members, contributing to dealing with cross-border security issues, developing transport infrastructure that fosters regional and national links in the region.

Cooperation in the Mekong River Commission (MRC)

The Mekong River Commission was established as the Mekong Commission in 1957, and became the Provisional Committee for the Mekong River Basin Research Coordination in 1978. In 1995, four countries shared the Mekong River lower basin (Vietnam, Laos, Cambodia and Thailand) signed the Mekong River Basin Sustainable Development Cooperation Agreement and established the Mekong River Commission - MRC including Council, Joint Committee and Secretariat. Member States have established National Mekong Committees to further assist the Commission in carrying out its duties. The Mekong River Commission is responsible for promotion, coordination the management and development of water and related resources in a sustainable manner for the common good of nations and the well-being of the community by implementing carry out strategic activities and programmes, providing scientific information and policy advice.

The first Mekong River Commission Summit took place solemnly in April 2010, with the participation of member countries and strategic partners as China, Myanmar, countries and international donors such as the United States, Japan, France, Germany, Australia, Belgium, Finland and New Zealand, Luxembourg, European Union - EU, ASEAN, WWF (World Wide Fund for Nature), World Bank and Asian Development Bank. The Conference adopted the Hua Hin Joint Statement, which strongly commits to cooperate and promote sustainable development among the 4 member countries; using and management of water resources and related resources of the lower Mekong River; affirming the Commission's great achievements in the past 15 years. The Declaration highlighted four important issues: Food security; energy and hydropower development; mitigating the impact of climate change; increasing the participation of social organizations in the development of plans and processes for decision-making.

In April 2014, the Second Mekong River Commission Summit (MRC) opened in Ho Chi Minh City, Vietnam, with the participation of the high-level delegation of 4 member countries (Cambodia, Laos, Thailand, Vietnam) and the two dialogue partners as China, Myanmar and representatives of development partners and observers[21]. With the theme "Water, energy and food security in the context of climate change in the Mekong River Basin" the conference focused on the current outstanding issues in Mekong cooperation; reviewing and evaluating the results achieved during the implementation of the Hua Hin Declaration in 2010 and proposing measures to promote the sustainable management, use and development of the Mekong River[22] in the coming time.

Economic cooperation of the three rivers Ayeyawad-Chao Praya-Mekong (ACMECS)

ACMECS was established in November 2003 in the framework of economic cooperation among 5 countries of Vietnam, Laos, Cambodia, Myanmar and Thailand in order to strengthen joint and bilateral economic cooperation and exploit and promote comparative advantages among regions, member countries, improve competitiveness, narrow development gaps. At the first ACMECS Summit held in Bagan, member countries adopted the Bagan Declaration and ACMECS Action Plan, which outlined five areas of cooperation: Facilitation trade and investment; Industrial-agricultural cooperation; Traffic tourism cooperation and Human resource development. Up to now, there have been 7 times of summits, ACMECS has 7 areas of cooperation including: Trade-investment; Agriculture; Energy industry; Traffic; Travel; Human resource development; Health Care. At the fifth ACMECS Summit taking place in Laos in 2013, the Leaders adopted the Vientiane Declaration and the ACMECS Action Plan for the 2013-2015 period. Thereby further linking ACMECS cooperation with the process of building the ASEAN Economic Community 2015 and implementing the Master Plan on ASEAN Connectivity, enhancing the competitiveness, role and position of ACMECS countries in global production and supply chains. The ACMECS-6 Summit was held in June 2015, the Leaders noted the achievements made in implementing the Action Plan for the period 2013-2015, especially in transport connectivity and facilitation benefit for trade and investment between the five countries, development of transnational economic corridors such as East - West Economic Corridor (EWEC), Southern Economic Corridor (SEC), developing green tourism, and cooperation in Agriculture[23].

With the goal of making ACMECS a leading destination for investment and tourism, forming a unified production base in the ACMECS region, especially in border areas, ACMECS countries, including Vietnam, Laos and Cambodia have taken advantage of the new development opportunities offered by the ASEAN

Economic Community and free trade agreements. With the initial successes as above, ACMECS is considered a relatively effective channel of cooperation among 5 Southeast Asian countries to narrow the gap of economic development between the parties.

Economic cooperation and integration between Vietnam-Laos-Cambodia-Myanmar (CLMV)

The first CLMV conference was held in 2004 in Vientiane (Laos). At the conference, the leaders of the four countries adopted the Vientiane Declaration on Cooperation and Economic Integration among CLMV countries. The declaration highlighted the areas of cooperation: trade and investment, agriculture, industry and energy, transportation, information technology, tourism, human resource development and health care. At the second CLMV conference was held in 2005 in Kuala Lumpur (Malaysia), leaders discussed Action plans to implement the Vientiane Declaration, including short-term and medium-term plans. At the third conference was held in 2007 in Cebu (Philippines), the leaders decided to adjust the action plan to accelerate cooperation in all areas. The fourth conference was conducted in 2008 in Hanoi (Vietnam) on the same occasion as ACMECS III Summit. At this conference, the leaders of the 4 countries approved the CLMV Collabourative Project List of 58 projects, and decided from 2008, the CLMV Summit will be held every 2 years respectively in each country in the order of the Latin alphabet and on the same occasion as the ACMECS Summit[24].

At the CLMV 6 Summit was held in Vientiane (Laos) in March 2013, leaders of CLMV countries emphasized their commitment to strengthening the traditional friendship and mutually beneficial relations between the four countries. They have assessed the implementation of projects and action programmes since CLMV 5 meeting in Phnom Penh in 2010 and discussed future cooperation directions to narrow the development gap between the four CLMV countries and the remaining ASEAN countries, fulfilling the goal of building the ASEAN community by year 2015. CLMV-6 also agreed to strengthen cooperation in the near future, focus on promoting cooperation on trade, investment and tourism; implemented the signed agreements in bilateral and multilateral frameworks among CLMV countries, continue to apply the "one-stop-one-stop" model at other border gates to facilitate trade and investment activities; promptly implement the Roadmap for building the ASEAN Community[25] and the ASEAN Master Plan on connectivity to accelerate the integration process in ASEAN. At the same time, CLMV-6 has promoted to traffic connections, making the best use of the corridors in the region such as EWEC, NSC (North - South Corridor) and South Corridor, facilitating traffic on the links between Laos, Myanmar and Vietnam and promote the implementation of the CLMV Multilateral Agreement on Air Services.

CLMV-7 (2015) is an opportunity for member countries to be proud of achievements achieved in the previous nine years of cooperation to promote exchanges between CLMV member countries. This year (2015) is a very important year for establishing the ASEAN Economic Community (AEC), so that member countries of CLMV can jointly accelerate the process of establishing AEC. Next, on October 26, 2016, in Hanoi (Vietnam), The 8th CLMV Summit was held under the theme "Seizing Opportunities, Shaping the Future". The leaders agreed to carry out both domestic economic reforms, maintain macroeconomic stability and create favourable business environment, and proactively integrate more deeply into the regional and global economy. The leaders also agreed to take concrete measures to strengthen the economic and market cohesion of the four countries, towards a seamlessly connected region.

It can be seen that, up to now, the CLMV Development Quadrilateral cooperation mechanism has achieved many achievements, especially the goal of poverty reduction and narrowing the development gap between countries. CLMV Cooperation between the four countries is a necessary condition and an important factor for the integration process of Vietnam and ASEAN, helping to maintain peace, stability and sustainable development in the region.

Vietnam-Laos-Cambodia and Thailand in multilateral cooperation mechanisms

Vietnam-Laos-Cambodia and Thailand have together participated in cooperation initiatives with many multilateral cooperation mechanisms by country group, such as: Indochina Comprehensive Development Forum since 1993; Cooperation between ASEAN and Japan established a Working Group on Economic Cooperation between Cambodia, Laos, Myanmar and Vietnam (1994); ASEAN-Mekong Basin Development Cooperation (AMBDC) (1995); Mekong-Ganges cooperation (MGC) (2000) including 6 countries of Laos - Myanmar-Thailand-Cambodia-Vietnam-India. These countries focus on four areas of cooperation: tourism, culture, and education and transportation links to have a solid foundation for future trade and investment cooperation in the region.

Vietnam-Laos-Cambodia attaches importance to developing cooperation and association within the framework of multilateral mechanisms, such as Asia-Europe Cooperation Forum (ASEM) (1996), Asia Pacific Economic Cooperation (APEC) (1989), Pacific Economic Cooperation Conference (PECC), ASEAN + 1 subregional cooperation (formed in the 70s and 80s of the last century), ASEAN + 3 (1997), Asian cooperation Dialogue (ACD) (2002), East Asia Summit (EAS) (2005)... which is a strong driving force to promote regional cooperation and integration in East Asia.

OUTLOOK FOR RELATIONS BETWEEN VIETNAM, LAOS, CAMBODIA AND THAILAND TILL 2030

Firstly, the politics and security-defense cooperation between four countries will continue to be maintained and expanded in the direction of cooperating with ASEAN to together solve non-traditional security issues such as countering terrorism, transnational crime, religious conflict and separatist movements, economic security, environmental security, human security, poverty, natural disasters... Political and security - defense cooperation between the four countries will take place both bilateral and multilateral, through ARF and outside the ARF framework. The countries and ASEAN have developed the ASEAN Security Community (ASC), later changed to ASEAN Political - Security Community (APSC) as one of the three pillars of politics - security, economy, socio- culture that plays an important role for peace and security in Southeast Asia and the whole Asia-Pacific region.

Secondly, it is cooperation and integration in the field of economy of the four countries. The countries want to integrate with other ASEAN countries in order to develop the ASEAN Economic Community (AEC) from now to 2030. The cooperation and integration of investment and finance are also an important priority direction between Vietnam - Laos - Cambodia and ASEAN, which will focus on strengthening and promoting investment and opening up capital markets more and less constraints to capital flows; faster implementation of AIA programme from now to 2020 and vision to 2030.

In order to create a breakthrough in economic integration, Vietnam - Laos - Cambodia together with ASEAN focus on implementing the rapid integration programme for 12 identified priority sectors. In the coming years, ASEAN will design to apply the principle of "majority" in combination with the principle of "10-X" and gradually implement the principle of "2 + X" that has been noted in the ASEAN Charter, Agreement CEPT, ASEAN Framework Decree, and in the SEOM conference. Besides, in the short and medium-term perspective, Vietnam - Laos - Cambodia and ASEAN countries remain prominent extrovert economic cooperation organizations. That is good at heavily export markets like Vietnam, Laos and Cambodia. That is also reason why promote the trend of some ASEAN countries, including Vietnam - Laos - Cambodia to seek Bilateral Free Trade Agreements (BFTA) with non-bloc countries. At the same time, Vietnam-Laos-Cambodia together with ASEAN have strengthened the function of dispute resolution in the region by strong sanctions and a regional institution is given full authority.

Third is cooperation and linking on culture - society, science - technology and environment. In the coming years, Vietnam, Laos, Cambodia, Thailand and ASEAN countries strongly focus on the implementation ASEAN Socio-Cultural Community (ASCC). Therefore, countries will invest a lot of resources in basic and advanced education, training, science and technology development, job creation and social protection. The cooperation will create conditions for qualified and skilled workers to freely find jobs and jobs in any country in the ASEAN community, contributing to making for ASEAN is not only a common market for trade but also a common market for goods production.

Besides, the countries and ASEAN have actively solved environmental issues, transnational pollution, poverty reduction, socio-economic inequality, Vietnam - Laos - Cambodia and Thailand. In the future, they are increasingly cooperating for building a healthy ASEAN without drugs, without pandemics; together act for an ASEAN spirit... to build and protect ASEAN together.

The cooperation on science and technology between Vietnam - Laos - Cambodia and Thailand will be promoted in the direction of: Regional coordination for scientific and technological research and exploitation on the basis of promotion the advantages of each countries; countries will together benefit from the whole region for the results of scientific and technological research and exploitation under the common principles and conditions; methods of managing and organizing to research science and technology on the principle of opening up the whole region, making countries comply with common regional regimes and standards, conducting scientific exchange and cooperation - technology in accordance with the general planning of the region, ensuring copyright for inventions and industrial property...

Conclusion

In the current period, in the face of rapid changes in the regional and global situation, especially the strong impact of globalization, Vietnam - Laos - Cambodia and Thailand have been promoting together policy of foreign affairs in directions of diversification and multilateralization in international relations, but still give high priority to the development of comprehensive relations between the four countries. Vietnam - Laos - Cambodia and Thailand relation is a dynamic and coherent political-economic entity playing an increasingly important role in ASEAN with achievements in the cooperation and linkages between four countries over the past time. Although facing still many great challenges, the relationship between Vietnam - Laos - Cambodia and Thailand is opening a new opportunity to upgrade to a new height, which is contributing to the realization of the construction and developing the ASEAN Community.

Based on achievements, the 4 countries are fully capable of strengthening and further developing the traditional friendship, special solidarity and comprehensive cooperation. In addition, the four countries active link in the implementation of bilateral and multilateral cooperation programmes and within the framework of cooperation in the Mekong sub-region. The relationship, solidarity and cooperation, mutual assistance between Vietnam - Laos - Cambodia and Thailand will continue to be strengthened and developed to both depth and width, practical and effective. In particular, Vietnam's position has been increasingly affirmed with great influence in the region, becoming an important link in regional and international relations.

Notes

1. Import and export reaches nearly 200 billion USD at https://customsnews.vn/import-and-export-reaches-nearly-200-billion-usd-1110.html
2. Laos-Vietnam trade over 1 billion USD in 2018 at http://www.xinhuanet.com/english/2019-01/11/c_137736223.htm
3. *Ibid.*
4. Ly Thi Tran and Simon Marginson, Internationalisation in Vietnamese Higher Education, Springer, 2018.

5. *Ibid.*
6. https://reliefweb.int/report/lao-peoples-democratic-republic/bomb-clearing-efforts-laos-slow-due-shortage-funds
7. https://www.vir.com.vn/vietnam-and-cambodia-target-5-billion-in-two-way-trade-turnover-70965.html
8. https://customsnews.vn/iron-and-steel-imported-significantly-from-china-while-heavily-exported-to-cambodia-12803.html
9. Vietnam and Cambodia target $5 billion in two-way trade turnover at https://www.vir.com.vn/vietnam-and-cambodia-target-5-billion-in-two-way-trade-turnover-70965.html
10. Vietnam Education Information Portal
11. Việt Nam-Cambodia joint victory commemorated at https://vietnamnews.vn/politics-laws/483248/viet-nam-cambodia-joint-victory-commemorated.html#2qtSWoY9iY8GLpBh.97
12. Vietnam, Cambodia boost postal, telecoms, ICT cooperationhttps://en.nhandan.org.vn/scitech/sci-tech/item/7242102-vietnam-cambodia-boost-postal-telecoms-ict-cooperation.html
13. https://www.wemakescholars.com/scholarships-for-cambodian-students-to-study-in-vietnam
14. Davenport, T. (2014). Southeast Asian Approaches to Maritime Boundaries. Asian Journal of International Law, 4(2), 309-357. doi:10.1017/S2044251313000313
15. https://customsnews.vn/thailand-vietnams-largest-trade-partner-in-asean-8414.html
16. https://vietnamnews.vn/economy/568987/fdi-inflows-into-viet-nam-surge-in-11-months.html
17. https://theaseanpost.com/article/rise-vietnams-tourism
18. https://theaseanpost.com/article/what-clv-development-triangle-area
19. Ibid.
20. Greater Mekong Subregion (GMS) at https://www.adb.org/countries/gms/main
21. http://www.mrcmekong.org/news-and-events/news/mrc-launches-new-website-3rd-summit/
22. http://www.mrcmekong.org/news-and-events/speeches/mrc-hua-hin-declaration/
23. http://www.mfa.go.th/main/en/news3/6886/90570-BANGKOK-DECLARATION-OF-THE-8TH-AYEYAWADY-%E2%80%93-CHAO-PH.html
24. Chap Sotharith, Development Strategy For CLMV in The Age of Economic Integration At http://www.eria.org/RPR-2007-4.pdf
25. https://issuu.com/livetradingnews/docs/aseanreport

References

1. Nguyen Hoang Giap, Nguyen Huu Cat and Nguyen Thi Que: *Current ASEAN cooperation, linking and participation of Vietnam*, Political theory Publishing House, Hanoi, 2008 (from p. 13 to p. 57; p. 145-p. 175).
   (Nguyễn Hoàng Giáp, Nguyễn Hữu Cát, Nguyễn Thị Quế: *Hợp tác liên kết ASEAN hiện nay và sự tham gia của Việt Nam*, Nxb. Lý luận chính trị, Hà Nội, 2008 (từ tr.13 đến tr.57; tr.145-tr.175).
2. Nguyen Hoang Giap, Nguyen Thi Que (Editor), *Vietnam joined ASEAN from 1995 up to now: Achievements, problems and prospects*, Political theory Publishing House, 2012.

(Nguyễn Hoàng Giáp, Nguyễn Thị Quế (Chủ biên), *Việt Nam gia nhập ASEAN từ năm 1995 đến nay: Thành tựu, vấn đề và triển vọng*, Nxb. Chính trị quốc gia, Hà Nội, 2012).

3. Nguyen Hoang Giap, Nguyen Thi Que, *Vietnam Foreign Policy in the Renovation Period*, Political theory Publishing House, 2013.
   (Nguyễn Hoàng Giáp, Nguyễn Thị Quế, *Chính sách đối ngoại Việt Nam thời kỳ đổi mới*, Nxb. Lý luận chính trị, Hà Nội, 2013).
4. Nguyen Hoang Giap, Nguyen Thi Que, Mai Hoai Anh (Editor), The relationship between independence, autonomy and international integration in Vietnam today: Theoretical and practical issues, Political theory Publishing House, Hanoi, 2015.
   (Nguyễn Hoàng Giáp, Nguyễn Thị Quế, Mai Hoài Anh (Chủ biên), Mối quan hệ giữa độc lập, tự chủ và hội nhập quốc tế ở Việt Nam hiện nay: Những vấn đề lý luận và thực tiễn, Nxb. Lý luận chính trị, Hà Nội, 2015).
5. Vu Duong Ninh (Editor), *Vietnam in the changing world*, Hanoi National University Publishing House, Hanoi, 2017.
   (Vũ Dương Ninh (Chủ biên), Việt Nam trong thế giới đang đổi thay, Nxb. Đại học Quốc gia Hà Nội, 2017).
6. Nguyen Thi Que (Editor), *Foreign policy of big countries in the current period*, Hanoi National Political Publishing House, Hanoi, 2015.
   (Nguyễn Thị Quế (Chủ biên), *Chính sách đối ngoại của các nước lớn trong giai đoạn hiện nay*, Nxb Chính trị quốc gia, Hà Nội, 2015).
7. Nguyen Xuan Son, Thai Van Long, (chief editor), *Foreign relations of ASEAN countries*, Hanoi National Political Publishing House, Hanoi, 1997 (from p. 122 to p. 136).
   (Nguyễn Xuân Sơn, Thái Văn Long, (chủ biên), *Quan hệ đối ngoại của các nước ASEAN*, Nxb Chính trị quốc gia, Hà Nội, 1997 (từ tr.122 đến tr.136).
8. Nguyen Hong Son, ASEAN Economic Community (AEC) - Content and Roadmap, Social Sciences Publishing House, Hanoi, 2011 (p. 71-102, p. 127).
   (Nguyễn Hồng Sơn, *Cộng đồng kinh tế ASEAN (AEC) - Nội dung và lộ trình*, Nxb Khoa học xã hội, Hà Nội, 2011 (tr.71-102, tr.127).

11 The Relationship Between Vietnam and Regional and International Organizations

Van-Huong Le and Thi-Hong-Hoa Vu

ASEAN and Vietnam's Participation

General information about ASEAN

The Association of Southeast Asian Nations (ASEAN) was established on August 8, 1967 with five initial members (Thailand, Indonesia, Malaysia, Singapore, and the Philippines) and gradually developed into a comprehensive and co-operative organization, including all the ten Southeast Asian countries. Currently, ASEAN is transforming itself into a new development stage, officially becoming the ASEAN Community on December 31, 2015, aiming to build a "*tolerant, law-based, people-oriented, taking people as a center* Community" that is on the legal basis of the ASEAN Charter[1] and ASEAN Community Vision 2025[2].

Community formation is not only meaningful for ASEAN's governments but also brings many practical benefits to ASEAN's people. For Vietnam, the Community formation is important because this event marks the 20-year journey of Vietnam to join ASEAN and international integration. ASEAN Community has entered its fourth year of implementation and is in the midst of implementing the ASEAN Community Vision 2025, with a focus on implementing Master Plans on all three pillars: *the Political-Security Community, the Economic Community and the Socio-Cultural Community*; expanding and deepening foreign relations, strengthening ASEAN's central role in the regional structure that is shaping; strengthening connectivity and narrowing the development gap through the Master Plan on ASEAN Connectivity (MPAC) 2025 and Initiative for ASEAN Integration IAI Work Plan III (2016-2020). Up to now, (2019), ASEAN has achieved some encouraging results on all three pillars of the Community[3]. Economic growth of member countries continued to be stable, expected GDP in 2019 reached 4.9%, total GDP was estimated at USD 3,000 billion[4].

In 2019, ASEAN continues to promote cooperation and association under the theme of "*Promoting partnerships for sustainability*" on the basis of promoting the results achieved in previous years. Specific priorities for implementing the Topic of the Year include: *Political – security:* strengthening

ASEAN capacity to address security challenges such as terrorism, transnational crime and cyber security; increasing diplomatic capacity to prevent, promote cooperation in border management, maritime cooperation, diplomatic and defence cooperation, sustainable security. *Economics:* focusing on ASEAN digitization, adaptation with the industrial revolution 4.0, strengthening connectivity, facilitating trade, services, investment, sustainable economic development, completing RCEP negotiations, linking regional initiatives. *Socio-culture:* promoting cooperation towards people and ensuring human security through cooperation programmes on social welfare, environmental protection, disaster management and response to change climate, promoting lifelong education, promotion ASEAN cultural identity, promoting cooperation to adapt to population aging, developing human resources to meet the requirements of the industrial revolution 4.0.

In addition, ASEAN continues to implement an opening foreign policy, striving for maintaining a balanced relationship, mutually beneficial cooperation with its Partners, actively strengthening the mechanisms initiated and chaired by ASEAN, contribute to strengthen opening, transparent, rule-based regional structures with ASEAN as a central role. Accordingly, the ASEAN and the EU agreed with upgrading relations to become Strategic Partners on the principle (at the 22nd ASEAN-EU Foreign Ministerial Meeting, January 2019); actively implementing the strategic partnership with Russia (upgrading the ASEAN-Russia Summit in November 2018), successfully organizing activities within the ASEAN-Japan Day in Vietnam (June/2019); actively preparing for High Level to celebrate 30 years of ASEAN-Korea relations (November 2019); cooperating under the theme of ASEAN-China Media Year 2019. ASEAN has adopted the documents of ASEAN's common views on the Indo-Pacific, especially to complete the first draft document of Code of Conduct (COC) on the East Sea at the ASEAN Foreign Ministers' Meeting and the partner countries from July 29 to August 3, 2019. This is the basis to promote self-reliance and the central role of ASEAN in the context of increased strategic competition among powers.

However, ASEAN still faces to many challenges from both inside and outside: the level of cohesion, operational efficiency of limited apparatus; the internal status of member countries is still complicated with the impact of strategic competition between powers and limited ability to solve issues affecting the region. Issues such as the situation of Rakhine State, Myanmar, East Sea (SCS) are still the hot point attracting attention of outside powers to this region. This threatens to ASEAN's solidarity, unity and centrality. The increasing competition, friction between major countries on the one hand creates location for ASEAN, but on the other hand, also places the central role of ASEAN and the mechanisms led by ASEAN in the new challenges. Intra-ASEAN economic links are still lax, the process of negotiating the Regional Comprehensive Economic Partnership (RCEP) is still difficult, not easy to achieve the target by the end of 2019 as planned.

Vietnam's participation and its role in ASEAN

Vietnam officially joined ASEAN on July 28, 1995 on the occasion of the 28th ASEAN Foreign Ministers' Meeting (AMM-28) in Brunei. However, the process of participating in ASEAN has been started before, namely: in July 1992, Vietnam joined the Treaty of Amity and Cooperation in Southeast Asia (TAC) and became an observer of ASEAN; since 1993 Vietnam participated in regular consultation meetings with ASEAN on the occasion of the ASEAN Foreign Ministers' Meeting, participating in ASEAN cooperation programmes and projects in five areas: science - technology, environment, health, culture - information, social development. In 1994 Vietnam became one of the original members of the ASEAN Regional Forum (ARF), the first regional forum to discuss political and security issues played key role by ASEAN.

The decision to join ASEAN was the first breakthrough step of Vietnam's regional and international integration process. ASEAN has always been a pillar, a strategic priority in Vietnam's independent, autonomous, multilateral and diversified foreign policy. The 12th National Party Congress once again affirmed the policy and guideline "Proactive, positive and responsible with ASEAN countries to build a strong Community". For more than two decades participating in ASEAN cooperation, Vietnam plays a pivotal role in determining the goals and formation of major ASEAN decisions; has an important contribution to ASEAN's general and strong development as following:

Vietnam has contributed to ASEAN expansion. Immediately after joining, Vietnam has actively promoted admission of Cambodia, Laos and Myanmar into ASEAN, fulfilled the idea of an ASEAN including 10 Southeast Asian countries, and created new changes in dialogue within ASEAN and addressing regional issues. Besides, Vietnam successfully organized the 6th ASEAN Summit in Hanoi (December 15-16, 1998) with important results, including the Hanoi Action Programme, contributing to development orientation of the Association and overcome the regional financial crisis at that time. Subsequently, the relevant Ministries, branches as well as the National Assembly and people's Organizations have also hosted the successful organization of many important conferences/activities of ASEAN at different levels and sectors, contributing to part promoting ASEAN cooperation. In particular, Vietnam has successfully completed the role of ASEAN President in 2010 with great and substantive results, contributing to promoting the "enforcement culture" and concretizing an important step to form ASEAN Community 2015 as well as enhancing the role of ASEAN.

In addition, Vietnam coordinates with member countries to build other important orientations and decisions of ASEAN such as ASEAN Vision 2020 (1997) and ASEAN Vision 2025 (2015); Declaration ASEAN Concord II (2003), formation of the ASEAN Community, ASEAN Charter (2007), Roadmap for ASEAN Community (2009-2015); Master Plan on ASEAN Connectivity (MPAC) and the Initiative for ASEAN Integration (IAI) on narrowing the development gap; successfully undertook important rotating missions in ASEAN such as the

Chairman of 6th ASEAN Summit (1998), Chairman of the ASEAN Standing Committee (2000-2001), actively coordinating relations between ASEAN and important partners such as the US, Russia, EU, India and now Japan; important contributions to the process of formation, expansion and consolidation of institutions chaired by ASEAN such as the East Asia Summit (EAS), the ASEAN Defense Ministers Meeting Plus (ADMM +) etc.

From 2016 up to now, ASEAN's successes have made a significant contribution to Vietnam, especially contributing to the early implementation of ASEAN Community Vision 2025 in order to make ASEAN links become more extensive and play a more important role in the region. The relevant Ministries and Agencies in Vietnam have developed projects, programmes and plans to implement ASEAN's Vision and Master Plans with of the three pillars. Notably, Vietnam actively launched many new proposals and developed its role in ASEAN, received the acclaim and support of another countries, including the adoption Declaration of ASEAN Regional Forum (ARF) on strengthening cooperation between maritime law enforcement forces; completing the list of 26 priorities activities to implement the ASEAN-India Action Plan for 2016-2018; chairing negotiations on ASEAN-Japan Comprehensive Economic Partnership Agreement; chairing the Investment Group representing ASEAN in the negotiations for the Regional Comprehensive Economic Partnership Agreement (RCEP); chairing and co-chairing many activities such as 12th ASEAN Ministerial Meeting on Health, Senior Officials Meeting and Joint Working Group on DOC Declaration, ASEAN Traffic Police Forum... On the basis of Vietnam-Laos special friendship, Vietnam has actively supported Laos to successfully undertake ASEAN Chairmanship 2016.

In the context that ASEAN is under influence of many factors on solidarity, prestige and position in the region, Vietnam has made efforts to consolidate solidarity, unity and the role of ASEAN in regional issues, in handling traditional and non-traditional security challenges, as well as problems arising in relationships with partners; and at the same time promoting practical cooperation in important regional mechanisms and forums initiated and led by ASEAN, such as the East Asia Summit (EAS), the ASEAN Regional Forum (ARF), and ASEAN Defense Ministers Meeting Plus (ADMM +). In the East Sea issue, Vietnam actively exchanged and coordinated with other countries to create consensus in ASEAN and between ASEAN and its partners on ASEAN's role and the common interests of all the countries in order to maintain peace, stability, security, maritime and air safety in the East Sea; promote the East Sea issue in ASEAN documents and conferences with positive content; emphasize the full and effective implementation of the DOC Declaration and soon complete Code of Conduct COC.

Besides, Vietnam has been in the forefront of regional economic integration, being one of the two countries with the highest implementing rate of commitments in the Master Plan to build the ASEAN Economic Community (AEC) (with 95.5%, second to Singapore). Vietnam is also actively involved in promoting the development/implementation of intra-regional economic cooperation agreements between ASEAN and its Partners; contributing collabourative initiatives in areas such as supporting small, medium and micro enterprises; trade facilitation, e-commerce development, strengthening connectivity and narrowing the development gap in ASEAN. In addition, Vietnam actively participates in and proposes practical cooperation initiatives aimed at the people, including contents on social welfare, support for vulnerable people, education, health, disease prevention, environmental protection, climate change response and at the same time actively promote propaganda and promotion of ASEAN among the people.

Currently, the situation in the world and the region is posing many new challenges and requirements for ASEAN like that to consolidate solidarity and unity; to maintain a central role and create new momentum and vitality for Community. Therefore, ASEAN must improve on institutions, enhance efficiency and renew cooperation contents to express the vitality and bright future of the Community. Vietnam is willing to contribute in all aspects, affirming the image of a prestigious, proactive, active and responsible member under the common roof. In order to realize the ASEAN Vision 2025, Vietnam will continue to further promote its role, promote real cooperation areas, bring specific benefits to each member state's people; actively implement and integrate Master Plans in ASEAN Vision into specific action programmes of ministries, branches and localities on international integration; make appropriate investment in resources and further promote propaganda, raise awareness so that the ASEAN Community is more and more attached and close to every citizen and business; and above all, to maintain solidarity, unity and values principles that have made ASEAN's identity and success.

Relations between Vietnam and the United Nations

Overview of the United Nations organization

The United Nations (UN) was officially established on October 24, 1945 when the UN Charter was ratified by China, France, the former Soviet Union, the United Kingdom, the United States of America and the majority of signatory nations. Immediately after the devastating destruction during the World War II, the lofty mission specified in the UN Charter is to prevent the scourge of war. In order to fulfill that mission, member states set the UN's primary goal to maintain international peace and security, and to identify other important goals for UN operations to strengthen friendly relations among nations; to promote cooperation to solve international issues related to economics, societies, culture, humanitarian issues and human rights. Countries also give the UN a central role to regulate the actions of nationalities towards those common goals.

The establishment of the UN reflects the burning desire on the world of peace, stability and overall development of nationalities who had just undergone suffering due to wars, while also reflecting new volume force comparisons, that is the rise of the Soviet Union and the United States become the two poles of the world.

Up till now, the UN has undergone 70 years of development, becoming the most extensive global organization with the participation of almost all of the planet's independent nations. The role and activities of the UN are expanded in all aspects, its efforts to work towards implementing the goals and objectives have been set, thereby bringing positive and great impacts on international life and each ethnic group.

From the 51 member states when it was founded, the UN now has 193 member states and becomes a comprehensive system consisting 6 main agencies[5], many auxiliary agencies, 20 professional organizations and 5 economic – society Committees that is located in regions, dozens of funds and programmes, operating in all areas from conflict resolution and prevention, disarmament and non-dissemination, anti-terrorism, protection of the tyranny accident, environmental protection and sustainable development, promoting democracy, human rights, gender equality, economic and social development.

With important achievements, the UN is recognized by the international community as a global organization that plays a very important role in international political life and is an indispensable foundation for a peaceful, more prosperous and fair world.

After 70 years of operation, the UN has proven itself to be the largest, most diverse, reputable and large-scale global organization. This good result reflects the aspirations and persistent struggles of peoples and progressive forces who wish for a world of peace, cooperation and development, at the same time rooted in the urgent demands of the multilateral cooperation to be able to cope with major global challenges. Countries and groups of countries always attach importance to this mechanism in promoting their interests and implementing foreign policies. However, due to the process of UN formation and development reflecting the context and comparing forces around the world, affected by the interests of nations, besides financial difficulties and resource mobilization force, so the UN's operational efficiency in many areas is limited, unable to respond to new global changes and challenges as well as changes in the comparison of internal forces, especially the increase in number of members, in some cases ineffective, lack of transparency, abuse and application of double standards to pressure and intervene. The main challenges facing the UN are: challenges to the reputation of the UN; challenges in undertaking international peace and security maintenance after the Cold War; challenges in solving global issues such as poverty, debt, development gap, habitat degradation, population explosion, dangerous diseases and epidemics, as well as transnational crime activities.

In this situation, the reform of the United Nations in a comprehensive and systematic manner, in accordance with the new international situation, is an objective requirement. So far, the members have agreed that the UN should be reformed to strengthen its role, efficiency and democratization. The UN reform includes three main contents: Reform of the UN apparatus (the General Assembly, the Security Council, the Economic and Social Council, and the

Trusteeship Council, International Court of Justice,), reorganizing the Secretariat and working methods of the UN. The issue of development and implementation of the UN Millennium Development Goals.

Looking back 70 years of existence and development, the UN has experienced history with many ups and downs; beside limitations, UN achievements are outstanding. The UN increasingly proves itself to be an indispensable organization in world politics. The growth of the UN is due to the right goals in accordance with the aspirations of peace, independence, development and social progress of the peoples.

Relations between Vietnam and the United Nations

Vietnam officially joined the United Nations (UN) on September 20, 1977. Since then, Vietnam's relations with the UN have been growing. Immediately after joining the UN, Vietnam enlisted the support and approval of the UN member states to the UN General Assembly 32 (1977) ratifying Resolution 32/2 calling on countries and international aid organization for helping Vietnam to rebuild after the war. On the other hand, Vietnam also committed itself to contribute funds, capital, personnel assistance and technology of the UN to serve the socio-economic development of the country. The UN became a forum for Vietnam to implement the requirements of foreign policy.

Vietnam's becoming a member of the United Nations has an important political-legal significance, affirming the full position of an independent, united Vietnam in the international arena, opening a new era for implementing external activities in general and multilateral foreign affairs in particular. The position and role of Vietnam at the UN has increasingly improved. Vietnam has also actively and positively coordinated with non-aligned and developing countries to protect the basic principles of the UN Charter such as the principle of sovereignty equality, non-intervention internal work of other countries, not usage or threaten the usage of force and protect the interests of developing countries, including Vietnam. Vietnam enters a new stage of development, promoting this relationship and further improving the effectiveness of the use of UN resources to directly serve socio-economic development goals is very necessary.

The process of Vietnam joining the UN can be divided into the following stages:

Period 1977-1986: Vietnam officially joined the UN in 1977, but some international organizations have provided aid to Vietnam since 1975. During this period, Vietnam had to deal with severe consequences of the war, to reorganize the poor and backward economy and step by step restore production. The UN has actively helped Vietnam address many multifaceted difficulties with a total aid of more than US $ 500 million[6]. Major donor organizations include: United Nations Development Programme (UNDP), World Food Programme (WFP), United Nations Children's Fund (UNICEF), United Nations Population Fund (UNFPA), and United Nations High Commissioner for Refugees (UNHCR), and the World Health Organization

(WHO). These organizations have significantly supported the investment of the Vietnamese Government in social development issues, focusing in the areas of education, health, care and protection, mothers and children health, and population and family planning.

Cooperation with the UN has contributed favourable conditions to improve the level of technology and promoting science and technology acumen in Vietnam, recovering and building a number of production facilities, increasing the capacity of development. At the same time, in the context of embargoes, cooperation with the UN facilitates for Vietnam to access to aid from many Western countries.

Period 1986-1996: In this period, Vietnam implemented the renovation policy in which the most important task was to carry out economic policy and social policy reform. Until the end of the 1980s, the UN accounted for nearly 60% of total aid to Vietnam, except from socialist countries. During this period, UN grants to Vietnam reached over USD 630 million. Since the early 1990s, many countries in the Organization for Economic Cooperation and Development (OECD), international and regional financial institutions resumed aid to Vietnam, but the UN still accounts for 30% of external technical assistance.

During this period, a number of organizations have raised support levels such as the International Fund for Agricultural Development (IFAD), the United Nations Educational, Scientific and Cultural Organization (UNESCO), the United Nations Industrial Development Organization (UNIDO). A number of other organizations have also started direct aid activities such as the UN Drug Control Programme (UNDCP), the United Nations Environment Programme (UNEP), the International Labour Organization (ILO) and more countries as well as monetary and financial institutions such as the World Bank (WB), International Monetary Fund (IMF), Asian Development Bank (ADB) participating in various types of multi-bilateral mixed projects.

Collabourative projects are a significant source of support for Vietnam in building development policies, improving the management capacity of agencies and staff qualifications in the process of implementing innovation policies. At the same time, the UN continues to make valuable contributions to improving production technology skills, developing scientific and technical human resources, and addressing other social issues of Vietnam.

Period 1997-2011: During the period 1997-2000, the UN gave priority to the areas of poverty reduction and social policies; development reform and management; environmental and natural resource management; and aid coordination, state management and resource mobilization.

In the 2001-2005 period, the UN has three main priorities: furthering reform, poverty reduction and sustainable development. At Vietnam Government's request, the UN strongly shifted technical assistance to support reforms in economic policies and institutions, state-owned enterprises, public administration, law, and early planning for public investment, banking system development, and expanding into other areas like HIV/AIDS prevention and other dangerous diseases; support the implementation of grassroots democratic regulations, implementation of equal rights for men and women, organizing annual Consultative Group meetings on donors, etc. The main priorities in this period are to promote reform and consultancy in the development or revision of many important laws, poverty reduction, support for the implementation of Programme 135, integration with the implementation of the Millennium Development Goals (MDGs), to support in efforts forces to protect nature, to raise people's awareness about the environment, to develop strategies and policies, to improve natural resource management capacity, environmental management and biodiversity. In the period of 2006-2011, UN aid to Vietnam reached over 400 million USD[7]. During the period of 2007-2011, Vietnam Government wanted to implement multilateral foreign policy, diversify international relations, make friends with all countries, so Vietnam took advantage of the United Nations forum as a basis to strengthen relations with organizations in the United Nations system, expand bilateral and multilateral relations with countries and international organizations. The most outstanding activity during this period was that Vietnam successfully completed its duties as a non-permanent member of the UN Security Council for the 2008-2009. This is the first time Vietnam has joined the UN's most important agency on international peace and security in the context that the UN Security Council must deal with massive workloads due to the emergence of complex security issues. In addition, there are new global security challenges and the negative impact of the most severe global financial-economic crisis in modern world history.

Vietnam actively negotiated and became an official member of the Chemical Weapons Convention (CWC) in 1998, participated in negotiations and was one of the first countries to sign the Comprehensive Nuclear Test Ban Treaty (CTBT) in 1996, joined and became a member of the Disarmament Conference (CD) in 1996. In addition, Vietnam soon participated in the preparation process for major conferences such as the NPT Review Conference 2000, 2005 and 2010; Conference on fighting small arms illegal trade in 2001, 2003 etc.

Vietnam also participates in UN policy-making mechanisms, such as serving Vietnam's position as Vice President of the UN General Assembly in 1997, joining the United Nations Economic and Social Council (ECOSOC) (1998-2000).

Vietnam not only performs well the task of attracting aid from UN development organizations but also actively builds forms of cooperation and participation in these organizations. The tripartite cooperation model (initially between Vietnam, FAO and Senegal on rice cultivation) has been expanded and applied widely, considered a model for South-South cooperation. Vietnam are also actively involved in the UN system through being a member of the Executive Board of UNDP/UNFPA (term 2000-2002), ECOSOC (1998-2000). During this period, Vietnam actively coordinated with UN development organizations to implement the "One UN" pilot initiative, highly appreciated by the donor community.

Period 2012-2016: Within the framework of the Unified Action Initiative – Delivery as One UN (DaO), the Government of Vietnam and the UN are actively coordinating the implementation of the next UN One Plan for the period of 2012-2016, in accordance with the draft Socio-Economic Development Plan (SEDP) and Vietnam's Socio-Economic Development Strategy (SEDS). This general plan prioritizes three main areas: quality of growth, social protection and access to social services; enhancing voice and improving public governance. An important component of the Unified Action Initiative - One UN is a Common Home, concretized by the construction of the One United Nations Green House in Hanoi. This is the first environmentally friendly UN House, inaugurated on the occasion of UN Secretary General Ban Ki-Moon visiting Vietnam in May 2015. As one of the eight pilot countries implementing the Unified Action Initiative in the world, this initiative of Vietnam has contributed to improving operational efficiency and strengthening the systematic cohesion of UN organizations in Vietnam in general.

Since January 1, 2014, Vietnam has officially become a member of the Human Rights Council (2014-2016). In June 2014, Vietnam for the first time sent forces to participate in UN peacekeeping activities. Currently, Vietnam is taking the role of ECOSOC member for the 2016-2018.

The cooperation between Vietnam and the UN is a good example of development cooperation between UN member states as well as on the role of the UN in promoting international cooperation to address economic and social issues as well as culture and humane. Although the total amount of UN aid to Vietnam over the past 30 years has been just over USD 2 billion, it has been enormously significant because the UN focuses on supporting many essential areas of economic development and building institutions, laws, solving many urgent social issues. The UN has also assisted Vietnam in the most difficult periods after the war in the context of encirclement and embargo. This cooperation has achieved good results and positive effects, meeting the requirements of Vietnam on socio-economic development in each period. These results will facilitate the joint efforts of Vietnam and the UN to overcome the shortcomings, expand and improve the effectiveness of cooperation on both sides, actively support the industrialization and modernization of Vietnam and contribute to improving the role of the UN in the new period.

Period 2017-2019 and Strategic Plan to 2021 - The New Joint One Strategic Plan for the 2017-2021 period between Vietnam and the United Nations (Cooperation programme in the framework of the One UN Initiative) was signed on July 5, 2017. This programme focuses on supporting the Government of Vietnam in implementing the Socio-Economic Development Plan for 2016-2020 and Sustainable Development Goals (SDGs). The programme includes four priority areas: *Investing in People; Ensuring adaptation to Climate Change and sustainable environmental development; Promoting Prosperity and Partnership; Strengthen Justice, Peace and Comprehensive Administration.* The total budget of this Programme is expected to be 423,348,650 USD, of which 96,254,080 USD from the regular budget; 68,135,684 USD from other funding sources and 258,958,886 USD need to continue to mobilize[8].

Vietnam has been actively involved in the development and implementation of UN international treaties as well as on joint efforts to promote the UN's role as a fair, effective and equitable global multilateral institution what responses to the common aspirations of mankind. In 2017, Vietnam is one of the first 52 countries to sign the Treaty on the Prohibition of Nuclear Weapons and in 2018, Vietnam is the 10th country to ratify this Treaty. Vietnam has also sent 27 military officers and is preparing to send a second-level field hospital to participate in UN peacekeeping activities. Vietnam has officially been elected as a non-permanent member of the UN Security Council for the term 2020-2021 and in 5/2018 has been unanimously nominated by the Asia-Pacific Group as a candidate of the Group in this position (election took place in June 2019).

On June 7, 2019, at the United Nations Headquarters in New York, USA, the United Nations General Assembly elected Vietnam as a non-permanent member of the Security Council for 2020-2021 term with a record high number of votes - 192/193 votes. This is an important recognition and appreciation of the international community for Vietnam's role and contribution to international and regional work; expressing Vietnam's position and prestige in the international arena. With 15 members including 10 non-permanent members, the Security Council is one of the six main organs of the United Nations, given the leading responsibility for maintaining international peace and security. Following the first term in 2008-2009, this is the second time Vietnam has been elected as a member of this agency. Vietnam's decision to stand for a Security Council comes from peaceful foreign policy, respect and a strong commitment to UN goals and a desire to contribute more to the joint efforts of the international community to promote the role of the UN in international political life, especially in maintaining international peace and security. With the desire to truly become a *'Partner for Sustainable Peace"*, in the next two-year term, Vietnam will have the opportunity to proactively propose, promote its initiatives, to have an independent voice, autonomy, respect for cooperation and dialogue with all member states, reflecting the interests of countries in the activities of the Security Council; actively contribute to the Security Council to be more transparent and effective in maintaining peace and security in the world. As a rule, Vietnam will officially assume the role of non-permanent member of the UN Security Council from January 1, 2020.

Vietnam's Relationship with APEC

General information about APEC

The Asia-Pacific Economic Cooperation Forum (APEC) was established in 1989 with the goal of strengthening the economic and political ties between member economies of the Pacific District. Through 30 years of establishment and development, APEC continues to affirm as a leading regional economic integration mechanism, taking initiative and leading to promote the trend of economic liberalization, trade and investment in the region and around the world, making an important contribution to economic growth and maintaining peace, stability, cooperation and development in the Asia-Pacific region. APEC cooperation focuses on three main pillars: trade liberalization and investment, business facilitation and economic-technical cooperation. APEC's most important and transparent commitment to date, adopted at the Second Summit (Indonesia, 1994), is to fulfill the initial Bogor objectives on trade and free and open investment for developed member economics in 2010 and developing member economies in 2020.

Among the 21 APEC members[9], there are 3 largest economies in the world, 9 members of the 20 major economies (G20) and many emerging and dynamic development economies, representing about 39% of the world's population, contributing 59% of GDP and 49% of global trade[10].

APEC operates on the principle of consensus, voluntary and non-constraint; no Charter or no regulations. APEC uses the concept "economy"; senior leaders of members are collectively referred to as economic leaders.

APEC's annual activities include: Summits; the Inter-ministerial Minister for Foreign Affairs and Economic Affairs Conferences specialized on trade, finance, small and medium enterprises and other areas such as structural reform, human resource development, tourism, food security, women and economy, health, energy, transport transportation, information and communication; 5 Senior Officials Meetings, with many conferences and seminars of Committees, Working Groups and other working-level mechanisms under government, scholar and enterprise channels.

Up till now, APEC has achieved many outstanding and substantial achievements on all three pillars of cooperation: *Regarding trade liberalization and investment:* from 1989 to 2015, the total value of APEC trade increased 7 times from nearly 3 trillion USD to about USD 20 trillion, the average tax rate of the region decreased nearly 3 times from 17% to 5.6%[11]; *Regarding business facilitation*: the cost of commercial transactions in the region decreased significantly through 5% reductions in 2006, 2010 and 10% in 2015[12]; *Economic and technical cooperation*: Each year, APEC provides funding for about 150 cooperation projects and developing capacity with a total value of up to USD 23 million.[13]

Entering the fourth decade of development when the world is in the context of fast and profound changes under the impacts of the fourth industrial revolution, APEC is currently implementing major cooperation strategies and programmess including: Quality Growth Strategy to 2020, the new Agenda for Structural Reform (RAASR) to 2020, the Services Competiveness Roadmap to 2025, the Overall Connection Plan to 2025, the comprehensive development agenda on economy and finance, society to 2030, the framework for human resource development in the digital era to 2025. Members are discussing to build APEC Vision after 2020 to contribute to maintaining the region's role, to be a driving force and global economic integration, improving operational efficiency, affirming status as leading economic forum in Asia-Pacific, orienting activities towards people and businesses more and more.

In a hyper-connected world, Asia-Pacific continues to be a leading dynamic development center, with an important strategic geographic and geo-economic location, a driving force of growth and linking the global economy, a key political center of the world. As the leading mechanism of economic integration in the Asia-Pacific region, APEC continues to pioneer to promote trade, investment, connectivity and promote strongly leadership in global economic management, implement Sustainable Development Goals by 2030 and respond to common challenges. Entering the fourth development decade, given the rapid and profound changes of the world and region, under the strong impact of the fourth industrial revolution, APEC is transforming fundamentally, increasingly expanding its co-operation in a more practical way, for the benefit of people and businesses.

Participation in APEC and Vietnam's role

On November 14, 1998, in the capital of Kuala Lumpur, Malaysia, Vietnam officially became a member of the Asia-Pacific Economic Cooperation Forum (APEC). This event marked an important step in the process of international economic integration of Vietnam as well as a premise to increase Vietnam international economic integration to the global level with joining the World Trade Organization (WTO) in 2007. Joining APEC also shows Vietnam's determination to actively contribute to promoting peace, stability, cooperation, and trade and investment liberalization in the region.

Since joining APEC, Vietnam's per capita income has increased more than 5 times, from US $ 363 in 1997 to US $ 2,300[14]. On a broader scale, in the past 35 years, the world has experienced an increase in material wealth and a reduction in income inequality at an unprecedented level. This is mainly a result of the integration process of nations into the global economy, a remarkable achievement. Globally, humanity has lost about 1900 years to double its income from about $ 500 to $ 1,200[15]. While some people are fortunate to live in countries with earlier double income levels, the key is that in most modern history, the people' living level in the world has remained almost unchanged for centuries. This achievement is due to the stable environment established with the efforts of regional and global institutions. While ASEAN builds awareness of respect for existing territories, APEC and other global institutions further promote market opening. In addition, processes in Asia-Pacific have fundamentally created confidence so that governments tend to reform firmly in pursuit of agendas, on the basis of realizing that this is a general status of countries.

Global trade reform and participation has helped Vietnam achieve an average annual income increase of more than 5% to become a current middle-income economy and is expected to achieve a high average income (over $ 20 America one day) in 2026, 40 years after the beginning of the renovation. At the time of reform, Vietnam's per capita income is equivalent to that of other "slow" countries such as Cambodia and Laos. After 30 years of innovation and integration, Vietnam's per capita income is significantly higher than those of the two countries and is rapidly catching up with some ASEAN founding members. The possibility of this forecast becomes a reality depending on both Vietnam's reform process as well as a favourable external environment.

In the process of accompanying APEC, Vietnam has made active and proactive contributions of Vietnam to the APEC Forum, contributing to promoting peace, stability, cooperation, regional economic integration and maintenance. APEC's role is the leading economic linkage mechanism in Asia-Pacific. In particular, the most outstanding thing is that Vietnam is one of the few members who have twice successfully assumed the role of APEC homeowners (2006 and 2017).

As the chair of Vietnam, at the High-Level Week in November 2006 in Hanoi, APEC Leaders for the first time identified the prospect of forming the Asia-Pacific Free Trade Area. Ocean (FTAAP). This is an important decision, laying the foundation for the strategic vision of regional economic integration. At the same time, the Hanoi Action Programme aims to implement the GoGo Goals, the APEC Comprehensive Reform Package, cooperation commitments on human security, human resource development, structural reform, and support. Assisting the developing members to improve their integration capabilities... are also considered as timely and effective solutions to APEC issues faced at that time. The results of the 2006 APEC Year with the spirit of "Towards an active community for sustainable development and prosperity" have contributed to creating more impetus to boost APEC cooperation in a more effective and dynamic way.

Nearly 11 years later, in 2017, Vietnam was trusted by members to host APEC for the second time. This responsibility puts us ahead of many challenges, especially in the context of 2017 being considered as one of the most difficult times for the Forum, with the strong rise of protectionism, populism, and combating inequalities under globalization as well as challenges of climate change, social inequality, and aging population. In such a difficult context, with bravery and intelligence, with determination and consensus, Vietnam have organized outstanding success in the 2017 APEC Year with nearly 250 events, culminating in the 25th APEC High Week in the dynamic and modern coastal city of Danang.

"*Doi Moi*" and participation in global trade have helped Vietnam achieve an average annual income increase of more than 5% to become a current middle-income economy and is expected to achieve a high average income (over 20 USD/day) in 2026, 40 years after the "*Doi Moi*". At the beginning of "*Doi Moi*", Vietnam's per capita income is equivalent to other "slow" countries such as Cambodia and Laos. After 30 years of "*Doi Moi*" and integration, Vietnam's per capita income is significantly higher than Cambodia and Laos, and is rapidly catching up with some ASEAN founding member countries. The possibility of this forecast becomes a reality depending on both Vietnam's reform process as well as a favourable external environment.

In the process of accompanying APEC, Vietnam has actively and proactively contributed to the APEC Forum and has been promoting peace, stability, cooperation, regional economic integration and buttressing APEC's role as the leading economic linkage mechanism in Asia-Pacific. In particular, the most outstanding thing is that Vietnam is one of the few members who have twice successfully assumed the role of APEC Chair (2006 and 2017).

At the High-Level Week in November 2006 in Hanoi, the first Vietnam as host country, APEC Leaders for the first time identified the prospect of forming the Free Trade Area of the Asia-Pacific (FTAAP). This is an important decision laying the foundation for the strategic vision of regional economic integration. At the same time, the Hanoi Action Programme aims to implement the Bogor Goals, the APEC Comprehensive Reform Package, cooperation commitments on human security, human resource development, structural reform, and assisting the developing members to improve their integration capabilities... are also considered as timely and effective solutions to APEC issues faced at that time. The results of the 2006 APEC Year with the theme of "Towards a Dynamic community for sustainable development and prosperity" have contributed to creating more impetus to boost APEC cooperation in a more effective and dynamic way.

With the theme of "Creating New Dynamism, Fostering a Shared Future" Vietnam has chaired and coordinated with members to promote many great cooperation contents, arouse new motivations for sustainable, creative and inclusive growth, promote trade liberalization, investment and regional connectivity, strengthen APEC's leadership in global economic and trade governance and respond to shared challenges. The Declaration of the 25th APEC Summit and the Inter-ministerial Minister for Foreign Affairs and Economic Affairs together with the attached documents have contributed to maintaining the momentum of cooperation, association and APEC core values of promoting trade and free investment, opening and supporting for the multilateral trading system. The role and contribution of Vietnam are particularly valued high when Vietnam presides over the initiation of discussions on the building of the New Vision for the APEC Forum after 2020. Besides, the imprint of Vietnam is also expressed through success of the first Dialogue between APEC Leaders, ASEAN and Vietnam that positively contributed to promoting the formation of a The Comprehensive and Progressive Agreement for Trans-Pacific Partnership (CPTPP) on the occasion of APEC High-Level Week in Da Nang. The success and attraction of Vietnam are also reflected in the records of the participation and contribution of the business community on the occasion of APEC High-Level Week, notably the APEC Business Summit with the participation of more 2,100 leading businesses in the regions and world, and Vietnam Business Summit were the first held in Vietnam.

It can be said that the successes and the imprints of Vietnam through two host APEC affirmed active, positive and utmost responsibility in participating in shaping regional economic links, maintaining the role of Asia-Pacific as the driving force of global economic integration and growth. Vietnam is one of the most active members in proposing for initiatives and projects, with more than 100 projects in many fields. Many of those initiatives are evaluated in a practical way, meeting the common interest, especially in overarching development, human resource development in the digital era, facilitating cross-border e-commerce, green, sustainable and creative MSMEs, food security and climate change, rural and urban development...

Vietnam also has many contributions in managing APEC activities through taking the position of Executive Director of the APEC Secretariat (2005-2006), Chairman/Vice Chairman of many Committees and many key Working Groups such as Committee on Trade and Investment, Budget Management Committee, Small and Medium Enterprises, Health Working Groups, responding to an emergency... In the period 2016-2018, Vietnam have taken on the role of Chairman, Vice Chairman of 18 Committees, APEC Working Group and ABAC, highly appreciated by the members.

In addition, the role of Vietnamese enterprises in APEC cooperation is increasingly enhanced. Vietnamese enterprises have actively participated, proposing many recommendations to APEC Leaders and Ministers. In particular, in the 2017 APEC Year, Vietnamese enterprises contributed their intelligence, effort and directly participated in many activities, affirming their maturity, integration capacity, roles and responsibilities for APEC cooperation as well as regional economic links.

Moreover, Vietnam plays a key role in the development of the regional trading system. Notably, Vietnam is a member of both TPP and RCEP. Along with a few other economies, Vietnam is in a position to assess whether the provisions of the two agreements will promote the economy to integrate more deeply with the region, or to force the economy to choose one of two agreements. A more special feature is that Vietnam is the only economy in the region that has signed a trade agreement with Russia or can reflect a purely pragmatic approach to the need to reach every market. Whatever the reason, unlike other economies, with its network of trade agreements, Vietnam is in a position to contribute a unique perspective on the progress of the regional trading system.

Vietnam's Role in Trade and the Partnership Agreements

The Trans-Pacific Partnership Agreement (TPP) was signed between 12 countries on February 4, 2016 in Auckland, New Zealand after 5 years of negotiations with the aim of integrating Asia-Pacific economies. At the end of 2016, after President Donald Trump was elected, the US officially withdrew from this agreement according to Donald Trump's new policy. On November 11, 2017, TPP Ministers have reached a basic agreement for the TPP-11 agreement and unified the new name for the agreement–The Comprehensive and Progressive Agreement for Trans-Pacific Partnership (CPTPP). Despite facing many challenges, the trend of cooperation and economic linkage continue to be promoted along with competition policies, increasing the influence of major countries and the need for economic development and diversification relations between emerging and developing economies. Asia-Pacific is at the forefront of the trend of cooperation and economic integration with various forms of multi-level cooperation. In particular, the CPTPP has become effective since

December 30, 2018 that expresses the determination of regional economies to pursue trade liberalization based on laws, opening, justice, inclusiveness and benefits to all parties involved.

On March 8, 2018, Vietnam and its partner countries signed the CPTPP Agreement, which is a new generation Free Trade Agreement (FTA) with a broad commitment and highest standards that our country has participated in. The CPTPP Agreement has 11 member countries with a total GDP value of about USD 10 trillion, accounting for 13% of global GDP. On November 12, 2018, the National Assembly of Vietnam officially ratified the CPTPP Agreement. Participation in CPTPP helps Vietnam to demonstrate its strong commitment to innovation and comprehensive and extensive international integration; at the same time, create opportunities to promote foreign economic relations and improve market economy institutions in Vietnam. However, the changes in the regional and global economic and trade profile have had a multifaceted impact on Vietnam. On the one hand, Vietnam has the opportunity to expand and diversify export markets, attract resources to serve socio-economic development, promote and deepen cooperation with major countries and important partners of Vietnam. On the other hand, Vietnam is at risk of being affected by trade-economic friction of powers and changes in the external environment, especially in the areas of trade, finance - currency, and climate change, geopolitical tensions... In the period from now to 2030, Vietnam will basically complete the implementation of commitments under the framework of FTAs and many economic cooperation frameworks which Vietnam has participated in. Along with 10 other member countries, Vietnam signed the Comprehensive Partnership for Trans-Pacific Partnership Agreement (CPTPP) and is one of the seven countries that approved the first new generation Free Trade Agreement (FTA) in the world, affirming Vietnam's role as a link in important economic links in the region.

Along with CPTPP effective from 14 January 2019 and the signing of EU-Vietnam Free Trade Agreement (EVFTA), Investment Protection Agreement (IPA on June 30, 2019, can confirm the fullness and depth of international economic integration of Vietnam.

According to the EU, EVFTA is the most ambitious free trade agreement that the EU has ever negotiated with a developing country. The signing of the Agreement affirms the shared interests of Vietnam and the EU in jointly contributing to promoting international economic integration, trade liberalization, equal, transparent and rule-based investment. The early approval by EU members to sign EVFTA and IPA has affirmed that the EU highly appreciates the role and position of Vietnam, attaches great importance to bilateral and comprehensive cooperation and bilateral cooperation, and is the result of a close and effective coordination process among agencies of the both sides. This is the basis for Vietnam and EU to continue the process of approval for early agreements to take effect in the coming time. Along with the PCA, EVFTA and EVIPA have marked an important step in Vietnam-EU comprehensive partnership and cooperation. Bilateral economic and trade cooperation has shifted from a basic status that Vietnam receives EU supports to develop, eradicate poverty and transform the economy into an equal co-operative partnership, mutually beneficial cooperation with the commitments of a "new generation" free trade agreement (FTA).

As the agreement has a deep and comprehensive commitment, covering the economics, trade, investment and sustainable development issues, EVFTA and EVIPA will open up great opportunities for the two sides to maximize their potential and complement each other, boost trade exchange and investment, promote sustainable development, thereby contributing to deepening and creating long-term benefits between the two parties. According to many studies, EVFTA will help Vietnam's GDP to increase by 4.6% and Vietnam's exports to the EU will increase by 42.7% by 2025; EU GDP is estimated to increase by 29.5 billion USD and exports increase by 29% in 2035. Thus, EVFTA and EVIPA bring very specific and practical economic benefits to the economy, enterprises and people of both Vietnam and EU.

It can be said that signing EVFTA and EVIPA is one of the important historical moments in the 30-year process of developing Vietnam - EU relations. That is the new milestone contains great cooperation opportunities but also requires a lot of shared efforts. In the coming time, when EVFTA and EVIPA are approved by the National Assembly of Vietnam and the European Parliament to officially put into operation, it will make an important contribution to Vietnam-EU partnership and comprehensive cooperation to reach new high level, contributing to peace, stability, development of both sides and of Asia – Europe region and the world. This can confirm that Vietnam is really entering into integration phase, a comprehensive and extensive international economic integration expressed as follows:

Firstly, Vietnam is becoming more closely connected with the world, being the leading open economy in Southeast Asia, a link in the links of important regional and inter-regional economy. Participation in "new generation" FTA agreements, especially CPTPP and EVFTA, is an important breakthrough of Vietnam's international integration. With 16 FTAs in which are implemented, negotiating and preparing for ratification, Vietnam has become the focal point of a deepening and comprehensive FTA network covering 59% of the world population, 61% of GDP and 68% of total trade demand, contributing to increasing the integration of benefits with most of the world's leading economic centers.

Secondly, from 2019, Vietnam entered the stage of implementing key international economic commitments, including "new generation" FTAs. This is the period when Vietnam fulfilled its commitments in many important economic cooperation frameworks such as ASEAN - China Free Trade Area (ACFTA) and ASEAN - Hong Kong Free Trade Agreement (AKFTA). Vietnam is among the group of first countries to implement the CPTPP and the "new generation" FTA with a broad commitment and highest standards ever in our country, opening a market of 10 trillion USD, accounting for 13% of global GDP. Participation in CPTPP and EVFTA shows Vietnam's strong commitment to innovation and comprehensive, extensive international integration, creating opportunities to promote foreign economic relations, perfecting the market economy institution, and at the same time demonstrate active participation and contribute to promoting multilateral, open, law-based international trading system.

Third, Vietnam participates in the process of shaping new regional and global structures with a new mind. In the World Economic Forum (WEF) in January, 2019, Vietnam was the first country in Southeast Asia to sign a Cooperation Agreement with WEF to build the Fourth Industrial Revolution Center in Vietnam and connect the Center with another Fourth Industrial Revolution Centers of WEF in the world. This affirms determination of Vietnam to become an "innovative nation", a deep integrated economy with the global economy. Invited to attend the 14th G20 Summit at Japan in June, 2019, Vietnam and 20 leading economies discussed and searched solutions to common problems of the world economy, maintaining order and promoting international economic cooperation and linkages, meeting the interests of all economies. With role Vice Chairman of APEC Vision Group, Vietnam are actively working with APEC members to build a new vision for the Forum in the post-2020 period. In the role of ASEAN's President 2020, and with almost absolute credibility of the international community for the role of a impermanent member of the United Nations Security Council in 2020-2021, Vietnam is fully capable of actively contributing to the creating and shaping of regional and global structures, take advantage of additional resources for the breakthroughs development in coming time.

Thus, from a country with many difficulties in the wars and there were misunderstandings times of history, Vietnam's relations with regional and international organizations were extremely tense, hindering the process of integration and development of Vietnam. But by smart and effective diplomacy, Vietnam has gradually improved and had closed and effective relations with regional and international organizations. In the process of participating in regional and world playgrounds, Vietnam has made many contributions to promote international relations in a good way, especially respecting the settlement of disputes according to international law by peaceful solution. Thereby, Vietnam's position in the views of international and regional friends has been increasingly enhanced and classified as one of the new middle power in East Asia. With stable economic growth in the past years, political stability and maintaining social security, especially with the way of peaceful foreign relations and respecting for the interests of the parties..., Vietnam will continue to make important contributions to the general development of humanity.

Notes

1. Ratified in 2007.
2. Ratified in 2015.
3. Already and implementing 258/290 action lines in the Master Plan on Political-Security Community, 154/157 priorities in the Master Plan on Economic Community; carried out 954 actions of 109 strategic measures of the Master Plan on the Socio-Culture (Report of the ASEAN Secretary-General submitted to the ASEAN Summit 34).

4. According to the statistic of the Department of ASEAN, Ministry of Foreign Affairs of Vietnam.
5. Six main organs of the UN are responsible for various action areas: the General Assembly, the Security Council, the Economic and Social Council, and the Trusteeship Council, (officially terminating operations according to Decisions of the Summit in 2005), International Court of Justice and UN Secretariat.
6. https://nhandan.com.vn/vietnamlienhopquoc/
7. https://nhandan.com.vn/vietnamlienhopquoc/, accessed 10/8/2019
8. https://nhandan.com.vn/vietnamlienhopquoc/, accessed 10/8/2019
9. 12 founding members in 1989 include: Australia, Brunei, Canada, Indonesia, Japan, South Korea, Malaysia, New Zealand, the Philippines, Singapore, Thailand, the United States; 03 members joined in 1991: China, Hong Kong - China, Taipei - China; 03 members joined in 1993-1994 including Mexico, Papua New Guinea, Chile; 03 members joined in 1998, including Peru, Russia and Vietnam. APEC has suspended the admission of new members since 1998. Currently, many countries wish to join APEC such as India, Pakistan, Bangladesh, Sri Lanka, Macau, Mongolia, Laos, Cambodia, Costa Rica, Colombia, Panama, Ecuador.
10. APEC documents at a glance 2018.
11. https://dantri.com.vn/chinh-tri/tiep-tuc-thuc-day-hop-tac-lien-ket-kinh-te-khu-vuc-va-toan-cau-20181115102459689.htm, accessed 20/8/2019
12. https://dantri.com.vn/chinh-tri/tiep-tuc-thuc-day-hop-tac-lien-ket-kinh-te-khu-vuc-va-toan-cau-20181115102459689.htm, accessed 20/8/2019
13. https://dantri.com.vn/chinh-tri/tiep-tuc-thuc-day-hop-tac-lien-ket-kinh-te-khu-vuc-va-toan-cau-20181115102459689.htm, accessed 20/8/2019
14. Basic data on APEC economies, https://tuoitre.vn/nhung-so-lieu-co-ban-ve-cac-nen-kinh-te-apec-170323.htm, accessed 20/8/2019
15. Basic data on APEC economies, https://tuoitre.vn/nhung-so-lieu-co-ban-ve-cac-nen-kinh-te-apec-170323.htm, accessed 20/8/2019

References

ASEAN

1. Deputy Foreign Minister Nguyen Quoc Dung, *The article "Promote the realization of the ASEAN Community Vision 2025"*, the People's Newspaper, April 26, 2017.
2. Deputy Foreign Minister Nguyen Quoc Dung, *"Vietnam in the spirit of ASEAN Community"*, World and Vietnam Newspaper, 2/2018.
3. Nguyen Hoang Giap, Nguyen Huu Cat, Nguyen Thi Que, *"Current ASEAN cooperation and participation of Vietnam"*, National Political Publishing House, 2008.
4. Thuy Duong Duong, *"ASEAN Cultural and Social Community - Vision 2025"*, National Political Publishing House, April 2017.
5. Basic documents on ASEAN of ASEAN Department, Ministry of Foreign Affairs, Vietnam

United Nations

1. Documents on the Ministry of Foreign Affairs' Website, link: http://www.mofa.gov.vn/en/ctc_quocte/un/nr040819155753/nr060928134849/copy_of_ns0609 28102409/view

2. Documents on the Ministry of Foreign Affairs' website, link: http://www.mofa.gov.vn/en/ctc_quocte/un/nr040819155753/ns170503145947/view 3
3. *"General Secretary and President Nguyen Phu Trong congratulated Vietnam for being elected United Nations Security Council"*, the World newspaper, June 7, 2019 at the link: https://baoquocte.vn/tong-bi-thu-chu-tich-nuoc-nguyen-phu-trong-chuc-mung-viet-nam-trung-cu-hoi- dong-bao-an-lien-hop-quoc-95537. html
4. Basic documents about the United Nations and the Security Council of the Department of International Organizations, Ministry of Foreign Affairs

APEC, CPTPP

1. Book: *"20 years of joining APEC - The imprint of Vietnam's international integration"* compiled by APEC National Committee 2017, publishing license: 2019-2017/CXBIPH/13-92-TN in Public Media Trading Joint Stock Company.
2. Politburo Member, President of the Socialist Republic of Vietnam, Male Chairman of the 25th APEC Summit Tran Dai Quang, *"Success of APEC Year 2017 and High-Level Week with the role and position of Vietnam"*, Nhan Dan newspaper, November 26, 2017.
3. Pham Binh Minh - Politburo Member, Deputy Prime Minister and Minister of Foreign Affairs Ministry, *"20 years of joining APEC: From a strategic vision to Vietnam's imprints"*, Nhan Dan newspaper, November 14, 2018
4. Bui Thanh Son - Permanent Deputy Minister of Foreign Affairs Bui Thanh Son gave an interview with Vietnam Television Station about 20 years of Vietnam joining APEC (November 2018) at the link: https://www.youtube.com/watch?v = nV2FPqkZoyY
5. Nguyen Thi Thanh Hai, Human Rights Institute, Ho Chi Minh National Academy of Politics, *"Comprehensive and Progressive for Trans-Pacific Partnership Agreement and its impacts on human rights in Vietnam"*, The Journal of Communist, Vol. 920, June 2019.
6. Comprehensive and Progressive for Trans-Pacific Partnership Agreement, Plan forimplementation by link: http://cptpp.moit.gov.vn/?page=overview&category_id=ae16c761-9aca-4f55-b3e8-f3e43979bb59
7. Le Hoai Trung - the Party Central Committee member, Deputy Minister of Foreign Affairs, *"Multilateral foreign relations contributes to promoting integration and strengthening the country"*, the journal of External Information, link: http://tapchithongtindoingoai.vn/ly-luan-thuc-tien-kinh- nghiem/doi-ngoai-da-phuong-gop-phan-day-manh-hoi-nhap-quoc-te-tang-cuong-suc-20469, accessed 14/8/2019.
8. Bui Thanh Son - Deputy Minister of Foreign Affairs, "New motivation to raise the level of Partnership and Vietnam - EU Comprehensive Cooperation" by the link: https://baoquocte.vn/dong-luc-moi-nang-tam-quan-he-doi-tac-va-hop-tac-toan-dien-viet-nam-eu-96757.html
9. Basic documents about the United Nations and Security Council of the Department of Multilateral Economic Cooperation and Department of Economic Integration, Ministry of Foreign Affairs.

12 Vietnam's Soft Power in International Relations

Thi-Trang Le

Soft Power, Smart Power and Sharp Power

What is "Soft power"?

In the 90s of the twentieth century, the model of socialism in the Soviet Union and Eastern European countries collapsed, the Cold War ended, the world moved from confrontation to peaceful dialogue, cooperation, and development in the trend of globalization. From here, the nature of power has changed. Countries that want to achieve their goals need to change a new international behaviour in accordance with the trend of globalization, from confrontation to dialogue, peace and cooperation. The concept of soft power was born in that context. The hard power of a nation is clearly identifiable, through data on military potential (quantity and quality of the military, command capability, military theory and military equipment, especially weapons of great destructive power), economic potential (economic scale, GDP and economic structure). Hard power is an important source of power that helps nations defend their sovereignty, protect themselves from threats, and affirm their position in the world. But in today's global age, hard power does not determine everything, soft power is the great endogenous source in international relations.

Joseph S. Nye introduced the concept of soft power for the first time in the book "*Bound to lead: the changing nature of American power*"(1990). He established the connotation of the concept of "soft power" including: *First,* soft power is the attraction and fascination, rather than coercion or persuasion to promote the effect. *Second,* soft power reflects a nation's ability to set and build international institutions, which is the new form of power mentioned by new realism and liberalism. *Third,* the acknowledging soft power may be the recognition of value or institution, it can also be the recognition of international system judgment. Acknowledging power helps a nation achieve its legal status in the international arena[1].

Later, he continued to develop this concept in "*The Paradox of American Power: Why the World's Only Superpower Can't Go It Alone*" (2002). In particular, in 2004, his initial studies on soft power were upgraded to a theoretical system in the book "*Soft Power: The Means to Success in World*

Politics". He expressed that: Soft power is "*the second aspect of power, that is, a country may obtain the outcomes it wants in world politics because other countries – admiring its values, emulating its example, aspiring to its level of prosperity and openness – want to follow it*"[2]. "*From a behavioural perspective, soft power is attraction. From a resource perspective, soft power is the resource that produces this attraction*"[3]. Nye identifies three main resources for creating a nation's "soft power", namely a country's culture, political values and foreign policies. Thus, basically soft power is understood as the attraction, enticement, ability to influence and attract a nation to other countries through non-coercive methods in international relations.

In the twenty-first century, a major factor affecting international relations is the Fourth Industrial Revolution. The great achievements of this revolution have brought to human life convenient invaluable benefits, improving the quality of life and strongly liberating human labour. However, along with that is the competition on the cyber front and the possibility of a war of information, technology and high-tech weapons that threaten global security. Therefore, soft power is a basic factor to enhance national competitiveness as well as to expand the sphere of influence of a country in the region and the world. If a nation relies only on hard power, that cannot solve the problem but sometimes leave complicated and unpredictable consequences. Cultural soft power has become an important part of national synergy, playing a huge role in fulfilling the country's great goals, especially in international relations. Therefore, winning on an international chess board requires each country to understand and know how to promote its soft power.

Smart Power and Sharp Power

In the era of new science-technology revolution taking information as the key, soft power is able to bring into play its capabilities thanks to the global network (internet), digital television technology. Space and time limitations are no longer a big deal. The tools of hard power are difficult to reach the target and conquer it in the blink of eye. Therefore, the use of soft power proved to be superior to hard power[4]. The relationship between hard power and soft power is a reciprocal, dialectical relationship between each other. Hard power "can make a premise to promote "soft power", making "soft power" attractive. Soft power is an extension and expansion of hard power. If a country is weak in economy and defense capacity, it will be difficult to maximize its soft power, in which case, soft power factors such as political stability, social consensus, cultural attraction... will play an important role, offset the weakness of hard power, creating certain strong values in national development and international relations. In contrast, a country with strong economic and defense power but lacking the focus on soft power factors also minimizes its competition in international relations. Thus, a nation's synergy must be based on a strong combination of hard and soft power, the combined (current and potential) capabilities of military, economic, political, culture, ideology at home and the application of these capabilities in international political relations for the survival and development of the nation.

From the analysis of the essence and dialectical relationship between "hard power" and "soft power", J. Nye and the authors Chester A. Crocker, Fen Osler Hampson, and Pamela R. Aall developed the new term "smart power" in 2004. According to Nye, smart power is the ability to combine hard and soft power into a winning strategy. In other words, intelligent power is the ability to use hard and soft power to create strategies, policies, and ways of action to achieve the desired results. Thus, smart power is not a third type of power, but a combination or mixture of soft power and hard power. With such a spirit, smart power tends to rely on modern scientific and technological knowledge, so that it can create revolutionary changes in leadership and management. Smart power has thus become an important and powerful force in the modern world.

According to the authors Chester A. Crocker, Fen Osler Hampson, and Pamela R. Aall, "smart power involves the strategic use of diplomacy, persuasion, capacity building and projection of power and influence in the ways that are cos-effective and have political and social legitimacy- The key is to take advantage of military power and all types of diplomacy"[5]. It is the ability to identify contexts, take advantage of trends, and properly use hard and soft power to achieve the highest efficiency.

In the current information age, a new concept of power was born, which is "Sharp Power". "Sharp power" is a phrase given by the National Endowment for Democray-NED. Sharp power is a nation's reliance on "*subversion, bullying and pressure, which combine to promote self-censorship'. Whereas soft power harnesses the allure of culture and values to augment a country's strength, sharp power helps authoritarian regimes compel behaviour at home and manipulate opinion abroad*"[6].

Although sharp power and soft power operate in very different ways, it is difficult to distinguish the differences between them. All results relate to the way of selecting and staging information. In the current situation of the world, the global countries tend to cooperate bilateral and multilateral and develop together. Therefore, "hard power" of a nation in the world is no longer visible or threatening to force as strongly as before, especially among typical nations. The world is increasingly defined, the three sources of national power - military, economic and soft power - remain extremely important, even at varying degrees. If this trend continues to develop in international relations, the advantage will belong to the country that excels in information technology, communication and knows how to use its "soft power" to spread that superiority. Intelligence in the use of power is the understanding of potentials and national capacities and the clever use of it in international relations to achieve the set goals.

Sources of Vietnamese's Soft Power

Vietnam is a country with a long-standing culture, imbued with national identity, united in diversity and pervasive, attractive to the world

Over thousands of years of building and defending the country, the people of Vietnam have formed a long-standing culture, united in diversity and imbued with national identity, making culture an important endogenous resource for the socio-economic development of the country. Vietnamese culture is the result of creative labour, the tenacious struggle for national construction and defense of the Vietnamese ethnic community, as a result of exchanging and absorbing the quintessence of many world civilizations in order to ceaselessly perfect yourself. Vietnamese culture has molded the soul, temperament, bravery of the Vietnamese people, radiating the glorious history of the nation. Over 1,000 years of colonization and anti-domination, the Vietnamese people are not only assimilated but also creative in localizing cultural elements from the outside, selectively absorbing to build up a culture that has both the depth of the regional cultural infrastructure and the bold characteristic of the preeminent identity of our nation. Vietnam was not assimilated by Han civilization, on the basis of Chinese characters, Vietnamese people created Nom scripts... With its special geopolitical position, Vietnam is located at the junction of exchanges between civilizations in the world, which is a stop not only for nations on the path to conquering the world, but also is the intersection of the great religions, beliefs, ideologies and cultures of mankind. In a process of exchange and extensive acculturation with China, India, Southeast Asian countries to the contacts and transformations when meeting French culture in the nineteenth century, western twentieth century and globalization in the twenty-first century, Vietnamese culture today has a new face, national spirit and humanism have risen to a new level, the value system and national consciousness are "filters" to decant turbidity, creating a firm orientation for modern Vietnamese culture.

The Resolution of the Fifth Plenum of the Central Executive Committee of the 8th Plenum "*On building and developing an advanced Vietnamese culture imbued with national identity*" outlined the sustainable values and the quintessence of the communists. fellow ethnic groups of Vietnam, that is: "*passionate patriotism, nationalistic will; solidarity, a sense of community connecting individuals - families - villages - Fatherland; kindness, tolerance, great affection, morality; diligence and creativity in labour; sophistication in behaviour, simplicity in lifestyle* "[7]. The national cultural values formed in the historical and cultural process are the strength to unite the community, so that the people can overcome the harsh challenges of history in the thousands of years of building and defending the country. That is the cultural soft power that Vietnam is continuing to develop in the current context.

Entering the trend of globalization and international integration, Vietnamese culture attracts and spreads its strong attractiveness in the eyes of international friends. Through cultural diplomacy activities, the cultural values of the nation are introduced, promoted, helping the world to better understand the country, people and culture of Vietnam. The United Nations Educational, Scientific and Cultural Organization (UNESCO) has recognized that Vietnam has many types of heritages: world natural heritage (Ha Long Bay, Phong Nha-Ke Bang National Park, Trang An scenic complex, etc.); world cultural heritages; documentary heritage and mixed heritage,... Vietnam also owns intangible cultural heritages (Quan Ho, Ca Tru, Bai Choi, folk songs for example, Xoan singing, Mau worship religion, Hue royal court music, Tay Nguyen gong culture space,...). To date, Vietnam has had 27 heritage sites recognized by UNESCO and is the country with the most world heritage sites in Southeast Asia. The picture of Vietnam's heritage is the representation of a nation rich in identity, dynamism, creativity, openness and incessant integration, exchange and exchange of cultural and civilized values of humanity. On the other hand, the overseas Vietnamese community with a strong striving and the mind to think about the homeland is always closely connected, helping the international community to consolidate awareness and understand correctly and understand clearly about In Vietnam, turning that power into a fulcrum and solid support for Vietnam not only in socio-economic development but also in international relations.

Through cooperative activities and cultural exchange programmes on various scales, Vietnam's image is promoted with a more comprehensive beauty. Vietnam has become an ideal destination to attract international friends. According to the evaluation of HSBC Bank on "*The most livable and working places in the world 2019*", Vietnam is ranked the Top 10 most livable and working places in the world for the first time[8].

Countries	*Ranking 2019*	*Ranking 2018*
Switzerland	1	8
Singapore	2	1
Canada	3	4
Spain	4	13
New Zealand	5	2
Australia	6	6
Turkey	7	22
Germany	8	3
UAE	9	9
Vietnam	10	19

Top 10 countries where the best places to live and work in 2019 (Source: HSBC)

Society and People to People Contacts

Vietnam is known to the international community for its image of a courageous and fierce people in the struggle against foreign aggression; At the same time, it is also a peace-loving people, friendly with the peoples in the region and the world... These are cultural values that imbued with national identity, at the same time, have pervasive power and appealing to the international community.

After thousands of years of being dominated by Chinese feudalism, hundreds of years of being conquered by the French colonialists, the Vietnamese people still exist and develop as an independent nation. It is the national spirit, the heroic and resilient quality in the struggle to defend the Fatherland, which has brought admiration from international friends about a small nation but did not yield to any great powers. People are always united by long-standing cultural and historical traditions. Professor E. Tin-pho (American Air Force General Staff Academy) admitted: "*In 1975, the United States left a home. The country was born and brought up by the United States for more than two decades of collapsed, because the Vietnam War of the United States has long been defeated. It failed because the enemy had devised a better military strategy, a war awareness strategy on a broader scale, regarded as a cultural phenomenon closely associated with social and economic aspects, politics, diplomacy as well as military. Air force - America's greatest strength is crippled by "cultural winds" of history and culture*[9]. The heroic and resilient qualities have formed a great strength to help the Vietnamese people overcome many challenges. The patriotism of the Vietnamese people has been formed since the time of Van Lang, through a long history reinforced one more step and raised into a spirit of sacrifice and fight, determined to regain national sovereignty. Patriotism is the spiritual product of the entire nation, the strength of community cohesion, and the "soft power" that is skillfully applied in practice and expressed through the many majestic ancient poems, as Nguyen Trai summarized: "Bring great cause to overcome brutality. Get people to change violence instead". Thus, patriotic ideology plays a key role in Vietnam's spiritual values table. Patriotism is expressed in the spirit of self-giving for good cause, in the determination to win and retain national sovereignty.

President Ho Chi Minh, the beloved leader of our people, has inherited and developed Vietnam's soft power to new heights and combined fluency and dialectic of soft power with hard power to create intelligent power. Ho Chi Minh said: "*First is fighting with tactic. Second fight by diplomacy. Third is fighting with troops*[10], "*after the matter of defense, diplomacy is a necessary issue for an independent country* "[11]. Therefore, he asserted: "*Strength is gong and diplomacy is reputation. Gong has a loud voice*"[12], so "*if we want to win diplomacy, we have to praise our strength*"[13]. Immediately after the birth of the Democratic Republic of Vietnam, Ho Chi Minh emphasized: "*Our people have a passionate patriotism. It is our precious tradition. Since ancient times, up to now, when the Fatherland was invaded, that spirit is excited, it forms a wave. Extremely powerful, huge, it passes through all the dangers, difficulties, it engulfed all the flood of water selling and flood*"[14]. Thus, Ho Chi Minh succeeded in promoting the power of people's diplomacy, praising the strength of the masses in the early days of communist democracy. Implementing the policy of the Communist Party of Vietnam and President Ho Chi Minh, the Vietnamese people want to be like one heart, unite to fight against victory, protect territorial integrity, and unify the Fatherland.

From the practice of national liberation and national defense, the Vietnamese people have set a shining example of patriotism, revolutionary heroism, etc. and received the admiration and support of the world's progressive people. Up to now, the world still reminds of Vietnam as a phenomenon, a miraculous story, but hidden behind the characteristic of the national spirit is the strength of the people, the will of the nation and the patriotism of each person, is the just cause of the cause of defending the Fatherland. It is "soft power" in the master protection country's sovereignty, territorial integrity, besides military and political power, contributes to preserving peace and security in the region and the world.

Projecting Vietnam's Soft Power

The tolerance and generosity of the Vietnamese people is also expressed in the spirit of willingness to forgive and open the honourable escape route for the enemies when they have failed on the battlefield to quickly end the war, avoiding damage loss for both sides. In modern times, Vietnam is willing to close the past to build a good diplomatic relationship, mutually beneficial on the basis of respecting each other's independence, sovereignty and territorial integrity.

In the 4,000-year history of national construction and defense, our nation has experienced 22 wars against foreign invaders. But when it won, Vietnamese people are willing to forgive, resolving resentment, treating with the spirit of humanity, create a normalized relationship after the war, "of faith and resentment", remove hatred by the peaceful, flexible, cooperative measures of respect for the nation between the two sides, coexist and development.

During the war of aggression against Vietnam, from the feudal dynasties of China (Han, Tang, Tong, Nguyen, Minh, Thanh...) to superpowers in the world (France, Japan, the USA), many powerful generals attacked Vietnam, but failed at the power of patriotic tradition, of the great unity of the whole people... When they were pushed into the world, Vietnam is ready to open a way for the enemy to retreat in honour. During the resistance war against the Ming army (China), hen the Ming army was in a difficult position, the Lam Son insurgents paved the way for "filial piety" for them, provided food, horses and boats to let the defeated generals and soldiers return with their wishes. "Extinguish all war forever, open the everlasting peace". In the twentieth century, the Vietnamese people had to face the wars of aggression by two superpowers in the world, France and the United States. Upholding the tradition of fighting against foreign invaders, the Vietnamese people continued to defeat the strategies of France and the United States, creating resounding victories in the world, typically the Dien Bien Phu victory in 1954, Great victory in spring 1975... Having won the decisive victories on the military front, Vietnam was ready to open diplomatic fronts with France and the United States to quickly end the war, avoiding the lowest level of damage for both sides. In the good faith of Vietnam, the Geneva Agreement of 1954 and the Paris Agreement of 1973 were signed, restoring peace in Vietnam. War invalids and prisoners of France and the United States during the Vietnam War were also concerned and were freed to return to their homeland. This makes the opponent pay attention and revolt. As a result, Vietnam has transformed from former enemies into partners, including both comprehensive and strategic.

Americans admire and praise the Vietnamese generosity and generosity. After the war, many American veterans came to Vietnam with anxiety, fear of being chased, and revenge... But in the spirit of openness, tolerance and generosity of the Vietnamese people, they were excited and self-reliant when come back to Vietnam. The presidents of USA such as: Bill Clinton, G. W. Bush, Barack Obama, and Donal Trump were surprised at the openness, tolerance and hospitality of the country and its people. This is hard to do in any other former enemy nation of the United States. Before the change of Vietnam after the war, they surprised and constantly promoted about a new Vietnam for the whole world.

Currently, before the complicated developments in the South China Sea, in order for international friends to understand the legitimacy of defending national border sovereignty, Vietnam is ready to ignore China's aggressive moves on South China Sea to negotiate on the basis of respect for international law, including the 1982 United Nations Convention on the Law of the Sea, the Declaration of Conduct in the South China Sea between ASEAN and China, on all forums. bilateral and multilateral, regional and international in order to control disagreements, and at the same time seek basic, permanent solutions to all disputes. This action of Vietnam has received the sympathy and support of international friends.

The lesson of the spirit of tolerance, that magnitude always promotes strength in diplomatic activities, historical reality has eloquently demonstrated that rightness. Overcoming the limits of interests, the friendship between peoples, between nations will promote foreign cultural activities to enter the hearts of people, towards the high values of all humanity, sharing and helping each other, improving the "humanity and humanity" in international relations, overcoming differences, creating similarities and consensus in international exchange and cooperation. The image of a Vietnamese nation resiliently struggling in tolerance, tolerance, generosity and humanity in the conduct has been strongly attracted to countries around the world and internationally recognized, becoming a source. important force of Vietnam's soft power in international relations.

Relation between Economics and Soft Power

During more than 30 years of Doi Moi (1986-2019), the world has witnessed dramatic changes of Vietnam. Vietnam has risen from a poor, backward country, severely devastated by the warto become a country with impressive economic growth.

So far, Vietnam has built up material-technical facilities and socio-economic infrastructure to gradually meet the cause of industrialization and modernization, creating an environment to attract social resources. for development. The face of the country has changed a lot, the economy maintains a fairly high growth rate, the potential and scale of the economy increases (reaching the middle-income threshold), people's lives are gradually improved; at the same time creating demand and motivation for all sectors of social life, the team of businessmen and entrepreneurs have become an important force to implement the modern and industrialized nation. Basic macroeconomic stability, inflation under control. The innovation efforts over the past 30 years have helped the investment environment continually improve, thereby attracting more and more investment capital for development. The economic structure of Vietnam has initially shifted towards modernization. Under the leadership of the Party, the ideology and policies of developing a socialist-oriented market economy have been institutionalized into laws, creating a legal corridor for the economy to operate effectively. Thirty years of renovation is also a long-term process of international economic integration on many levels, in various forms, in accordance with the principles and standards of the global market. Over the past years, Vietnam has become a bright spot of the world on many fronts such as economic growth, investment, business and tourism destinations, having a say in many bilateral and multilateral fora, especially near It successfully organized the Second US-Korea Summit, participated in the candidacy for the non-permanent member of the United Nations Security Council and especially will assume the chairmanship of ASEAN in 2020. That is strengthening trying and asserting the soft power of a nation that aspires to rise for peace and prosperity.

This achievement has increasingly confirms the Party's right leadership as a decisive factor in the success of innovation, encouragement of the people to continue to respond, making an important contribution to maintaining political stability - society, continuing to promote the cause of national comprehensive renovation with higher strides. These achievements have been recognized and considered as an advantage of Vietnam when promoting the soft power in the trend of integration, participating in international relations in the region and the world. Thus, the economic achievements that Vietnam has achieved after more than 30 years of renovation have transformed and resonated into the nation's combined strength, becoming an important source of soft power and a solid foundation. for international relations in every aspect of the country.

Track II Diplomacy

Vietnam's soft power is known through the personal charisma of the greatest people in history. In particular, we can mention the ideology, values, personality of some outstanding figures such as: Tran Nhan Tong, Nguyen Trai, Nguyen Du,

Ho Chi Minh, Vo Nguyen Giap and many cultural people and celebrities. other prominent of the country.

Nguyen Trai (1380 -1442) was a great thinker, cultural celebrity, distinguished military, politician and talented diplomat of the Vietnamese nation. He lived in a period of turbulence, tribulation and anxiety in history, which was also the pivotal period of the two historical cultural routes of Vietnam. During the Le dynasty, he was the first ruler to build the Le dynasty in his heart. His life and career associated with the Lam Son uprising. Nguyen Trai affirmed that the border of Vietnam had a right to stand apart from the North and he considered it the ultimate goal of Vietnamese. With a strategic vision, Nguyen Trai has shown the ability of diplomatic relations cleverly, flexibly, consistently in principle but always shows humility. People's ideology, taking people as the root, always putting the interests of the people first has been accompanied throughout the struggle for national liberation, national reunification and going beyond the direction of building a human society, the name of the national hero and cultural celebrity Nguyen Trai, has really transcended national borders and integrated into the quintessence of cultural values of mankind.

Vietnam has two outstanding generals, Hung Dao Vuong Tran Quoc Tuan (XIII century) and Vo Nguyen Giap (XX century), who are honoured by the world as one of the most outstanding generals. Tran Quoc Tuan's victory over the might of the Mongols was one of the greatest victories in the history of the world. Therefore, he was voted by the world as one of the 10 most famous generals in the world of all time. In modern times, the world knows Vo Nguyen Giap - General Commander of the Vietnam People's Army, who has defeated the forces of the world's two superpowers, France and the United States, culminating in the victory of Dien Bien. Covered in 1954 and a great victory in the spring of 1975. As a talented organizer, General Vo Nguyen Giap gradually built the Vietnam People's Army from 34 in December 1944 into an army of over one million. people in 1975. Dien Bien Phu victory In addition to the victory of the strategy direction, on the organization of military activities, the strategic skill of military art, the basic issue is based on the strength of national culture. This cultural power is inherited from the rich cultural traditions of the nation, existing as a continuous flow from tradition to modernity. Vo Nguyen Giap is a special, rare case of both Vietnam and the world in the twentieth century. Not only famous as a genius general of all eras, he is also known and respected by the people of the world as a talented general - virtuous, literary - martial, but one of the bright faces of Vietnamese culture.

In the twentieth century, the country of Vietnam also had an outstanding person, who was strongly attracted to international friends, which was President Ho Chi Minh (1890-1969). President Ho Chi Minh was honoured by UNESCO as an outstanding cultural celebrity for his important and multifaceted contributions in the crystallized cultural, educational and artistic fields of the Vietnamese national cultural tradition. symbolizing the aspirations of peoples, affirming their cultural identities and the desire to enhance mutual understanding among peoples. It can be said that in the history of modern world, few leaders have been as knowledgeable about human culture as deeply as Ho Chi Minh. In the course of revolutionary activities, Ho Chi Minh absorbed and collected the quintessence of humanity selectively and creatively applied such quintessences to the specific conditions of the country and the people. clan; At the same time, he has great merit in spreading the national culture to the whole world. Ho Chi Minh became the symbol of Vietnamese culture, personality, personality, intelligence and soul, Eastern culture and human civilization. The person symbolizes a harmonious combination of cultures to "radiate a culture of the future".

During his lifetime, President Ho Chi Minh said that the soft power of a nation can only be achieved when in national culture, values and policies, the direction and fulfillment of the eternal aspiration of humankind are liberation and development. higher and higher for people, towards peace and civilization. "Independence - Freedom - Happiness" is an immutable goal of Vietnam. Therefore, the Vietnamese revolution has received strong international support for great victories. The reality of Vietnam's revolution from 1945 to now shows that, through Ho Chi Minh's activities, the world knows Vietnam better, sympathizes with the Vietnamese people in the struggle for national liberation as well as in national construction. That is the soft power of Vietnam with the attraction and strong persuasion to the peoples of the world. The great magnitude of his diplomatic ideas and great contributions to the culture of the country and mankind has been recognized worldwide. President Ho Chi Minh's legacy has become a guideline for the foreign policy of our Party and State, and has become a part of Vietnam's "soft power" in international relations.

Realistic Assessment about Vietnamese's Soft Power

When discussing Vietnam's soft power, in a 2007 press interview, Professor Joseph Nye affirmed: Vietnam has many things that can attract and attract other countries, such as the famous the history of struggle for independence to protect the sovereignty, the successful transition to an economy with impressive growth... This has helped increase Vietnam's soft power. The most attractive point of Vietnam's soft power now lies in the spirit of autonomy, national independence and economic development. Vietnam has 3 main resources to create soft power: national culture, national value system and national policies. It can be seen in which cultural soft power plays an important role. The source of cultural soft power is ultimately the beauty, the core values of a persuasive people to the international community, especially in sensitive situations involving interests. national and regional peace environment.

The soft power of Vietnamese culture is known for its image of a patriotic, courageous, resilient people, but rich in altruism, tolerance, friendliness and peace-loving. Those are sustainable values, able to spread and have the ability to gain and deeply touch countries around the world.

The world is in a period of strong regionalization and globalization. In the current strong bilateral and multilateral diplomacy, Vietnam has been chosen as the venue for diplomatic activities, international events of different sizes and sizes. Vietnam hosted the 2017 APEC organization following the success of APEC 2006, which showed Vietnam's increasing prestige, new vision and position in international relations. The support and active participation of regional and international countries attending APEC 2017 will be a lever to help Vietnam develop its soft power, demonstrating its active, leading and responsible roles. Leading economic forum for cooperation in the Asia-Pacific region. The success of the APEC Summit will enhance Vietnam's leading role at the ASEAN Summit in the Philippines that follows.

A series of international events took place in Vietnam such as welcoming the General Secretary, Chinese President Xi Jinping to visit and work with our country right after the 19th National Congress of the Chinese Communist Party; welcomed US President Donald Trump, the first US President to visit Vietnam at the first year in office; successfully organizing the World Economic Forum in Hanoi on all 3 aspects: content, security, connectivity; organizing the 26th Annual Meeting of the Asia-Pacific Parliamentary Forum (APPF-26) with the theme "Parliamentary partnership for peace, creativity and sustainable development"; In 2018, Vietnam was nominated by the Asia-Pacific group (including 54 members) at the United Nations to be the only candidate of the group to be a non-permanent member of the Security Council (Security Council). 2020-2021; and many more regional and continental events... In particular, in 2019, the fact that US President Donal Trump and North Korean President Kim Jong Un chose Hanoi as the venue for the 2019 US-Korea Summit, once again confirming the position of Vietnam. The international public acknowledges that Vietnam's efforts to contribute to the US-Korea summit are not only meaningful to political politics but also help international friends to better understand the country, its people and its potential. of Vietnam. The value of promoting Vietnam's image is immense when more than 2600 international journalists are present in Hanoi to report on this historic meeting. Clearly, if compared with the other major countries in the world, Vietnam's hard power potential is somewhat inferior but in return, the cultural soft power is extremely large. Lessons learned from the early years of renovation and international integration are lessons on promoting the potential of cultural potential in society, human liberation, combined with flexible and flexible foreign policy. active, open but in principle has brought a new position to the Vietnamese people in the world politics.

Conclusion

Vietnam is a peace-loving country, and the Vietnamese are friendly and kindly. Vietnam has a stable political environment, a well-developed economy and an open foreign policy, and a diversified and attractive culture for tourists. Therefore, Vietnam has an important ground value to promote its soft, intelligent and sensitive power. Speaking at the 29th Diplomatic Conference with the theme "Improving the effectiveness of foreign affairs and international integration - Successfully implementing the Resolution of the 12th Party Congress", opening on August 22, 2016 In Hanoi, Nguyen Phu Trong- General

Secretary of the Communist Party of Vietnam affirmed that the success or failure of diplomacy depends on the strength and position. Power and position here are expressed not only in physical strength but also in "soft power". That is the righteousness in our career; is the great power of national unity; The unanimous support of the people who love peace and justice in the world. It is also the clever implementation of foreign policy and direction as an art following the great ideas of President Ho Chi Minh. General Secretary Nguyen Phu Trong emphasized: We must promote those values to create a "brand" for the nation, to attract the outside world, to contribute to raising the spirit of national self-respect, confidence in communicating and widely promoting Vietnam's cultural values to the world.

In order to have soft power, we must first build this nation to prosper, create happiness for the people, build a good relationships and belief with all countries. Over the past years, Vietnam has become a bright spot of the world on many fronts and recognized. Therefore, Vietnam's position in the international arena has been increasingly enhanced. With the consensus and efforts of the entire Party, army and people, the goal of peace and common prosperity of the region and the world, Vietnam will increasingly develop and fulfill the dream of "parity with the great powers of the five continents" as expected of the great President Ho Chi Minh.

Notes

1. Joseph S. Nye Jr, Bound to Lead: The Changing Nature of American Power, pp. 5-6.
2. Joseph S. Nye Jr, Soft Power*: The Means to Succcess in World Politics,* New York: Public Affairs, 2004, pp. 5.
3. Joseph S. Nye Jr, Soft Power*: The Means to Succcess in World Politics*, pp. 5.
4. Luong Van Ke, *Method of determining national synergy, Journal of Americas today,* No. 9-2007 and Factors of national synergy, Journal of Americas today, No. 10-2007.
5. Crocker, Chester A,; Hampson, Fen Osler; Aall, Pamela R. (2007), *Leashing the Dogs of War: Conflict Management in a Divided World,* US Institute of Peace Press. pp. 13.
6. Joseph S. Nye Jr. (2018), *"China's soft and sharp power"*, accessed on 25/9/2019, https://www.aspistrategist.org.au/chinas-soft-sharp-power/
7. Communist Party of Vietnam: *Document of the Fifth Conference of the Central Executive Committee Session VIII,* Ha Noi: National politics Press, 1998, pp. 56.
8. Leading the People Online: *Vietnam reached the Top 10 most livable and working countries in the world,* https://dantri.com.vn/kinh-doanh/viet-nam-lot-top-10-nuoc-dang-song-va-lam-viec-nhat-the-gioi-ly-giai-the-nao-20190708195840166.htm, accessed on08-07-2019.
9. Led by Tran Van Binh (2005), "Ho Chi Minh's thought and cultural viewpoint are the spiritual foundation of society", Nhan Dan Newspaper on 14 May 2005.
10. Ho Chi Minh: *Complete episode,* Ha Noi: National politics Press, 1995, vol. 3, pp. 514.
11. Communist Party of Vietnam: *The Complete Party Document,* Ha Noi: National politics Press, 2001, vol. 8, pp. 290.
12. Ho Chi Minh: *Complete episode,* Ha Noi: National politics Press, 1995, vol. 4, pp. 126.
13. Communist Party of Vietnam: Directive of the Central Executive Committee on the

resistance to the national construction, November 25, 1945," Ha Noi: National politics Press, vol. 8, pp. 27.
14. Ho Chi Minh: *Complete episode*, Ha Noi: National politics Press, 2012, episode 7, pp. 38.

References

Vietnamese

1. Anh Pham Ngoc, *Cultural diplomacy in the context of integration*, Journal of Political Theory, No. 7/2015. (Phạm Ngọc Anh, *Ngoại giao văn hoá trong bối cảnh hội nhập*, Tạp chí Lý luận chính trị, số 7/2015).
2. Bao Hoang Chi (2012), *Crossing Vietnamese culture and policies*, National Political Press, Hanoi. (Hoàng Chí Bảo (2012), *Giao thoa văn hóa và chính sách Việt Nam*, Nxb Chính trị Quốc gia - Sự thật, Hà Nội).
3. Binh Do Thanh, Thanh Van Ngoc (co-editor) (2012), *Modern international relations - new issues*, National Political Press, Hanoi. (Đỗ Thanh Bình, Văn Ngọc Thành (đồng chủ biên) (2012), *Quan hệ quốc tế thời hiện đại - những vấn đề mới đặt ra*, Nxb Chính trị Quốc gia, Hà Nội).
4. Binh Le Thanh (editor) (2012), *Cultural interference and diplomacy in Vietnam*, National Political Press, Hanoi. (Lê Thanh Bình (chủ biên) (2012), *Giao thoa văn hóa và chính sánh ngoại giao Việt Nam*, Nxb Chính trị Quốc gia, Hà Nội).
5. Ministry of Foreign Affairs (2008), "*Cultural diplomacy for a Vietnamese identity in the international arena*", Proceedings of the Workshop, World Press, Hanoi. (Bộ Ngoại giao (2008), "*Ngoại giao văn hóa vì một bản sắc Việt Nam trên trường quốc tế*", *Kỷ yếu Hội thảo*, Nxb Thế giới, Hà Nội).
6. Ministry of Foreign Affairs, *Steering Committee of cultural diplomacy*, Summary report on cultural diplomacy in 2010, 2011, 2012, 2013, 2014, 2015. (Bộ Ngoại giao, Ban chỉ đạo công tác ngoại giao văn hoá, *Báo cáo tổng kết công tác ngoại giao văn hóa năm 2010, 2011, 2012, 2013, 2014, 2015)*.
7. The Government of the Socialist Republic of Vietnam (2015), *Foreign Cultural Strategy to 2020, issued together with the Prime Minister's Decision No. 210/QD - TTg of May 8, 2015*. (Chính phủ nước Cộng hòa Xã hội Chủ nghĩa Việt Nam (2015), *Chiến lược văn hóa đối ngoại đến năm 2020*, ban hành kèm theo Quyết định số 210/QĐ - TTg ngày 8/5/2015 của Thủ tướng Chính phủ).
8. Chuong Pham Hong, *Ho Chi Minh with Vietnamese soft power*, Journal of Political Theory No. 12/2017. (Phạm Hồng Chương, *Hồ Chí Minh với sức mạnh mềm Việt Nam*, Tạp chí Lý luận chính trị số 12/2017).
9. Doan Do Quy (2009), "*Communication and promotion of cultural diplomacy*", Journal of Communism, (797), pp. 42-47. (Đỗ Quý Doãn (2009), "Thông tin truyền thông và việc đẩy mạnh ngoại giao văn hóa", *Tạp chí Cộng Sản*, (797), tr. 42-47).
10. Vietnam Communist Party (1998), Document of the 5th Conference of the Central Executive Committee, Session VIII, Truth Press, Hanoi. (Đảng Cộng sản Việt Nam (1998), Văn kiện Đại hội Hội nghị lần thứ 5 Ban Chấp hành Trung ương khóa VIII, Nxb Sự thật, Hà Nội).
11. Ky Pham Huy (2014), *The issue of improving the cultural soft power in Vietnam today*, Journal of Political Theory, No. 359. (Phạm Huy Kỳ (2014), *Vấn đề nâng cao sức mạnh mềm văn hoá ở Việt Nam hiện nay*, Tạp chí Lý luận chính trị, số 359).
12. Phuong Thi Nguyen Thu (chief editor) (2015), *The power of Chinese soft cultural*

impacts on Vietnam and some East Asian countries, National Political Press, Hanoi. (Nguyễn Thị Thu Phương (chủ biên) (2015), *Sức mạnh mềm văn hóa Trung Quốc tác động tới Việt Nam và một số nước Đông Á*, Nxb Chính trị Quốc gia - Sự thật, Hà Nội).

13. Phuong Thi Nguyen Thu (2014), *Vietnam's cultural soft power and policy options*, Journal of Culture and Arts, No. 359 (5). (Nguyễn Thị Thu Phương (2014), *Sức mạnh mềm văn hoá và lựa chọn chính sách của Việt Nam*, Tạp chí Văn hoá Nghệ thuật, số 359 (5)).
14. Su Pham Quoc (2013), *"Honouring the national identity in cultural diplomacy"*, Journal of Culture and Arts, (344), pp. 7-12. (Phạm Quốc Sử (2013), *"Tôn vinh bản sắc dân tộc trong ngoại giao văn hóa"*, Tạp chí Văn hóa Nghệ thuật, (344), tr.7-12).
15. Thanh Song (2014), Cultural diplomacy with the issue of increasing "soft power" of Vietnam in integration and development, Journal of Political Theory No. 4/2014. (Song Thành (2014), Ngoại giao văn hoá với vấn đề gia tăng "sức mạnh mèm" của Việt Nam trong hội nhập và phát triển, Tạp chí Lý Luận Chính trị số 4/2014).
16. National Committee for International Cultural Development Decade (1992), *World Decade of Cultural Development*, Ministry of Culture and Information, Hanoi. (Uỷ ban Quốc gia về thập kỷ quốc tế phát triển văn hóa (1992*), Thập kỷ thế giới phát triển văn hóa,* Bộ Văn hóa Thông tin, Hà Nội).
17. Viet Pham Thai (2012), Diplomatic culture of theoretical basis, international experience and application, Political - Administrative Press, Hanoi. (Phạm Thái Việt (2012), Ngoại giao văn hóa cơ sở lý luận, kinh nghiệm quốc tế và ứng dụng, Nxb Chính trị - Hành chính, Hà Nội).
18. Yen Thi Nguyen Thuy (2014), *Cultural diplomacy with the role of soft power*, Journal of Culture and Arts, No. 361 (7). (Nguyễn Thị Thuỳ Yên (2014), *Ngoại giao văn hoá với vai trò là sức mạnh mềm*, Tạp chí Văn hoá Nghệ thuật, số 361 (7)).
19. Prime Minister, *Decision No. 208/QD-TTg on approving the cultural diplomacy strategy by 2020*, February 14, 2011. (Thủ tướng Chính Phủ, Quyết định số 208/QĐ – TTg về việc phê duyệt Chiến lược ngoại giao văn hoá đến năm 2020, ngày 14 tháng 2 năm 2011).
20. Ke Luong Van, *Method of determining national synergy*, Journal of America today, No. 9-2007. (Lương Văn Kế, *Phương pháp xác định sức mạnh tổng hợp quốc gia*, Tạp chí *Châu Mỹ ngày nay*, số 9-2007).
21. Ke Luong Van, *Elements of national synergy*, Journal of America today, No. 10-2007. (Lương Văn Kế, *Các yếu tố cấu thành sức mạnh tổng hợp quốc gia*, Tạp chí *Châu Mỹ ngày nay*, số 10-2007).

English

1. Commings Mitoln (2003), *Culture Diplomacy and Unisted Stated Governement*, Center for Arts and Culture, USA.
2. Harvey B. Feigen Baun (2002), *Globalization and Cultural Diplomacy*, Issue Paper on Art, Culture, The National Agenda, Center for Arts and Culture, George Washington University, Washington, DC.
3. Joseph Nye (2004), *"Soft Power: The means to sccess in World politic"*, New York: Public Affairs.
4. Marta Ryniejska- Kieldanowicz, *Cultural Diplomacy as a Form of International Comunication*, www.instituteforpr.org.
5. Mai Thi Dang Thu, Vietnam's soft power - a case study of Vietnamese cultural diplomacy towards ASEAN, A Thesis Submitted to the Victoria University of Wellington in Partial Fulfillment of the Requirements for the Degree of Master of

International Relations (MIR), Victoria University of Wellington 2015.
6. Chapman, Nicholas (2017), *Mechanisms of Vietnam's Multidirectional Foreign Policy*, Journal of Current Southeast Asian Affairs, 36, 2, pp. 31–69.
7. Lauren Saltiel (2014), *Cultural Governance and development in Vietnam*, Published by Pennsylvania Journal of International Law, USA.
8. http://whc.unesco.org/en/statesparties/vn accessed August 16, 2019
9. https://ich.unesco.org/en-state/viet-nam-VN accessed August 16, 2019
10. http://www.unesco.org/new/en/communication-and-information/memory-of-the-world/register/access-by-region-and-country/vn/

13 Vietnam as a Middle Power: Does is Fulfill the Criteria?

Thi-Hue Quach

Criteria and Role of a Middle Power

Criteria for a middle power

According to the *Britannica* dictionary, a middle power is a state that holds a position in the international power spectrum that is in the "middle"—below that of a superpower or of a great power, but with sufficient ability to shape international events[1]. So which criteria are used for categorizing a state into the group of middle powers? Some studies lay down the criteria for identifying a middle power which include geostrategic position, economic strength, military strength, national capacity, leadership capacity and international prestige[2]. Some other studies suggest that a middle power needs to confirm its position in the region and internationally on four factors which are quantitativeness, function, behaviour and identity[3]; or it needs to focus on five criteria which are national capacity, position in the world order, standard values on state-social organization, main interests of domestic classes, and characteristics of external relation policy[4]. Despite many different interpretations, in general, the middle powers need to meet the following criteria: national strength and capacity; diplomatic acts and conduct, international prestige; identity and value.

National strength and capacity indicators include area, population, geopolitical position, natural resources, economic scale, military strength, science and technology, environmental quality, etc.[5] to measure the nation's hard power and locate its position in the international hierarchy. The Lowy Institute's *Asia Power Index* (Australia) comprises 114 indicators of power[6]. If a country ranks in the mid-range or higher for most of these indicators, it has the prospect of joining the group of middle powers. However, it should be noted that strength and the ability to convert strength into specific competencies are not the same[7]. A nation's strength is relative and dependent on the correlation with other countries in each specific situation.

Regarding *diplomatic acts and conduct and international prestige*, according to A. F. Cooper, R. A. Higgott and K. R. Nossal in the "*Relocating Middle Powers: Australia and Canada in a Changing World Order* (Vancouver: University of British Columbia Press, 1993)", whether a country is considered a middle power mainly depends on its diplomatic conduct, for example, it often presents itself as a good member of the international community through its mediating role that contributes to the settlement of international conflicts, peacekeeping, economic development, humanitarian aid, etc.[8] A middle power attaches great importance to international laws and considers it a key tool for identifying and securing national interests[9]. Where international laws do not help fulfilling this goal, the middle power prioritizes the development of codes of conduct accepted by all parties, including large countries[10]. While respecting the laws, the middle power also has a practical approach (expectation governance) in the application process, reflected in the choice of the case, time, and legal aspect in fighting for and protecting national interests, especially those related to large countries. Middle powers often pursue *niche diplomacy* to assert their superior position, role and reputation. With moderate resources, if they want to take up a special position, they need to focus on issues that other small and medium-sized countries pay little attention to or issues that are not controlled by great powers. Middle powers are often active in diplomacy, taking part in resolving common issues instead of restricting attention to urgent and direct issues. Although not involved in any international conflict, middle powers have political opinions and real participation more frequently than countries which have similar characteristics (such as similar level of income) but do not belong to the group of middle powers. On the other hand, the middle powers tend to find ways to reduce conflicts by working with other countries with the same viewpoint on an issue through multilateral arrangements and institutions.[11]

Regarding *identity and value*, the final way to assess whether a country is a middle power is to consider its speech, argument or identity in external relations because how a country's policy planners plan its external policy will determine the country's identity. This will have a great impact on the country's diplomatic conducts in international relations, thereby impacting the international community's assessment and recognition of its role, its position. To distinguish the middle powers from other countries, researchers often rely on the following characteristics. Attaching significance to the role of diplomacy. Supporting the multilateral approach, encouraging other countries to have the same viewpoint, respecting international laws, codes of conduct and normative values, and opposing imposition and unilateralism. Having flexible diplomacy to consider specific situations before making decisions. Not challenging the change of the status quo, not reconsidering or radically changing the international system, but supporting reforms within the system.

To sum up, the basic criteria for assessing whether a country is a middle power include strength, capacity, diplomatic behaviour, level of influence, and identity and value in the international system. In particular, national strength and capacity are necessary conditions while criteria regarding function, behaviour, diplomatic conduct, international prestige, and identity and value in external relations are sufficient conditions for a country to be considered a middle power.

Classification of middle powers

According to scholar Eduard Jordaan of Singapore Management University, the middle powers can be divided into two groups: traditional middle powers and emerging middle powers. Despite many things in common, these two groups also have differences[12] listed in the table below:

Classification of Middle Powers

Classification	*Traditional middle powers*	*Emerging middle powers*
Economy	High income	Middle - high income
Society	Emphasis on equity	Acceptance of relative equity
Politics	Social democracy	Democratization
Diplomacy	Low regional influence, unclear tendency of regional integration, no attempt to create an identity different from that of other countries, easy to compromise with pressures of global reform, attaching importance to the global political and economic system	Desire to have strong regional influence and integration, creating an identity different from that of other countries, reforming without radically changing the global system, attaching importance to regional economy and politics
Examples	Australia, Canada, Norway, Sweden	Argentina, Brazil, Nigeria, South Africa, Turkey, Indonesia

Source: Le Dinh Tinh, The goal of becoming a middle power and diplomatic outlook of Vietnam after 2030, *International Research Journal*, Issue 2 (113), June 2018.

The table above shows that whether it is a traditional or emerging middle power, regardless of the approach taken, the criteria for a middle power include both internal and external factors, specifically, reaching certain levels of economic development and capacity for state and society organization, as well as the role and position of diplomacy. The influence level of middle powers is not equal to that of superpowers but slightly higher than the other countries.

The role of a middle power in international relations

Middle powers play an important role in international relations. Currently, scholars and analysts often classify certain countries as middle powers, typically, India, Canada, Australia, Sweden, South Korea, Brazil, South Africa, Turkey, Indonesia and Vietnam[13]. To prove the power of middle powers, researchers often cite the establishment of the G20 group in 1999 including seven G7 countries and thirteen other members (Argentina, Australia, Brazil, China, India, Indonesia, Mexico, Russia, Saudi Arabia, South Africa, South Korea, Turkey and the European Union). The advent of the G20 is the "most vivid" example of the alternation in the global balance of power[14]. With the establishment of the G20, middle powers can have a significant impact on the process of building the agenda or gathering forces, which is no longer the "exclusive" product of superpowers and large countries. Earlier, in the 1980s of the twentieth century, Australia played the role of regulating trade relations between the US and the EU, between the US and Japan, in favour of building a multilateral free trade system based on general principles. After its advent, the G20 has reached important agreements to adjust the content and manner of cooperation for many international financial institutions, reflecting the interests of both poor and rich countries[15].

The four middle powers including Japan, India, Indonesia and Australia will have a population of 1.64 billion, GDP of USD 9.13 trillion and defense spending of about USD 123 billion; compared to the US population of 316 million, GDP of USD 16.78 trillion and defense spending of USD 640.21 billion; or China's population of 1.36 billion, GDP of USD 9.18 billion and defense spending of about USD 188.64 billion[16]. Thus, in terms of capacity, in many situations, superpowers still need the participation of a middle power or a group of middle powers in dealing with regional issues. US Secretary of State Hillary Clinton once suggested that Jarkata assume leadership in resolving the South China Sea issue to Indonesian Foreign Minister Marty Natalegawa[17]. Foreign Minister Marty then explained that "leadership" here did not mean encroaching on the interests of other countries but an attempt to lead in order to avoid any situation that is too biased towards any disputing party. The US chose Indonesia because it was considered a middle power with a "cautious" and "balanced" viewpoint, not directly involved in the dispute and had diplomatic capacity[18].

In fact, superpowers can work together to set up international institutions and lead cooperation processes. However, those institutions would be unlikely to work in the long run without the active participation of middle powers. In the process of building a security structure in the Asia-Pacific region, middle powers and ASEAN (as a mid-sized entity whose economic scale currently ranks seventh and is forecasted to rank fourth in the world by 2050), are significant factors. That role is reflected in the efforts to mediate and harmonize interests of ASEAN in a central role with all the remaining countries, including large ones. As for large countries, with the goal of "sharing responsibility", taking advantage of the cooperation with other countries including middle powers in the free and open Indo-Pacific strategy, the Donald Trump administration is now proposing that the "allies" and "partners" in the region perform their role and make more contributions. China is also expressing the need to find partners in implementing and coordinating the Belt and Road Initiative. It would be difficult for both the US and China to achieve their goal without the participation and consensus of the countries in the region, especially the middle powers. To further illustrate the role and influence of Asian middle powers in the current world situation, scholar Chietigj Bajpaee offered the following evidence. Despite being the winner, the Philippines was suddenly no longer interested in enforcing the Permanent Court of Arbitration's decision on China's claim on the South China Sea, making the legal process seriously delayed. Despite pressure from China, North Korea and South Korea, they still decided to deploy the system of Terminal High Altitude Area Defense

(THAAD). Indonesia strongly shifted towards prioritizing maritime security in defense strategy. As such, the middle powers are more independent and have more action space[19]. Chietigj Bajpaee also said that Vietnam was one of the "countries driving the strategic change" in Asia[20].

Middle powers often act as the bridge between richer countries with stronger potentials and poorer and weaker ones. For example, Canada, Australia and South Korea act as a catalyst to strengthen North-South cooperation between less developed countries and the G20, G7/8 or BRICS[21]. The connecting and harmonizing role middle powers is increasingly important in the context of global and regional changes in the global balance of forces. Meanwhile, existing international institutions controlled by many large countries are often slow to adapt to this change. Notably, the International Monetary Fund (IMF), World Bank (WB), and International Atomic Energy Agency (IAEA) have yet to reflect the role of emerging countries and middle powers in their governance, membership and voting mechanism[22]. One of the consequences of not or slowly reforming existing institutions is that emerging countries can establish new institutions, such as China's establishment of Asian Infrastructure Investment Bank (AIIB) besides Asian Development Bank (ADB) to support the implementation of the Belt and Road Initiative (BRI).

The middle powers have made an important contribution to maintaining regional stability by supporting the ban on the proliferation of nuclear weapons, maintaining the stability of international economic order, reducing intergovernmental debt, and banning anti-personnel mines, etc. In 1998, eight non-governmental organizations joined forces to set up the *"Middle Power Initiative"* and emphasized that a middle power is "a country that plays a significant economic and political role, is internationally respected, and opposes nuclear arms race"[23]. Middle powers actively express their viewpoint on many international and regional issues, especially the hot spots like the South China Sea. These countries will not accept the solutions that the large countries settle with each other. Therefore, ASEAN countries attach great importance to multilateral agreements and mechanisms, and building an order based on laws, openness and tolerance, in which ASEAN plays a central role. As for assistance in increasing capacity, middle powers such as India, Japan, Australia and South Korea have made significant contributions to coastal states in the region.

The most defining characteristic of middle powers is that they attach special importance to values of peace, dialogue, respect for laws, settlement, agreement, and multilateral institutions. In comparison, big countries are thought to be more inclined to approach multilateralism with a more pragmatic principle and more selective way. For instance, although not allowed by the UN Security Council, the US carried out military attacks against Iraq (in 2003) and Siri (in 2017 and 2018). China maintained the "Three Noes" policy in the case brought by Philippines to the Permanent Court in 2016 (not acknowledging the Court, not agreeing with the Court's conclusion, and not enforcing the Court's decision). Unilateralism is primarily a product of a large country and is often not accepted by the middle powers. At the other end, small countries are often more cautious than middle powers when approaching multilateral arrangements due to their concerns that the national sovereignty may be affected and the ability to enforce commitments may be limited. Statistics show that small countries like Vanuatu, Costa Rica, Gabon hardly participate in multilateral institutions. Of course, there are exceptions, for example, Singapore or Austria, countries which are small in size and population but very active. Vatican City has an area of only 44 km^2 but has a great influence on many countries and over one billion Christians in the world, etc.

Will Vietnam's Dream of Becoming a New Middle Power in Asia a Reality?

Since 1986, after more than 30 years of implementing the guideline in innovating the country under the leadership of the Communist Party of Vietnam, economic, political, cultural, social, diplomatic, defense and security activities of Vietnam have made great progress. Vietnam's power is confirmed, and the country is increasingly influential in the region and the world. Compared with the criteria for a new middle power presented above, which includes national strength and capacity, behaviour and conduct, international influence, national identity and value, Vietnam basically meet the criteria for a new middle power. Specifically:

Vietnam's strength and capacity have had breakthrough development.

In terms of area and population: Compared to other countries in the world, Vietnam ranks 68th in terms of area. As of April 1, 2019, Vietnam's population reached 96,208,984 people, becoming the 15th most populous country in the world, ranking 3rd in Southeast Asia after Indonesia and the Philippines[24]. Boston Consulting Group predicted that after 2020 the middle class in Vietnam would double in number[25]. At this rate, it is likely that half of Vietnam's population is in the middle class by 2030.

The geopolitical importance of Vietnam: While the regional political landscape tends to disperse, the economic landscape tends to converge. The market economy is operating very strongly in the countries of the region, creating a growing demand for connection and trade among countries and among regions. Meanwhile, Vietnam is located next to the "backbone route" of the regional economy, especially the southern and central regions are in the "hinge" area between the sea and mainland, right in the geometric center of Southeast Asia. These are the key conditions for Vietnam to play an important role in the regional and international seaborne trade system that runs through these sea routes. The promotion of Vietnam's geopolitical advantages can work out in two ways. One way is to be the "gateway" to the sea of inland Asia. The other is to act as the "bridgehead" on land of the seaborne and airborne trade routes through the South China Sea. Geopolitical advantage is of strategic importance to the destiny of a country. The prosperity of a nation depends very much on its ability to exploit and take advantage of its geopolitical advantage. In the current political-economic situation of the world, a new world order is emerging, in which Vietnam is in a relatively central position amid disputes among large countries and regional economic connections.

In the 21st century, Vietnam is still a country with a special position on the world political chessboard, a factor affecting the geopolitical order. This was very soon predicted by Zbigniew Brezinski, Samuel Huntington and Robert Templer[26], but in the 1990s not many people, even US strategists, really paid attention. The 21st century is considered the century of Asia-Pacific. When this region became the center of economic power with the fastest and strongest growth in the world, Robert Templer and strategists of the Center for a New American Security (CNAS) analyzed further and acknowledged Vietnam's geostrategic position[27].

The history of Vietnam in the 20th century demonstrated that the cause of the wars of national defense and liberation was inseparable from the country's geopolitical position. Most famous scholars who wrote about the war believed that the American war in Vietnam (1954-1975) was the war of ideology. Today, in relation to the US strategy of pivoting towards Asia-Pacific and in relation to China's ambition towards the "Chinese Dream", Vietnam's geostrategic position is once again becoming important beyond the will of all parties.

It can be seen that among Southeast Asian countries, Vietnam has the most important strategic position in the South China Sea. It is the intersection of national interests of many great powers such as the US, China, Japan, Russia, India, etc. Considering the ambition and reach of large countries at present, Vietnam is on the strategic chessboard of four large countries including China, the US, Japan and India. For China, the South China Sea is of vital importance. 80% of China's imported oil as well as most of the common goods traded between China and Europe and the Middle East travel through the South China Sea. Therefore, China has strengthened its control over the East Sea and made an impact in Southeast Asia with the ambition to carry out the "Chinese Dream" towards becoming the world's No. 1 power and the region's leader, making large countries like the US, Japan and India fix their eyes on the South China Sea and seek countermeasures. For Japan, the South China Sea is of extremely vital importance. 90% of Japan's consumed oil and most of the goods traded between Japan and the Middle East and Europe must pass through the South China Sea[28]. Therefore, as long as China "exercises its sovereignty" in the South China Sea, Japan's "throat" will be in China's hands. The South China Sea, though not vital to the US, is still of strategic importance. It lies in the shortest route from the Pacific to the Indian Ocean. It is also the "main lifeblood" of the regional economy and of China, the major rival of the US and Japan (US's main ally in the region).

As superpowers are playing the role of "world leaders", the US naturally considers China's rise as a threat to the US position at the great strategic level. Japan and India are two regional powers that do not want China to become the "regional leader". Japan has entered into strategic alliance with the US and worked under America's "world leadership" to oppose China's "regional leadership". India has sought a more "liberal" position, but its strategic alliance with the US still dominates. On the Asia-Pacific power playground, the dispute over regional leadership between China and the of the US-Japan-India-Australia "diamond-shaped quadrilateral alliance" is emerging.

Vietnam is the country with the most geographical advantage in controlling the South China Sea. Among Southeast Asian countries, Vietnam is the most contiguous to China. Moreover, historically, Vietnam had extensive experience in maintaining diplomatic relation with China, especially diplomatic behaviours to ensure national interests and security. Since the late 1990s and early 2000s, China's rise has increased the strategic significance of the South China Sea, Southeast Asia and Vietnam on the international strategic chessboard. The US, Japan and India all want Vietnam to play a more active role in ensuring the South China Sea security for them and wish to make Vietnam their important ally in Southeast Asia in case the disputes among large countries become fierce. The attitude of nations, especially the powers, towards Vietnam, is a testament to Vietnam's unique geopolitical position. During the APEC Summit in November 2017, many politicians were lavish in their praise for Vietnam. US President Donald Trump did not hesitate to call Vietnam one of the "Great Miracles" of the world. As such, with its special geopolitical position and experience in implementing external affairs with personality, Vietnam is considered an important partner of many powers and the international community, and it can play an integral role in the powers' development of comprehensive relations in Asia-Pacific.

Regarding economic strength, since 1986, by implementing the guidelines on the country's comprehensive innovation under the leadership of the Communist Party of Vietnam, the country's economy has had tremendous development. From an outdated agricultural economy with 90% of the population engaged in agriculture and a low growth rate (in some years the growth rate was negative), Vietnam has had impressive development with the economic growth rate maintained at a high and stable level compared to that of the region and the world. On average, GDP only increased by 0.4%/year in the 1977-1980 period, but in the 1986-2015 period Vietnam's economic growth reached 6.65%/year, with an over 7% growth rate in 12 years and the highest growth rate of 9.54% in 1995. In 2018, GDP increased by 7.32%, reaching the highest growth rate in the past 10 years[29]. The latest report of the Asian Development Bank showed that Vietnam's GDP growth would reach about 6.8% in 2019. Vietnam's economic growth rate ranks second in Asia after China and India, and it is higher than that of South Korea, Thailand, Singapore, Indonesia, Malaysia and the Philippines[30]. Vietnam's economic development model has inspired other members such as Cambodia, Laos and Myanmar. According to DBS Bank's forecast, Vietnam's economy has the potential to grow by 6-6.5% in the next decade thanks to the strong foreign investment capital and productivity growth in the coming years. Mr. Irvin Seah, economic specialist of DBS Bank in Singapore stated that if this growth rate was maintained, Vietnam's economy would be larger than Singapore's economic scale in 2029[31]. Mr. Jim O'Neill, father of the BRIC concept and once the leading economist of Goldman Sachs, published in the Spanish Economist on April 21, 2019, in which he listed 11 economics with "the most promising future of the century" including South Korea, Mexico, Indonesia, Turkey, Iran, Egypt, Nigeria, the Philippines, Pakistan, Bangladesh and Vietnam[32].

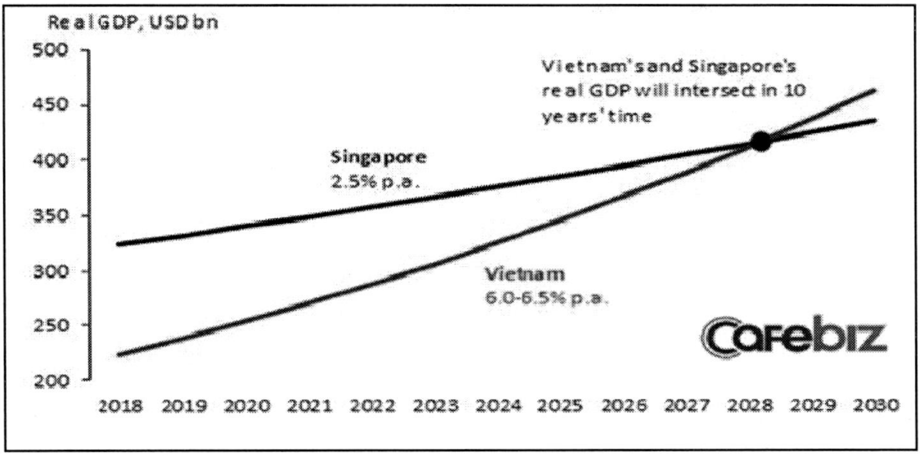

Chart 11: Vietnam Economy will be bigger than Singapore's by 2029
Source: Café biz. Will Vietnam's real GDP exceed that of Singapore from 2029? (USD billion)

Because of the economic development, the income per capita in Vietnam is increasing as well. Before 1986, Vietnam's average income was only USD 86/person/year and it was one of dozens of countries with the lowest GDP per capita in the world, etc. However, thanks to the country's innovation direction, Vietnam's income per capita is getting higher and higher. In 2005, it reached USD640/person/year, exceeding that of low-income developing countries (USD 500)[33]; by 2018 it increased to USD 2, 587[34].

Due to the stable economic growth, Vietnam's environment for business investment has experienced significant improvement, with the business environment ranking elevated by 14 levels to 68 from 82 over 190, competitiveness ranking elevated by 5 levels to 55 from 60 over 137 countries and territories, assessment of the prospects of Vietnam's banking system elevated to "positive" level from "stable" level[35]. By 2018, Vietnam has promoted economic, trade and investment cooperation with 224 markets in all continents[36]. Free trade has helped to increase Vietnam's import and export turnover to nearly USD 425 billion in 2017, four times higher than the turnover 10 years ago before Vietnam joined the WTO. Vietnam was considered one of the economies that are greatly open and successful in taking advantage of opportunities, especially ones from the new generation of Free Trade Agreement[37]. In 2018, the annual export turnover of goods reached about USD 244.7 billion, up 13.8% compared to that in 2017 (exceeding the target of 7-8% increase set by the National Assembly and the target of 8-10% increase set in the government's Resolution No. 01/NQ/CP dated January 1, 2018 on the tasks and solutions to implement the Socio-economic development plan and the State budget in 2018). Trade surplus reached USD 7.2 billion, the greatest ever.

Additionally, disbursed capital of foreign direct investment (FDI) projects set a record by reaching USD 19.1 billion, up 9.1% compared to that in 2017, becoming one of the "bright spots" in Vietnam's economic picture in 2018[38]. It was forecasted that Vietnam could enter the list of top 20 largest economies in the world after 2030. As forecasted by PWC (Price Waterhouse Coopers), by 2030, Vietnam could rank 29th in the list of economy rankings, surpassing the Netherlands, and by 2050 could rise to the 20th rank, surpassing Canada and Italy. Vietnam ranked 13th in the Lowy Institute's ranking of overall national capacity of Asian countries in 2018[39].

For new types of economy such as digital economy, sharing economy, Vietnam has also achieved the world's leading Internet growth. Vietnam's e-commerce in recent years has increased by 35%/year, 2.5 times faster than Japan[40]. What's important is that economy-wise Vietnam has demonstrated its effort to escape from the trap of the transition process or the middle-income trap[41]. Upon successful implementation of the Millennium Development Goals (MDGs), Vietnam can gradually change over from the recipient of development aid to the supporter of other countries. In the Agility Emerging Markets Logistics Index 2019, Vietnam is one of the top 10 countries. In the general assessment of Vietnam's economic influence, the Asia Power Index Report of Lowy Institute, a famous Chinese think tank, confirmed that "Vietnam ranked 10th in terms of economic influence in the Asia-Pacific region. Along with Malaysia, New Zealand and North Korea, Vietnam was the country with the fastest influence expansion in the region[42]. Vietnam has gradually become an important "link" in economic connections with the world's leading economies.

List of top 10 countries in the Emerging Markets Logistics Index 2019 of Agility

Ranking	*Country*	*Agility Emerging Markets Logistics Index 2019*	*Domestic Logistics Opportunities*	*Logistics Opportunities*	*Business Fundamentals*
1.	China	8.87	8.82	9.70	7.12
2.	India	7.39	8.09	7.20	6.35
3.	UAE	6.16	5.56	5.48	8.89
4.	Indonesia	6.09	6.32	5.94	5.94
5.	Malaysia	6.00	5.23	5.64	8.39
6.	Saudi Arabia	5.71	5.27	5.23	7.67
7.	Mexico	5.67	5.34	6.23	5.13
8.	Qatar	5.62	538	4.85	7.84
9.	Turkey	5.56	5.27	5.85	5.49
10.	Vietnam	5.48	4.88	6.12	5.31

The strength from innovation, efficiency improvement in the political system, and the implementation of democratic statue: Over 30 years of carrying out the innovation work, regarding the building and perfecting of the state apparatus, the achievements of great significance are the transition from the centralized socialist state model to the rule-of-law socialist state model, and the many results achieved in the implementation of democratic statue. This is a qualitative innovation in theoretical thinking on building and perfecting the state apparatus in the spirit of respecting the rule of law and caring about the legitimate interests of the people. The Communist Party of Vietnam maintains the leading role and confirms its position in the hearts of the people in the country as well as international friends. People can live in a democratic environment, so they are excited to contribute their efforts and wisdom to building an increasingly rich and civilized country.

Military and defense strength: The Vietnamese Army is one of the most experienced military forces in the world. Facing new higher requirements, Vietnam's military and defense capabilities are constantly improved by modernizing the army with priority given to Air Force, Naval Force, etc. Vietnam has become one of the countries with leading military power in Asia-Pacific, especially in Southeast Asia. The defensive capability to protect the nation cannot be underestimated because any enemy who is reckless enough to provoke war must pay a heavy price.

According to the world military rankings of the defense website Global Firepower (GFP), as of May 23, 2019, Vietnam ranked 23rd out of 137 countries and territories ranked. As for Southeast Asia, Global Firepower ranked a total of nine ASEAN countries (East Timor was not included in the list). Vietnam was in the dominant group of Southeast Asia, standing firmly at the 2nd position behind only Indonesia[43]. Vietnam's military position continues to be strengthened, performing well the task of protecting the Socialist Republic of Vietnam as well as participating in the implementation of international taks on the basis of respect for the law.

Top 5 countries with leading military power in Southeast Asia according to Global Firepower's ranking in which Vietnam ranks 2nd

The *Innovation Index* is also one of the most important bases for assessing the national capacity, especially in the context of the currently going strong scientific revolution 4.0. The number of scientific works published in Vietnam's ISI journals in the past 5-6 years has increased by 20%. Despite their modesty and not high starting point, the number of patents granted in Vietnam in the last 5 years has increased by 60%. According to the 2017 Global Innovation Index (GII 2017) conducted by the World Intellectual Property Organization (WIPO) in coordination with Cornell University (United States) and INSEAD Business Academy (France), Vietnam's ranking has elevated quite impressively, from the 59th out of 128 countries and economies to the 47th out of 127. This was the highest-ranking Vietnam had ever achieved. Vietnam also ranked 1st on the GII 2017 index among countries with low average income. Because of its creative potential, more and more foreign investors are choosing Vietnam to build technological startups, for example, Alt Inc.'s project to build Asia's largest center for developing artificial intelligence (AI) in Vietnam[44]. Many Vietnamese startup projects are highly valued in the region and the world.

Vietnam's diplomatic behaviour and conduct with regional and international influences

Vietnam is a particularly dynamic country in multilateral diplomacy - the leading sign of a middle power. This is reflected in the role and contribution of Vietnam in international and regional organizations. Vietnam joined ASEAN in 1995 and assumed the chairmanship of ASEAN in 1998. Vietnam is an active and proactive member in ASEAN. Vietnam can adjust its cooperation programmes within the CLV framework towards making greater contribution. As Thailand has been halfway through the ASEAN chairmanship, Vietnam has finalized the plans to successfully assume the ASEAN chair in 2020, to enhance the connection and close the gap between old and new members, with the wish for ASEAN to play a more active role in resolving international issues as well as further promoting ASEAN's centrality, etc.

Vietnam's maturity in multilateral diplomacy continues to be demonstrated with its participation in the World Trade Organization (WTO, 2007) and its good performance in the positions in various organizations of the United Nations system, for example, taking on the role of non-permanent member of the UN Security Council in the 2008-2009 period, Chair of ASEAN in 2010, hosting APEC in 2006 and 2017, and Chair of GMS in 2018. In two consecutive years 2017 and 2018, Vietnam was invited to attend the expanded G7 Summit. Especially, on June 7, 2019, at the headquarters of the United Nations, New York (United States), Vietnam was elected a non-permanent member of the UN Security Council in the 2020-2021 period, with a record number of votes in 75 years of UN development, 192/193 votes. During the 2008-2009 term, Vietnam made great contributions in an effort to resolve conflicts in hot spots around the world, promote peacekeeping activities of the Security Council, and strengthen the role of women in maintain peace and security, etc. As such, Vietnam's influence in regional and international relations is enormous. Firstly, Vietnam can act a *catalyst*, examples of which include the admission of Cambodia to ASEAN, admission of the US and Russia to the East Asia Summit, inviting ASEAN leaders to have dialogues with

APEC leaders in Da Nang city. Especially, Vietnam has become one of the catalysts in the future development of North Korea, particularly in matters related to economic and transition planning. Prior to the summit, Vietnam's role in supporting North Korea's future economic roadmap was widely discussed. US President Donald Trump even said that North Korea could be the next Vietnam, etc. Secondly, Vietnam can act as a *coordinator*. For example, Vietnam has been the country coordinating the ASEAN-China, ASEAN-US relations at many United Nations forums, regional and sub-regional forums. Vietnam can also act as the *subject that introduces initiatives* such as the initiatives within the framework of the United Nations, APEC, ASEAN, and sub-regional cooperation.

Vietnam's Multilateral Diplomacy[45]

Membership	United Nations, WTO, APEC, ASEM, ASEAN Community, La Francophonie, AIIB founders, etc.
Term membership	Non-permanent member of the United Nations Security Council (2008-2009); IAEA's Board of Governors (many times); United Nations Human Rights Council (2014-2016) (repeatedly participating in previous mechanisms); Economic and Social Council (ECOSOC) (2016-2018); World Heritage Committee (2013-2017); UNESCO Executive Board (2015-2019); Non-permanent member of the United Nations Security Council (2020-2021); United Nations Commission on International Trade Law (UNCITRAL) (2019-2025); etc.
Alternate or snap chairmanship	Senior Member of Francophonie (1997); Chairman of ASEAN 7 (1998); ASEM V (2004); APEC 14 (2006); ASEAN 15 (2010); WEF on East Asia (2010); Vietnam - Africa International Conference (2010); Vietnam - Latin America Forum on Trade and Investment (2012); IPU 32 (2015); APEC (2017); ASEAN 2020; etc.
Regional and sub-regional cooperation	GMS, LMI, LMC, MRC, CLV, etc.
Trilateral coopera-tion	Vietnam - Middle East, Africa - third partner; seismic surveys of China - Vietnam - the Philippines
New generation multilateral trade agreement	Comprehensive and Progressive Agreement for Trans-Pacific Partnership (CPTPP); EU-Vietnam Free Trade Agreement (EVFTA); etc. Vietnam has entered into 14 FTAs and is in the negotiation process of 2 FTAs, all of which are key FTAs of the region with a network of 58 partners including five permanent UN Security Council and accounting for over 80% of global GDP.
Security integration	Participating in United Nations Peacekeeping Operations since 2014; disarmament, anti-terrorism, expressed willingness to act as a mediator (North Korea); participating in regional security forums like ARF, Shangri La, ADMM+, etc.

Together with strengthening multilateral diplomatic relations, Vietnam also strengthens bilateral diplomatic relations and tripartite cooperation with dynamism and in the spirit of "pioneering, paving the way", "creating a framework" typical of middle powers' diplomacy. As a result, Vietnam has created a network of intertwined relationships, intermingled multi-dimensional and diverse interests with many countries in the world.

Vietnam's Bilateral Diplomacy as of February 2019

Diplomatic relation	189 countries
Economic, trade and investment relations	About 230 countries and territories
Comprehensive partners (13 countries)	South Africa (2004), Venezuela (2007), Chile (2007), Brazil (2007), New Zealand (2009), Argentina (2010), Ukraine (2011), United States (2013), Denmark (2013), Myanmar (2017), Canada (2017), North Korea (2018), Brunei (2019), Netherlands (2019)
Strategic partners (13 countries)	Japan (2006), South Korea (2009), Spain (2009), United Kingdom of Great Britain and Northern Ireland (2010), Germany (2011), Italy (2013), France (2013), Indonesia (2013), Thailand (2013), Singapore (2013), Malaysia (2015), Philippines (2015), and Australia (2018). (Strategic partner with Netherlands in certain fields)
Comprehensive strategic partnership (3 countries)	China (2008), Russia (2012), India (2016)
Special relation	Laos, Cambodia, Cuba
Comprehensive partner, Strategic partner	All P5 countries of the Security Council

Source: Compiled by author(s).

Therefore, in diplomatic relations, Vietnam has been performing increasingly well its role in the international community, especially in keeping peace and resolving international disputes; playing an important role in international organizations such as the United Nations, ASEAN, etc. Vietnam has developed from a country that only accepted the rules to a country that helps formulate the rules of the international system; especially, Vietnam's image as a country that loves peace, harmony and always respects international laws has been affirmed. As a result, Vietnam's position has been increasingly affirmed and acknowledged by the world. In ranking diplomatic influence of Vietnam, the Asia Power Index Report of Lowy Institute, China's famous think tank, affirmed that Vietnam, Malaysia, New Zealand and North Korea are the countries with the fastest expansion of influence in the region, of which Vietnam has had the most improvement in 2019[46].

Identity and value in creating Vietnam's position

Basically, Vietnam has effectively resolved the relation between integration and maintenance, creating national identity. Through the country's implementation of internal and external goals, Vietnam has been known worldwide as a Southeast Asian country who is independent, autonomous, self-reliant, peace and justice-loving, prioritizes relations with neighbouring and regional countries, advocates ASEAN taking the central role in the regional security structure being formed, is open-minded and integrates deeply, based on laws, towards meeting standards, achieving sustainable and humanitarian development, and building afair, democratic and civilized society. Accordingly, Vietnam is not a miniature China or imitate anyone's model as in the viewpoint of some scholars and a part of international media.

Vietnam earns increasing regional and international trust in promoting multilateral and sub-regional cooperation. Promoting the generally accepted common interests and values such as peace, stability and development, Vietnam has expressed its view that it can act as an intermediary in mediating and leading some cooperative processes[47]. Vietnam has clearly expressed its political views on many important issues like supporting denuclearization, supporting new-generation free trade, and promoting the building of regional and international orders based on law. Concerning bilateral diplomacy, Vietnam has made every effort to address the delicate, sensitive relationship between the non-ally policy and the building of genuine friendships and partnerships. This demonstrates the active but cautious and subtle approach and choice of Vietnam, consistent with the characteristics of a middle power.

Vietnam has created a consistent image of a country that respects common rules and normative values. For example, with respect to the Mekong problem, as a country at the very end downstream, Vietnam has expressed its position on upholding the principle to ensure water security and development goals in a fair, reasonable and sustainable manner based on good practices and international law; at the same time, respecting the legitimate development interests of other countries in the basin. Regarding the South China Sea issue, Vietnam is persistent and resolute in defending its sovereignty and principles but ready to show its willingness to cooperate to handle common challenges, in the spirit of respecting international law including UNCLOS 1982. It has actively participated in the building and implementation of a code of conduct, advocated the protection of "common interests" such as environment, fish source, security, safety, and navigation freedom. Vietnam's diplomacy is the perseverance, consistency, and respect for normative values in conduct such as peace, dialogue, equality, accompanied by the determination as well as a willingness to fight for legitimate interests when necessary.

Conclusion

In both theoretical and practical terms, Vietnam has basically met the criteria (capacity, behaviour, identity) to become a middle power. The Bangkok Post of

Thailand on June 11, 2019 confirmed that Vietnam was playing the role as Asia's middle power and was performing its role well both in the region and internationally, with stable politics and a strong economy. The Asia Power Index Report of Lowy Institute, China's think tank, emphasized that Vietnam ranked 13th in the aggregate power index and would soon rise to the 10th position[48]. In the coming time, Vietnam should proactively position itself as a middle power in its speeches and policy documents. Now that the criteria for a middle power have been met, Vietnam needs to adjust its diplomatic policy in order to continuously improve its position and influence in international relations. Vietnam's diplomacy should consider introducing into internal research, policy documents or external propaganda the positioning of Vietnam. To create a basis for implementation, this issue should also be included in the country's top-ranking official documents such as the upcoming 13th National Party Congress documents.

Notes

1. Bac, Meltem, "Middle Power", *Britannica*. Retrieved May 2, 2018, from https://www.britannica.com/topic/middle-power
2. Eduard Jordaan, "The Concept of a Middle Power in International Relations: Distinguishing between Emerging and Traditional Middle Powers", *Politikon: South African Journal of Political Studies*, 30 (1) (2003): 165-181.
3. Le Hong Hiep, "It's time for Vietnam to position itself as a "middle power?"". Retrieved August 16, 2018, from https://vietnamnet.vn/vn/tuanvietnam/dachieu/da-den-luc-viet-nam-dinh-vi-minh- la-cuoc-hang-trung-trung-469844.html
4. C. Holbraad, Middle Powers in International Politics (London: Macmillan, 1984); R. W. Cox, Approaches to World Order, with Timothy Sinclair (Cambridge: University of Cambridge Press, 1996); C. Pratt (ed.), 'Middle Power Internationalism and Global Poverty', Middle Power Internationalism: The North-South Dimension (Montreal: McGill-Queen's University Press, 1990); M. Neufeld, 'Hegemony and Foreign Policy Analysis: The Case of Canada', Studies in Political Economy, 48 (1995): 7-29.
5. Gregory F. Treverton, Seth G. Jones, *Measuring National Power*, RAND (Washington, DC., 2005): 10.
6. Lowy Institute, *Asia Power Index 2018*. Retrieved June 12, 2018, from https://power.lowyinstitute.org/
7. Ashley J. Tellis *et al.*, Measuring National Power in the Postindustrial Age: Analyst's Handbook (Santa Monica: RAND, 2000): 5.
8. A. F. Cooper, R. A. Higgott and K. R. Nossal, *Relocating Middle Powers: Australia and Canada in a Changing World Order* (Vancouver: University of British Columbia Press, 1993).
9. Ish-Shalom, Piki., *Democratic Peace: A Political Biography* (Michigan: University of Michigan Press, 2013).
10. R. W. Cox, *Approaches to World Order*, with Timothy Sinclair (Cambridge: University of Cambridge Press, 1996).
11. K. R. Nossal and R. Stubbs, 'Mahathir's Malaysia: An Emerging Middle Power?', in Cooper (ed.) (1997), p. 149-51.
12. Eduard Jordaan, "The Concept of a Middle Power in International Relations: Distinguishing between Emerging and Traditional Middle Powers", *Politikon: South African Journal of Political Studies*, 30 (1) (2003): 165-181.

13. Yilmaz, Suhnaz, "Middle Powers and Regional Powers", *Oxford Bibliographies*, 27/9/2017. Retrieved May 3, 2018, from http://www.oxfordbibliographies.com/view/document/obo-9780199743292/obo-9780199743292-0222.xml
14. Christian Downie, "Strategies for Middle Powers", *Australian Outlook* (9-6-2017). Retrieved April 23, 2018 http://www.internationalaffairs.org.au/australianoutlook/strategies-for-middle-powers/
15. "The Group of 20: The premier forum for international economic cooperation", 27/8/2013. Retrieved May 2, 2018, from http://www.canadainternational.gc.ca
16. Collected from Australian Department of Foreign Affairs and Trade and Stockholm International Peace Research Institute.
17. Bruce Gilley, "The rise of the middle powers", *The New York Times*, 10/9/2012. Retrieved May 3, 2018, from https://www.nytimes.com/2012/09/11/opinion/the-rise-of-the-middle-powers.html
18. Bruce Gilley, "The rise of the middle powers", *The New York Times*, 10/9/2012. Retrieved May 3, 2018, from https://www.nytimes.com/2012/09/11/opinion/the-rise-of-the-middle-powers.html
19. Chietigj Bajpaee, "Have Asia's Middle Powers Come of Age?", *The Diplomat* (7/10/2016). Retrieved April 23, 2018, from https://thediplomat.com/2016/10/have-asias-middle-powers-comes-of- age/
20. Chietigj Bajpaee, "Have Asia's Middle Powers Come of Age?", *The Diplomat* (7/10/2016). Retrieved April 23, 2018, from https://thediplomat.com/2016/10/have-asias-middle-powers-comes-of- age/
21. Jongryn, Mo (ed), *Middle Powers and G20 Governance* (New York: Asan- Palgrave Macmillan Series, 2012).
22. Christian Downie, "Strategies for Middle Powers", *Australian Outlook* (9-6-2017). Retrieved April 23, 2018, from http://www.internationalaffairs.org.au/australianoutlook/strategies-for-middle-powers/
23. *Middle Power Initiative*. Retrieved April 25, 2018, from http://www.middlepowers.org/
24. According to TuoiTre Online, Vietnam has a population of more than 96 million people, is the 15th most populous country in the world. Retrieved July 11, 2019, from https://tuoitre.vn/dan-so-viet-nam-hon-96-trieu-nguoi-la-nuoc -dong-dan-thu-15-the-gioi-20190711110548628.htm
25. AmCham, "Viet Nam's middle class set to double by 2020: BCG". Retrieved June 22, 2018, from http://www.amchamvietnam.com/vietnams-middle-class-set-to-double-by-2020-bcg/
26. Huntington, Samuel P., The Clash of Civilizations and the Remaking of World Order, 1996, Pub. Simon & Schuste.
27. Kaplan, Robert D. (2014), Asia's Cauldron: The South China Sea and the End of Stable Pacific, Random House, New York, 2014, p. 256.
28. According to the Open Encyclopedia.
29. General Statistics Office of Vietnam: *Statistical Yearbook of Vietnam 2018*, Statistical Publishing House, Hanoi, 2018
30. National Center for Socio-economic Information and Forecast (2015), "Some highlights in economic growth in the 2011-2015 period". Retrieved from http://www.ncseif.gov.vn/sites/vie/Pages/motsodiemnhantrongtang-nd-17232.html
31. VnEconomy: Vietnam's economy is forecasted to surpass Singapore in 2029. Retrieved May 28, 2019, from http://vneconomy.vn/kinh-te-viet-nam-duoc-du-bao-vuot-singapore-vao-2029-20190528164123523.htm,
32. According to http://songoaivu.tiengiang.gov.vn/nghiep-vu-ngoai-giao/-/asset_

publisher/QSpp7P8RukDa/content/viet-nam-la-mot-trong-11-nen-kinh-te-co-tuong-nhat-ky-cua-the-ky-21

33. Vo Hong Phuc, *Socio-economic achievements over 20 years of innovation (1986-2005)*, Vietnam's 20 years of innovation, National Political Publishing House, Hanoi, 2006, p. 146.
34. Vneconomy, *The income per capita in 2018 reached USD2,587 USD*. Retrieved July 27, 2019, from http://vneconomy.vn/thu-nhap-binh-quan-dau-nguoi-nam-2018-dat-2587-usd-20181227152354l2.htm
35. After Moody, Fitch raises Vietnam's ratings. See more: ""Fitch raises Vietnam's credit outlook to "positive", *VnEconomy* (May 19, 2017). Retrieved from http://vneconomy.vn/tai-chinh/fitch-nang-trien-vong-tin-em-viet-nam-len-tich-cuc- 2017 0519102828827.htm
36. Retrieved from http://baodongnai.com.vn/bao-xuan-2019/201901/doi-ngoai-da-phuong-nang-cao-vi-the-dat-nuoc-2931088/
37. "TPP 11: How Asia took the lead in free trade", *Nikkei Asian Review* (3-7-2018). Retrieved June 22, 2018, from https://asia.nikkei.com/Spotlight/Cover-Story/TPP-11-How-Asia-took-the-lead-in-free-trade
38. Retrieved from https://vov.vn/kinh-te/kinh-te-viet-nam-nam-2019-se-co-them-dong-luc-tang-truong-moi-857770.vov
39. Lowy Institute, Asia Power Index 2018. Retrieved June 12, 2018, from https://power.lowyinstitute.org/
40. "Viet Nam's e-commerce market booming", *Viet Nam News*. Retrieved June 22, 2018, from https://vietnamnews.vn/economy/419533/viet-nams-e-commerce-market-booming.html#VKoLoT36epcKc7xG.97
41. Truong Ba Thanh, Bui Quang Binh, "Some solutions to innovate Vietnam's economic growth model during the period of stepping up industrialization, modernization and international integration", *Communist Review* (October 25/ 2016). Retrieved June 22, 2018, from http://www.tapchicongsan.org.vn/Home/kinh-te/2016/41643/Mot-so-giai-phap-doi-moi- mo-tang-truong-kinh-te.aspx
42. According to Cafebiz, "*Vietnam is among the countries with the fastest influence expansion in Asia-Pacific*". Retrieved May 29, 2019, from http://cafebiz.vn/viet-nam-nam-trong-nhung-quoc-gia-mo-rong-tam-anh-huong-nhat-khu-vuc-chau-a-thai-binh-duong-20190529191938816.chn
43. See also at https://www.globalfirepower.com/countries-listing.asp. Retrieved June 12, 2018.
44. "Alt Inc builds Asia's largest Artificial Intelligence Research Center in Vietnam", *ICT News* (October 22, 2016). Retrieved June 22, 2018, from http://ictnews.vn/cntt/phan-mem/alt-inc-gift-content-center-with-knowledge-of-knowledge-in-English-with-the-best-in-Vietnam-144827.ict
45. Listed here are only some typical examples of Vietnam's diverse and multilateral diplomatic activities.
46. According to Cafebiz, "*Vietnam is among the countries with the fastest influence expansion in Asia-Pacific*". Retrieved May 29, 2019, from http://cafebiz.vn/viet-nam-nam-trong-nhung-quoc-gia-mo-rong-tam-anh-huong-nhat-khu-vuc-chau-a-thai-binh-duong-20190529191938816.chn
47. For example, Vietnam is said to be on the shortlist for organizing the summit between the US President and North Korean leader Kim Jong-un in June 2018.
48. According to Cafebiz, "*Vietnam is among the countries with the fastest influence expansion in Asia-Pacific*". Retrieved May 29, 2019, from http://cafebiz.vn/viet-nam-nam-trong-nhung-quoc-gia-mo-rong-tam-anh-huong-nhat-khu-vuc-chau-a-thai-binh-duong-20190529191938816.chn

References

1. The Communist Party of Vietnam: *Documents of the 12th National Congress*, National Political Publishing House, Hanoi, 2016.
2. Pham Binh Minh: "Vietnam's position on the development path", in *Vietnam on the development path of development*, National Political Publishing House, Hanoi, 2016.
3. Le Hong Hiep: "Is it time for Vietnam to position itself as a middle power?". Retrieved August 16, 2018, from https://vietnamnet.vn/vn/tuanvietnam/dachieu/da-den-luc-viet-nam-dinh- vi-minh-la-cuong-quoc-hang-trung-469844.html
4. Tran Bach Hieu: *Political situation of East Asia in the 1991-2016 period*, National Political Publishing House, Hanoi, 2017.
5. Le Hoai Trung (Chief Editor): Vietnam multilateral diplomacy in the period of initiative and active international integration, National Political Publishing House, Hanoi, 2017.
6. Nguyen Vu Tung (Chief Editor): *Vietnam's partnership framework*, Academy of International Relations, Hanoi, 2007.
7. Le Dinh Tinh: "Discussing strategic thinking: Theory, practice and the case of Vietnam", *International Studies*, 4 (111), December 2017.
8. Le Dinh Tinh: "The goal of becoming a middle power and Vietnam's diplomatic prospects after 2030", *International Studies*, 2 (113), June 2018.
9. To Anh Tuan: "Vietnam's long way to the United Nations 1945-1977". *International Studies*, 1 (112), March 2018.
10. Vu Le Thai Hoang and Le Linh Lan: "The role of multilateral diplomacy in national diplomatic policy of middle powers: The case of Indonesia", *International Studies*, 97, June 2014.
11. A.F. Cooper (ed.). *Niche Diplomacy: Middle Powers after the Cold War*. New York: Macmillan,1997.
12. A.F. Cooper, R. A. Higgott and K. R. Nossal. *Relocating Middle Powers: Australia and Canada in a Changing World Order*. Vancouver: University of British Columbia Press, 1993.
13. C. Holbraad. *Middle Powers in International Politics*. London: Macmillan, 1984.
14. Eduard Jordaan. "The Concept of a Middle Power in International Relations: Distinguishing between Emerging and Traditional Middle Powers". *Politikon: South African Journal of Political Studies*, 30 (1) (2003).
15. Le Dinh Tinh. "The 2017 APEC Summit: A Game Changer for the Asia Pacific?". *Asia-Pacific Bulletin*, No. 405, (15-11-2017), East West Center, Washington DC.
16. Rory Medcalf and C Raja Mohan. "Responding to Indo-Pacific Rivalry: Australia, India and middle power coalitions". *Analyses*, (Lowy Institute, 8-8-2014).
17. Sung-Mi Kim. "South Korea's middle-power diplomacy: Changes and challenges". *Research Pater*. London: Chatham House,6-2016.
18. Tran Thi Bich, Yoichiro Sato. "Vietnam's Post-Cold War hedging strategy: A changing mix of realist and liberal ingredients". *Asian Politics and Policy* Vol. 10, No. 1 (2018).

Conclusion

Pankaj K. Jha

Vietnam's history is replete with examples of its national and civilizational character and it was one of the very few countries which integrated after bifurcation by the colonial interests. Therefore the resolve of the nation is much greater than many other countries which became independent in Southeast Asia during that time. The role of Vietnamese political establishment in developing social moorings and civil society fundamentals have been to a large extent shaped by the committed political leadership and the suffering that the country suffered in the hands of major powers including Japanese, French, Americans and subsequently Chinese. The only country which sustained its national character in the face of tremendous pressure and international stress. Vietnam's civilizational past does stress on the fact that they have been subjugated by their northern neighbours but it also reinforces that the Vietnamese kings have developed society and brought about fundamental changes in Vietnamese economy and governance.

Since the start of the 20th century Vietnam was seen as a country which was strategically located and was testimony to the power struggle during the Second World War which saw Japanese at its door step. Subsequent to the war French have tried to harness resources of the country but got defeated. US intervention in the process led Vietnam adopting the Communist welfare system and was the reason that it got closer to both erstwhile Soviet Union and China. The ideological underpinnings of the governance and political system still bear the marks of the communist ideology. However, following the dissonance with China in late 1970s and the covert operations that China had conducted to penalize Vietnam for close affiliation with former Soviet Union build the steely resolve of the country. The period of rapprochement between China and US also exposed the power dynamics in Asia. Vietnam was seen as the few citadels of communist influence in Asia following the defeat of communist parties across Southeast Asia. With time Vietnam made fundamental changes to its political structure and adopted socialism as the benchmark of social change of economic development. However, Communist party of Vietnam remained at the epicenter for such changes. In comparison to the constraints on internet access, Vietnam is relatively better in access to the virtual world.

Even before the disintegration of Soviet Union and the hardships face by the Eastern European countries, Vietnam embarked on the economic reforms programme in 1986. Vietnam brought about changes in governance and also economic changes so that corruption and inefficient methods could be weeded out. With one of the largest standing armies in Southeast Asia, Vietnam was seen as a threat by many of its neighbouring countries. However, with the resolution of the Cambodian crisis in 1991 and Vietnam's involvement into ASEAN led multilateral structures, it was believed that Vietnam was indispensable to the thought of ASEAN unity and ASEAN way. Following the entry of Myanmar, Laos and Cambodia into ASEAN multilateral mechanisms, the ASEAN Ten was complete. The ASEAN dialogue partner process also fulfilled its obligations by taking active interest in the region. The dialogue partners also increased over a period of time. The ADMM+, East Asia Summit were few examples along with ASEAN Regional Forum. The evolution of East Asia Summit showcased that dialogue partners can be effectively engaged in discussing security issues of the region. The development of growth triangles and exclusive export zones made ASEAN as one of the most successful multilateral organizations which was often compared with that of European Union.

ASEAN also embarked on building the political, social, security and cultural communt9y and also integrated countries into ASEAN Free Trade Area. Regional Comprehensive Economic Partnership (RCEP) which started negotiations in 2012 and concluded in 2019 was an attempt to bring together developing and developed economies of the region to create vast market and a large labour force together. The attempt was to develop complementarities and enjoy economies of scale and better production efficiency while catering to larger regional economic growth objectives.

Vietnam being a growing economy and enhanced trade profile would need to cater to the regional changes in both political and economic domain, and would have to secure its interests in a largely competitive space. The per capita income of the country still is around USD 2500 as per the World Bank reports and therefore it would have to accelerated market reforms and develop infrastructure to support Foreign Direct investment inflows. However, the poverty has declined considerably over a period of three decades. Vietnam's economic growth ranges between 7-9 per cent and inflation has been relatively low. The surge in FDI over the last five years shows that with the economies of scale reducing and the real wages decreasing within China, many multinational companies would like to seek Vietnam for establishing their manufacturing bases. Vietnam population is nearly 100 million and it enjoys the youth bulge. Its 70 per cent of population is below 35 years of age making it one of the most promising economies in Asia for cheap labour and skilled expertise. In the services sector and to have large white collar workers it needs to invest in higher education and develop a core workforce which can accelerate country economy through services sector growth. Industrialization in Vietnam has been not that efficient because of inefficient models of production and heavy reliance on primary sectors. The country need to take efforts to address climate change issues and also develop environment friendly production such as reducing use of marine plastics. The new trade models might also put the climate friendly production in the scheme of things. Vietnamese government have highlighted these issues and making a blueprint to address marine, water and air pollution on a priority level.

With regard to health parameters, Vietnam has done remarkably well in comparison to its neighbours with drastic fall in child mortality and pre and post-natal care. Maternal mortality ratio has reduced also and there is comprehensive health coverage for citizens. In terms of research on medicine and providing better health facilities to its citizens Vietnam would have to create a strong workforce of medical practitioners and service providers.

Over the period of last thirty years, Vietnam has improved relations with EU, US and Japan and has nurtured better relations with China, Russia and its neighbours. However, it still have to make choices between the new friends and old partners. In this context US is likely to become the strategic partner in near future but this new strategic permutation would annoy neighbours like china and friends like Russia. However, with deft diplomacy and clever strategic maneuvers Vietnam knows how to keep partners and enjoy the benefits of partnership. Comprehensive Strategic partnership with India is one such partnership which have been intensified and permeated into economic, political and defence cooperation. This have also helped Vietnam in training its pilots, technicians and also helping technicians for maintenance of sophisticated weapon systems. However, the two countries still need to figure out the cooperation in related fields such as joint research and joint development of military weapons. Brahmos has bene one of the nagging issues which still needs resolution in terms of exports to Vietnam.

The big question which needs to be answered is whether Vietnam has made itself eligible for the middle power tag in Asia. The answer lies in evaluating its political stability, economic growth, young population and defence forces which are undertaking military modernization on a comprehensive scale. However, Vietnam have two nagging issues with its larger neighbour China which includes the problems in the diversion and building of dams on Mekong river, and secondly the tensions which are recurrent in South China Sea. Vietnam has sustained and maintained its posture on the two issues but given the fact that its economy is growing and is getting close to western nations, the dynamics would get more complex in coming years. ASEAN as an organization has tried to steer clear of the South China Sea controversy and the 'Code of Conduct' (CoC) on South China Sea is still way off the horizon. The challenge is whether US can maintain international maritime order or would cede the role to Beijing. The issue would be critical for the region. Additionally, the ideological affiliation with China and the national interest might put the Communist party at cross roads with older generation maintaining attachment to China while newer generation seeking a new role in the Asian order. The Indo-Pacific construct is one which might be an enticing idea but for Vietnam any idea which jeopardizes its national security and interest is not a welcome move. Vietnam would have to sustain its role as an emerging economy and a rising middle power.

Contributors

Dr. Pankaj Jha is Associate Professor with Jindal School of International Affairs (JSIA), O P Jindal Global University. Dr. Pankaj Jha was Director (Research) with Indian Council of World Affairs for more than two and half years. He had worked as Deputy Director with National Security Council Secretariat (2012-2013) and was closely associated with national security apparatus in India. He has been member of high level delegations to UK, Israel and other countries. He has been the visiting fellow with Centre for International Security Studies, Sydney University (2009) and Institute for South Asian Studies, Singapore (2006). He has also given lectures and participated in high level dialogues in Germany, Belgium, China, New Zealand, and Australia. He has more than 60 articles/chapters/academic papers in books as well as refereed and non-refereed journals. He is regularly quoted in International Newspapers/Magazines such as Nikkei Asian Review, South China Morning Post, Bangkok Post, Gulf News and International Business Times etc. He has authored two books on *India and China in Southeast Asia: Competition or Cooperation* (2013) and *India and the Oceania: Exploring Vistas of Cooperation* (2016).

Researcher Thi-Dung Nguyen is working at the Bac Giang province college of politics. She successfully defended her bachelor's thesis of Philosophy in 2007 and a Master of Science Socialism in 2018. Dung is interested in social, theoretical and philosophical issues, regularly participates in specialized scientific research to serve teaching at the school. She has participated in writing monographs, chaired the topic, writing papers for seminars and was a member of many books on philosophy and social theory. She has also participated in many scientific topics on politics and economy. Up to now, she has some published articles in Vietnam with ISSN index and she is also a co-author of many books published in Vietnam with ISBN index.

Dr. Trong-Hung Vu is a main lecturer in Historical Institute of Communist Party of Vietnam at the Ho Chi Minh National Academy of Politics (HCMA). He has been working at Ho Chi Minh National Academy of Politics since 2008. He successfully defended his doctoral's thesis in The History of Communist Party of Vietnam in 2017. In Historical Institute of Communist Party of Vietnam at the Ho Chi Minh National Academy of Politics (HCMA), he teaches topics on the history of the Communist Party of Vietnam and researches the materials, curriculum and scientific works related to Vietnamese politics, the ideas of parties in Vietnam and the world. He has more than 100 published articles in Vietnam and the internationally. In which, there are 15 scientific works published in the specialized journals in Vietnam with ISSN index, some articles published on international websites and journals, 7 scientific works published at International

Scientific Conferences in Vietnam, as the Master of 3 scientific topics, written 69 speeches in the national scientific conferences, participated in writing 16 books. He has authored 3 books in Vietnam, such as: History of the Socialist Party of Quang Dong (1948-2018); History of the party of Hung Yen city (2005-2015); Historical force of Thach that district (1945-2019)... He is also a co-author of many books published in Vietnam.

Researcher **Le-Dung Phung** is working at the Institute of Political Economy at the Ho Chi Minh National Academy of Politics (HCMA). She has a master degree of Education in 2009 and a master degree of Political Economy in 2016. Currently, she is a PhD student at the HCMA. She is a co-manager of one Nation-level research project: "*Practical implementation of poverty reduction policy in Vietnam from 2001 to 2010; proposing some mechanisms, policies and solutions for poverty reduction from 2011-2020*"; manager of one Ministry-level research project: "*Model of socio - economic development of Southeast Asian countries and reference values for Vietnam*" and manager of an Institute-level research project: "*The Law of value in the Industrial revolution 4.0*". Moreover, she has participated in many scientific topics on polictics and economy. Up until now, she has 12 published articles in Vietnam with ISSN index and she is also a co-author of many books published in Vietnam with ISBN index.

Tuan-Thuy Nguyen is currently a researcher of the Institute of Religions and Beliefs at the Ho Chi Minh National Academy of Politics (HCMA); in 2010, she graduated with a good bachelor's degree in political education at Hanoi University of Education; and passed the civil servant exam at Ho Chi Minh National Political Academy. In 2012, she defended her Master of Philosophy. Currently, she is a Ph. D. student in Religious Studies. In the Institute of Religions and Beliefs at the Ho Chi Minh National Academy of Politics (HCMA), she researches and teaches topics on Religion and to study materials; textbooks and scientific works related to religion; especially Vietnamese Buddhism and religious legal entities. She is the author of many scientific works related to building the Communist Party of Vietnam; scientific works published in religious public journals in Vietnam with ISSN index, scientific works published at scientific seminars in Vietnam and the head of the Academy's scientific topic.

Dr. Truong-Thu Doan is a Senior Lecturer and Deputy Director of the Institute of Political Science (IPS) - Ho Chi Minh National Academy of Politics (HCMA). In 1995 Dr. Doan started his career at HCMA as a researcher and lecturer at the Institute of Scientific Socialism (ISS). From 2009 up to now, he has been working at the IPS as a Senior Lecturer on Political Theories. In 2017, Dr. Doan was assigned as Deputy Director of IPS. Dr. Truong-Thu Doan was awarded his PhD for a thesis on political philosophy at the Institute of Philosophy, Vietnam Academy of Social Sciences in 2006. He received training in the frame of Knowledge-based Management Programme of National Graduate Institute for Policy Studies (GRIPS) in Tokyo, Japan; Public Leadership in Sustainable Development course at Portland State University (PSU) and the Daniel K. Inouye Asia-Pacific Center for Security Studies (DKI APCSS) in Honolulu, Hawaii, USA. He worked on theories on gender equality under the supervision of UNDP as well as Vietnam National University (VNU). Gender equality in Vietnam is also a concern on his research as it witnessed his appearance on Workshop of UN Women - ASEAN on Advancing and Monitoring women's political participation in the ASEAN. He played the role of a trainer in courses on gender equality for the officers in all levels of Vietnam Communist Party and Government, for women and women candidates of Vietnam National Assembly and People's Assembly at multiple levels. He also takes on courses of Political Theories, Political Systems, Developmental Politics and Political Philosophy at the University of Social Sciences and Humanities (USSH) of Vietnam National University (VNU). He has written more than 20 articles, chapters, scholarly articles about scientific topics and journals refereed and non–refereed. He is the first author of the book *Vietnam Political Thought 1930-1945 (2018)* and author of *Human Rights in Social Progress (2019)*.

Dr. Thi-Hong-Hanh Nguyen is a lecturer in Vietnam Communist Party Building Institute, Political Academy Area 1, Ho Chi Minh National Academy of Politics. She successfully defended the dissertation on building the Communist Party of Vietnam in 2017. At the Vietnam Communist Party Building Institute, Political Academy Area 1, she has participated in teaching thematic history of Vietnamese Communist Party, building the Communist Party of Vietnam and researches the materials, curriculum and scientific works related to Vietnamese politics, the ideas of parties in Vietnam and the world. Till now, she has published many scientific works. Some of them were published in the specialized journal in Vietnam with ISSN index, some articles published on the site and domestic magazines. She has joined in many International Scientific Seminar in Vietnam. She is also co-author of many books published in Vietnam.

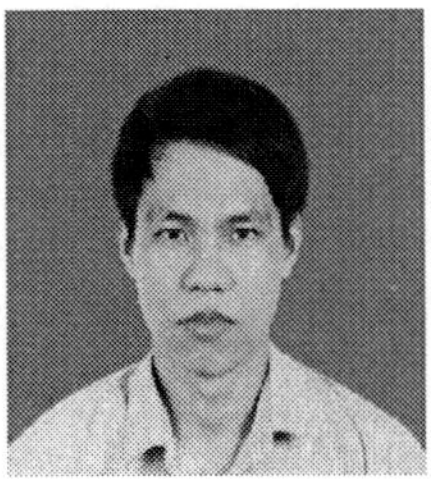

Mr Van-Son Nguyen is a researcher of the Institute of International Relations–Ho Chi Minh National Academy of Politics (HCMA) of Vietnam. He studied and graduated both bachelor's and master's degree in politics at Faculty of Political Science–University of Science, Society and Humanities–Vietnam National University, Hanoi. In 2014, he started his career at the Ho Chi Minh National Political Academy. From 2014 to present, he has focused his research on the fields of international relations and politics, especially those related to India, major countries in the world, Southeast Asia. He has had a number of studies published in prestigious journals in Vietnam with ISSN index. In 2018, he also participated in a book entitled: International Integration of Vietnam today: problems and breakthrough solutions. Especially in the last month of November 2019, he successfully defended grassroots science topics with the content: Strategic competition between India and China in the Indo-Pacific region and the counterpart of Vietnam, led by himself. Currently, he is focusing in-depth research on India.

Ms. Thu-Ha Nguyen is currently a PhD student at Hanoi University of Social Sciences and Humanities (USSH) - Hanoi National University, majoring in International Relations. Ms. Ha has participated in many seminars, conferences and forums on issues related to world politics and international relations. She is particularly interested in issues of China such as foreign policy, the leadership of the Chinese Communist Party, economic policy and more recently China's Belt and Road Initiative (BRI) and its impacts on the world and the region... With good foreign language skills (Ms. Ha has a master's degree in English issued in Vietnam), Ms. Ha is able to exploit and research specialized documents in both languages English and Vietnamese. Up to now, she has published many articles in Vietnam with the ISSN index. Ms. Ha also participated in a number of monographs, topics, books and presentations for domestic and international conferences.

Dr Thi-Hong-Mai Nguyen is a senior lecturer at the Party History Institute of Ho Chi Minh National Political Academy (HCMA). Ms. Mai has been working at the Ho Chi Minh National Political Academy since 1993 and successfully defended her PhD thesis in 2012. She has nearly 20 articles published in Vietnam with the ISSN index. She has also written 30 presentations for many international and domestic scientific conferences, including three articles submitted to the seminar between Vietnam and India, Vietnam and the Soviet Union. She is the Chairman of a ministry-level scientific topic: "The Party leads the struggle to protect the ideological foundation in the 1986-1996 period"; Chairman of 3 grassroots scientific topics: "Impact of the socialist system on the process of implementing the Socialist Revolution in Vietnam in the period 1960-1975"; Studying and identifying historical Party characters in the history of revolutionary struggle in the southwestern provinces of the South "; The process of implementing Directive 100 of the Party Central Committee Secretariat on the contracting of agricultural products from 1981 to 1988. In addition, Dr. Nguyen Thi Hong Mai has participated in many scientific projects and projects at State, ministry, grassroots level. Dr. Mai is the editor and co-author of 30 books on the history of the local Party Committee and central agencies and organizations published in Vietnam.

Researcher **Van-Huong Le** is currently working at the Ministry of Foreign Affairs of Vietnam and covering office works. From 2012 to 2015, he was an attacher at Vietnam Embassy in Canada. Here, he research on the diplomatic relationship between Vietnam and Canada. He also participated in organizing the 40th anniversary of diplomatic relations between Vietnam and Canada. In 2017, he had a master degree of Business Administration at National Yunlin University of Science and Technology, Taiwan. He just successfully defended his Master's thesis with the topic: "The technological competition between the America and China under President Donald Trump" in Institute of International Relations - Ho Chi Minh National Academy of Political in November 2019.

Mr. Le has participated in many external activities of Ministry of Foreign Affairs of Vietnam and scientific projects with topics on, politics and international relations, including 05 topics that have been accepted. At present, Mr. Le focuses on researching the relationship between the United State and China.

Researcher **Thi-Hong-Hoa Vu** has worked for the Ministry of Foreign Affairs of Vietnam since 2010. Currently, Ms. Vu is in charge of foreign press and external information. She assists Vietnamese and foreign correspondents to cover foreign affairs events and activities of Vietnam State and Party's Leaders. She has a master's degree in French language from Hanoi University in 2009. During the time at the Ministry of Foreign Affairs, as a press officer, Hoa participated directly in 10 external events held in Vietnam as well as internationally such as the ASEAN and APEC summits, Meet with Ambassadors from the Middle East and Africa.

Furthermore, Ms. Vu had participated in many the scientific researching projects of the Ministry of Foreign Affairs with topics on foreign press and external information as well as politics and international relations, including 02 topics that have been accepted. Beside Hoa also participated in other competitions which were organized by the Ministry of Foreign Affairs and the Central Propaganda Department. She won the prize in the contest of writing about Studying and following Ho Chi Minh's moral example (2013) or Paris Agreement (2015).

Thi-Trang Le is Master of Cultural Studies at the Ho Chi Minh National Academy of Politics (HCMA). Besides, she had two bachelor degrees of Culturology at Academy of Journalism and Communication (2013) and Political Science at HCMA (2015). Currently, she has been the lecturer and researcher at Institute of Culture and Development (HCMA). Her research interests are mainly focused on: urban culture, consumer culture, cultural industry, ethical culture, political culture and soft power in international relations. She has published 16 articles in with ISSN index and co-author of 3 books published in Vietnam related to soft power and cultural diplomacy. She also participated in international scientific conferences of soft power, cultural diplomacy in Thailand, South Korea and Vietnam. It is expected that in the near future, she will continue her research direction on cultural diplomacy and develop this topic at her PhD level.

Researcher **Thi-Hue Quach** is a lecturer in the Institute of International Relations at the Ho Chi Minh National Academy of Politics (HCMA). PhD student Quach Thi Hue has been working at Ho Chi Minh National Academy of Politics since 2015. PhD Hue defended her master's thesis in 2014 and is currently a PhD student in International Relations at the University of Social Sciences and Humanities (USSH) of Vietnam National University (VNU). She has been an editor of the Political Science Information Magazine of the Institute of Scientific Information of Ho Chi Minh National Academy of Politics for 2 years. Here, she was in charge of exploiting and editing foreign documents including English journals, articles, books, documents and scientific topics for researching and teaching politics, international relations, leadership, law... at the Ho Chi Minh National Academy of Politics (HCMA). Hue is currently a Lecturer in the International Relations Institute of Ho Chi Minh National Academy of Politics (HCMA). She has more than 20 published articles in Vietnam with ISSN index, some articles published on international websites and journals. She has participated in many scientific topics on politics and international relations, including 02 topics that have been accepted. Ms Hue is also a co-author of many books published in Vietnam.

Index